Black Days, White Nights

BLACK DAYS,
WHITE NIGHTS

Herman Carmel

HIPPOCRENE BOOKS
NEW YORK

Library of Congress Cataloging in Publication Data

Carmel, Herman.
  Black days, white nights.

  Includes index.
    1. World War, 1939–1945—Personal narratives, Jewish.
  2. Refugees, Jewish—Soviet Union—Biography.
  3. Carmel, Herman. I. Title.
  D810.J4C32   1984   940.53'15'03924   84-10866
  ISBN 0-88254-998-7

For my dear granddaughters

Rina and Abigail

Contents

Foreword by Elie Wiesel

IN OUR CENTURY, marked by hate and violence, testimony is the very sap and essence of literature.

For those who saw humanity driven to the limits of its possibilities in both good and evil, imagination must give way to realism.

Knowledge, said Albert Einstein, kills imagination. He may have been right. It is only with difficulty that the novelist invents situations and problems never experienced by himself or others. If someone needs evidence for this, let him read the memoirs of death camp survivors. Or Herman Carmel's autobiographical narrative.

Born in a little village of the Austro-Hungarian Empire, the author tells of his escapes from Cossack, German, and Russian. Like so many of his contemporaries, he seems to have spent his entire life running from country to country, from refuge to refuge, and from event to event.

What is his first memory? At five he overhears his mother whisper that the Cossacks are doing terrible things to Jewish women. He knows nothing about Cossacks, or about what Cossacks could do to Jewish women. But he knows that he should be afraid. This fear is to accompany him for many years. For other reasons, of course.

The rise of Nazism in Germany, then Austria. The complacency and indulgence of the Great Powers toward the Third Reich. The Munich Agreement. The invasion of Czechoslovakia. Worried, the Jews ask themselves what to do. Some flee, most remain. Doors are closed. How do you open them? Herman Carmel finds a way. Having relatives in Latvia, he takes his wife and seeks shelter there. Before departing, however, he gets to know the local Gestapo. Nothing really serious: a few insults and humiliations, a few hours, even nights, of panic. With an exit visa in their pocket, the couple leaves for Latvia, via Berlin and Lithuania. A careful observer, Carmel offers us a personal,

ix

yet almost journalistic, account of this unreal period before the storm. He writes of these times as he lived them, far from home, settled in a new career of teaching German to Red Army cadets. Does he sense war approaching? It even takes the Russians by surprise. The author follows them in the retreat to the Urals.

There a new life begins for him and his small family, now enlarged by the birth of a son. He depicts this world as few professional writers have done: his achievement never compromises his sincerity.

Thus, the reader will find in this book a valuable testimony of the Russians' life during the war. The stupid cruelty of some officials is to be seen, but so is the generosity, the humanity, of an officer, a physician, a waitress, and an anonymous passerby. Courage on one side, cowardice on the other.

As a foreigner, refugee, and Jew, Carmel has three counts against him. Yes, antisemitism has not disappeared, not even during the war. In the public square one may often hear Jews laughed at, or accused of all the vices on this earth. Luckily, in those times the Jews in Russia knew how to defend themselves. An antisemitic senior officer would be dismissed and punished. The real terror, for Jews and others, comes from elsewhere, from the secret police. People disappear into prisons and Siberia. Distrust is pathological. A word too many, or a misplaced smile, and freedom is no more.

Carmel, miraculously, knows how to attach himself to others. He makes friends almost everywhere. Most of them, of course, are Jews, refugees like himself as well as native Russians. Among those he befriends are some astonishing individuals, descendants of "Cantonists" who had been forced into 25 years of military service in the time of the Czar. And there are Zionists, a Jew from Palestine, talmudic scholars, lovers of Hebrew poetry, and Just Men disguised as peasants or merchants . . .

One must read this book, and read it well, to understand the tenacity of the Jewish people and their dedication to the fight for their collective memory. Some pages overwhelm us with truth, others with humanity. Those pages which describe his son's ailments, for example, are so solemn and admirable, the suffering discreet, so discreet.

Herman Carmel hardly asks for the reader's pity. His only aim is to inform, and maybe to move. He fulfills his role of witness honestly and well. How can we not be thankful to him?

Black Days, White Nights

1

Flight Before the Storm

ONE

I WAS LESS than five years old when the First World War broke out and have only a faint recollection of the vanishing good life. To be sure, I remember many events at the outbreak of war and during the ensuing years, and in the turbulent time thereafter. All of these stories crowd my memories and beg to be told. But the story I am now trying to relate is confined to the period starting with the Munich Agreement; I tell of my experiences under the Hitler occupation and particularly of my wanderings in the Soviet Union during the years of World War II.

There is, however, one childhood memory from the days of the First World War that has relevance to the story in this book, and I would like to tell it. Some months after the start of the war, I was standing with my father by a Habsburg officer who gazed fixedly through his field glasses at the Tisa River of my town of birth, Bedevla. After a while he handed the binoculars to my father and pointed where to look.

I did not grasp the meaning of Father's excited questions and the officer's terse answers, but I gathered from their words that there was a patrol of Cossack horsemen on the other shore.

I did not know then what a Cossack was, but I had heard that terrible word mentioned often. I still remember the frightened expressions on the faces of adults when they talked about the Jewish pogroms carried out by Cossacks in the territory already captured by the Russians. I recall vividly the whispers of my mother with the neighborhood women about the horrible things

3

the Cossacks perpetrated on Jewish women, and how they would hush their whispers when noticing us children within earshot.

I had no notion then of what it was that the Cossacks did to Jewish women, but I suspected that it must be something monstrous, for my two older sisters, like the other Jewish girls and younger married women in town, had already fled some days before to the safety of the hinterland. Only my ten-year-old brother and I remained with our parents. Mother gave me strict orders: "Play only in front of the house lest a Cossack grab you!" She did not need to warn me a second time; I hardly dared now to go farther than the porch by myself. I was sure that Cossacks were not human but cruel devils, about whom I had heard many scary tales from the older children.

As soon as Father came home with the bad news from the officer, we hurriedly loaded our bedding and other bundles onto a neighbor's wagon and left immediately, together with his family.

I have only a very hazy recollection of the journey of escape: I don't remember where we drove, how far we got, or how long we were away—whether it was only days or a much longer time—but the memory that has remained was connected with Cossacks.

Our neighbors had a little girl about my age, whose name I have long since forgotten. But I remember how, in order to frighten her, I told her that a Cossack was coming to get her. During the day we drove, and at night we slept in the wagon. One evening, as we were about to go to sleep in a forest, I crawled up behind her, pulled her hair and whispered in a husky voice, "I am a Cossack and have come to get you!" The girl was startled and began to cry loudly. I sneaked back under my cover and pretended to be fast asleep, but it did not help me much; my mother gave me a terrible spanking. This did not prevent me, however, from starting the next morning to scare the girl again with Cossacks. There is, apparently, a Cossack in all of us.

One morning I woke up and was surprised to find myself sleeping in my bed at home again. The Russian Army had been thrown back, and the front was now far away. Before long my sisters too returned home. But the fright of the Cossacks remained deep in my heart.

I got to see a Cossack in the flesh only later in the war, when they put up a camp for Russian prisoners of war near our town. The arrival of the prisoners caused a great sensation. The elderly Austrian soldiers marching the prisoners from the railroad station to the camp looked the other way when a prisoner would leave the column and hurry to a door to beg for food. I stood with Mother at the window and watched the prisoners pass. Then there was a light knock on the door. My mother gave me a piece of bread and said, "Go and give it to the poor hungry Cossack."

When I opened the door I saw standing there a bearded man with an emaciated face, wearing a strange tall fur hat, a shabby army overcoat and torn high boots. Shoving the bread quickly into his pocket, he mumbled something and ran back to the column. I felt rather disappointed that I was not scared of the Cossack at all.

On my subsequent visits to the prison camp I had a chance to see some more captive Cossacks. But my fear of them and the hasty escape from their pogrom and killings have remained in my memory. Years later, when I became a refugee from Hitler and was forced into exile, I recalled my first childhood flight from the Cossacks. That horror returned to me during the grillings by the Gestapo and then later by its Soviet counterpart, the NKVD.

* * *

Before parting from this sketchy reminiscence of my early childhood, however, I want to mention another episode in connection with that camp. There were some Russian Jewish prisoners in the camp. Though the Jews of our town were hungry themselves, they made every effort to bring the prisoners some kosher food, especially on the Sabbath and holidays. The adults, being prohibited by Jewish Law to carry things beyond the limits of the Sabbath *eiruv,* used to take along us younger children—whom the Law allows to do so—to carry the food to the camp.

As Passover approached, the *Seder* ritual and the supply of proper Pesach food became a serious problem. The leaders of our community, however, succeeded in persuading the commandant to release the Jewish prisoners into their custody for the holiday.

One of them was our guest for Passover. His name was Yitzhak, and he came from the city of Kremenchug. He was a likeable young man and soon became one of the family. For hours on end he would study the Talmud together with my father, and Mother went out of her way to give him the best food she could get under those difficult war conditions.

I got to like Yitzhak very much and used to cling to him and listen to the beautiful Hebrew songs he knew. I took a special liking to his military cap and was delighted when he allowed me to put it on. I went outside in it to show off to the children, parading up and down the street and giving the military salute to everybody I met. Once, however, it nearly got me, and Yitzhak too, into trouble. An Austrian soldier passed and I saluted him adroitly. He noticed the Russian cap on my head and started out after me. Scared, I ran and hid in the house. I deemed it prudent not to wear the cap outside anymore.

The developing flirtation between Yitzhak and my older sister did not escape my notice. It did not get, of course, any further than furtive exchanges of bashful glances and blushes. I am sure that my parents also were aware of this romance and that they would not have minded having him as a son-in-law, if his first name were not the same as my father's—a barrier to marriage according to Jewish tradition.

Some time after Passover Yitzhak was transferred to another camp somewhere in Austria. He kept exchanging letters with us for a long time, but then he suddenly stopped writing and we could not find out what happened to him.

World War I came to an end, and the Hapsburg Monarchy fell apart. During the ensuing anarchy and political disorder the town of my birth changed hands several times between Hungarian, Ukrainian and Rumanian armed forces until after the war it finally became part of the newly founded Czechoslovak Republic. Some years later, after drinking my fill of Torah and Talmud at several famous Yeshivas, I decided to leave my home town with its ancient Hasidic way of life and go West to imbibe secular knowledge and wisdom from the Czech fountains of higher learning.

TWO

At the time my sad story begins to unfold, my parents were not alive anymore. I was already married and had been teaching for several years at a gymnasium in Brno, the capital of Moravia. But after two decades of normalcy and peacefulness, life once again was getting out of joint.

It is pointless to brood about one's past nearsightedness and mistakes. But my mind involuntarily wanders back to the spring of 1938. After Hitler's *Anschluss* of Austria, my brother and an uncle in the United States sent me an immigration affidavit. They urged me to leave everything and come as soon as possible, but I procrastinated applying for the visa.

The reason for my delay was that my heart was not at all in emigrating to America. I was too deeply attached to the way of life Thomas Masaryk had created in democratic Czechoslovakia. In one of my letters to my brother, who kept urging me to come, I wrote half-jokingly that I would send him an affidavit to return home and get away from the deep depression and long lines of unemployed in America.

Chamberlain's envoy, Lord Runciman, was already in Prague and secretly twisting President Eduard Beneš's arm to cede the Sudetenland to Germany. But I, like most Jews in Czechoslovakia, lived in a fool's paradise and did not realize the seriousness of the approaching danger. I was firmly convinced that the Western democracies would never allow Hitler to harm the only genuinely democratic country in the heart of Europe. "It can never happen here," I assured myself.

Meanwhile, the Nazi clouds kept moving closer and closer. The pressure on Czechoslovakia grew. Toward the end of May I finally went to the American Consulate in Prague. "Just in case," I thought. There was a long line outside. When I managed at last to get inside, the secretary shook his head. "You have kept this affidavit for too long. The Czech immigration quota is already filled. I'm afraid you'll have to wait quite some time now for your turn."

In retrospect I have not really been able to rationalize my behavior. I did not feel too unhappy at the news in the consulate. I hoped—against hope perhaps—that the country would withstand the Nazi menace and that I would not have to leave at all.

In a sense I welcomed the delay; it would give me time to finish my studies for my Ph.D. degree at Masaryk University of Brno.

My wife Ida and I gave up our apartment and moved in with an elderly Czech widow across the park from the University. The large apartment, occupied only by the mother and her son, Tonda, was comfortable and quiet, and I could devote myself to my studies. Ida was studying medicine, so the closeness to the University was convenient for both of us.

The summer weeks were fraught with political tension; Hitler's open threats grew bolder. The Germans in Czechoslovakia were incited to disturbances and riots. My heart was filled with apprehension over the worsening crisis, but I had to worry about the examinations and preparing my doctoral thesis. I stayed holed up in my academic ivory tower, trying hard to concentrate on my work.

* * *

Tonda was a bachelor in his late thirties. Before long we became friends, and he would drop in often for a chat. He worked in an ammunition factory and was the first Czech proletarian I got to know closely. He was active in the Czech labor movement and an intelligent man. I was grateful to him for telling me about the mood of working people. It was heartening to hear that they stood united behind President Beneš and were ready to fight against German military aggression.

In September 1938 the crisis seemed to be nearing a climax. Under British and French pressure Beneš agreed to arbitration and a plebiscite in the disputed areas, but Hitler rejected this offer and insisted on immediate cession and virtual surrender. His storming at hapless Czechoslovakia became unbearable and Beneš ordered a general mobilization.

I remember vividly that event. It was evening; I was sitting in my room and chatting with Tonda when suddenly we heard an unusual bustle in the street. We walked to the window and saw many people hurrying by. We asked one of the passersby what happened, and without stopping he shouted back, "Haven't you heard it on the radio? Mobilization has just been ordered!"

When Tonda left I tried to go back to my work but was too

excited to concentrate, so I decided to go out. There had been many demonstrations across the country against yielding to Hitler and calling for mobilization. Now that it finally had come, I wanted to see how people reacted to it. I walked for hours through the streets. Groups of people were standing at the corners and talking about the mobilization. Gone was the boisterous excitement of the recent mass demonstrations. There was now rather a relief from the great tension. The Czechs took it with their sober sense of realism. Reservists came out of the houses with knapsacks or small valises, each of them hurrying to report to his military unit.

I returned home long after midnight. I tried to fall asleep, but sleep would not come. My heart was filled with concern over what was going to happen; the military odds were not exactly in our favor. Would the Western democracies stand by us? I had no military training whatsoever, but my conscience was bothering me; I felt that I could not remain a mere bystander in this fateful fight for the independence of my country.

In the morning I went to the Špilberk. It was the first time that I had been inside the old military fortress, in whose dungeons famous revolutionaries from all corners of the Hapsburg Monarchy had been tortured. In the Czechoslovak era it was no longer used as a fortress. I knew it only as a large wooded hill in the middle of the city, with a beautiful park at the top, where, at night, the soldiers from the garrison below met with the women of the night.

I did not get a chance to see the mysterious Špilberk dungeons, about which there were so many gruesome tales. Inside I was shown to a well-lit office. There was a line of men of all ages who had come there for the same reason I had—to offer their services to the army. I filled out a questionnaire. The major read it and told me to go home, back to my work, and wait to hear from him.

* * *

The tragic events of the Munich Appeasement are well known, and there is no need for me to elaborate on them. The Czech Army stood ready in strong border fortifications, and the government and people were willing to withstand Hitler. I believe that if Britain and France had rallied to our side then, the horrors of World War II would have been prevented.

To the misfortune of the world, however, the mediocre and nearsighted Chamberlain and Daladier left us in the lurch and made their pilgrimage to Hitler's Canossa. On September 30, 1938, they handed Hilter the only democratic state in Central Europe. The Munich tragedy was defined most succinctly by Beneš. "Our friends have decided without us against us." Chamberlain said with incredible fatuity that "If we have to fight it must be on larger issues." And waiving his treaty with Hitler upon his return to London, he declared, "I bring you peace with honor. I believe it is peace in our time." But Churchill warned prophetically that "Britain and France had to choose between war and dishonor. They chose dishonor. They will have war."

The aftermath of Munich was disastrous for Czechoslovakia. Despite his solemn promises that he did not want "one single Czech," Hitler annexed many regions with a decidedly Czech population, going beyond the frontiers allotted to him in the Munich Agreement. He cut through the communications arteries and disrupted the economy of the country, deliberately rendering her entirely dependent on Germany.

President Beneš resigned shortly after Munich and left for voluntary exile in the West. Czechoslovakia moved into the period of the Second Republic, as the truncated state was called in the half year between Munich and total occupation by Hitler.

The Second Republic did not write a glorious chapter in modern Czech history. The Munich tragedy shook the nation to its very foundations. Bitterly disappointed after the betrayal by the Western democracies, the Czechs turned their backs on the heritage of Masaryk and Beneš and renounced democracy. Cynicism began to erode the moral fiber of the national soul.

A new, reactionary government willingly fulfilled every German wish. Dubious characters of the lunatic rightist fringe took over the press and radio and dominated public life in general. It was distressing to observe the entire political climate change. Saddest of all, many former staunch democrats, totally demoralized, became turncoats.

Simultaneously, intensive anti-Semitic propaganda began.

The Jews were blamed for the entire Munich tragedy. Beneš and Masaryk were branded as "traitorous Jewish lackeys" who had led the nation down the path of democracy instead of moving to the side of Hitler, who—strange reasoning indeed—would have spared the Czechs. The Jews were the most convenient scapegoat to be thrown as a peace offering into the jaws of the Nazi Moloch. More and more anti-Jewish restrictions were gradually introduced into all facets of life.

The first victims of Munich were the Jews expelled from the territory annexed by Hitler immediately following the occupation. While the Czechs who fled from those regions were met as brothers and given all help to resettle in new places, the nearly 45,000 Jews were received with icy indifference, as if they were strangers and not citizens. Thus they were given to understand that they were not welcome any longer in their own country.

* * *

The oppression and humiliation of a nation brings out the worst and at the same time the best in people. The behavior of the Czechs toward the Jews in those days could be used as a barometer of moral standards. Most Czechs remained rational and did not forget who their real enemies were. But too many vented their suppressed hatred of the Germans on their helpless Jewish neighbors. Gradually the anti-Semitic mood in the Second Republic spread, and often one could hear cynical remarks and anti-Jewish insults.

I recall one unpleasant personal experience. There was a grocery store near us where we usually shopped. Some time after Munich I came in and remarked innocently how rapidly the prices were soaring lately. The owner, whom I had known as a quiet, friendly, middle-aged man, blurted out, "The cheek you have! You think you still live in your Jew-dominated First Republic. If you Jews don't like it here, why don't you all go to the traitor Beneš who ran away like a coward from the wrath of the Czech patriots?"

Far more saddening to me was the change in Tonda. Soon after Munich he began to avoid me. He barely responded to my greeting when we met occasionally in the corridor. Seeing that he was cool and aloof, I left him alone; I assumed that he was too overwhelmed by the national misfortune. One evening in November he came in unexpectedly. I noticed, however, that he felt uneasy. After some embarrassment he began. "You know that my mother and I have been taking a risk in letting you live with us. The neighbors call us 'Jew-lovers'. You'll have to pay a much higher rent."

I would have been less shocked if he had simply asked us to move. I might have interpreted it as a forced step to provide himself with an alibi in view of his past pro-Beneš activities. But to take advantage of our plight to extort more money from us— could this be the same Tonda as on the evening of mobilization? I was sad, shaken, but I controlled myself and said, "You don't have to worry; we'll move out as fast as we can."

In the next few days we moved back to our previous apartment, in the house of a Jewish family. It was far from the university and caused me much inconvenience, but I had become frightened of the nice Tondas.

Life for the Jews grew increasingly difficult. Every day there were new anti-Jewish restrictions in all facets of the economy, culture and education. At Masaryk University the policy was not uniform. While Ida, like all other Jewish students, had been expelled from the Medical College not long after Munich, the Philosophy Faculty, where I studied, resisted the introduction of the anti-Jewish laws even after the invasion.

* * *

The Jews themselves were divided in a broad spectrum of opinion, from the dark pessimists who tried to emigrate but could find no country that would admit them to the incurable optimists who went on believing that things were going to turn out alright in the end. How wide the divergence of outlook on the situation was, I had a chance to witness one evening in January 1939 at a social gathering of the faculty of the Jewish Gymnasium.

Some of my colleagues had been my teachers when I was a student at that school. After years of teaching there I still showed them the highest deference and did not want to rebut their views. There were among them wise professors and noted scholars in their fields, some of them leaders in Jewish life. But much of the talk I heard that evening stunned me by its naiveté.

One did not have to go far for proof to substantiate the suspicions that Hitler had evil designs on the rest of Czechoslovakia. I would like, however, to mention the story told by Braun, the teacher of Czech. He had just returned from a visit to a Moravian town, situated on the new border with Germany. He related that while the Czechs had put up a custom-house and other border markers immediately after Munich, the Germans failed to do so on their side. This was not an isolated case; it was the same all along the new frontiers. The people on the new borders deduced from it that the Germans did not want to bother putting up temporary buildings because they intended to occupy the whole country.

I remember the condescending smiles with which the wise professors received the young teacher's story. This and similar arguments of a few other teachers, who came out in support of Braun, were shrugged off as panicky conjectures. Berger, my mathematics and physics teacher, said, with his customary rashness, "That 'miserable corporal' would never dare to invade our country. Has he forgotten that France and Britain have guaranteed the safety of her new borders?"

He was readily seconded by my Latin professor, Markel, who quipped "It would be foolish of that 'sign painter' to incorporate ten million hostile Slavs when, as things stand now, they are his obedient slaves and out of sight, fulfilling readily all his commands." I noticed that Bruckmann, the director of the gymnasium, became fidgety about the blunt usage of epithets for Hitler. With his usual authority he diplomatically set about to end the touchy discussion. "Gentlemen, let us not jump to conclusions."

At that moment Deckstein, my philosophy professor, began clearing his throat. He was a veteran Zionist, friend of Martin Buber, A.D. Gordon and other contemporary Jewish thinkers. Despite all his theoretical knowledge about society, however, Deckstein remained the epitome of the absent-minded professor. I recall how some mischievous students used to ask him some question in class. Deckstein would launch into a lengthy discourse and be carried off light years away from the reality around him. Meanwhile, one of the students would sneak up to Deckstein's desk and "borrow" his notebook and, upon entering good marks for himself and his accomplices, would stealthily return it to its place. Deckstein never noticed what was going on.

As soon as the director finished, Deckstein began a long talk about the principles of Masaryk's teachings, exhorting us to participate in the struggle for the preservation of those principles. In the light of the sad reality outside, his lofty words sounded so irrelevant. But none of us seemed to have the heart to destroy the respected professor's beautiful world that did not exist anymore.

Suddenly there came an unexpected attack on this dream world. It was Drangsal, the teacher of religion. He mercilessly ripped that world apart. His acid rebuttal included personal insults of Deckstein and others, calling them hypocrits who did not live up to their Zionist preachings.

Drangsal was an eloquent man, but was considered an eccentric. The son of a rabbi in a Moravian town, he had received an ultra-orthodox education in Frankfurt, Germany, and was opposed to all modern ideas in Jewish life. Only those who met his specifications were considered by him to be Jews. I did not particularly care for him. He was conceited and readily became insulting to those who disagreed with him. That evening, however, I grudgingly admired him for having the audacity to shatter naive beliefs and to call things by their right names. His words caused embarrassment, but they also somehow cleared the atmosphere of illusions. A somber mood prevailed as we descended back to the sad reality.

Very few of my colleagues who were present at that gathering survived the Holocaust. The others, including Deckstein, perished in Theresienstadt and other German death camps. Strangely enough, it was Drangsal, to whom Zionism was anathema, who later joined an "illegal" transport to the Jewish Homeland. There, he published a considerable body of literary criticism. But in most of his writings his old prejudices against the *Ostjuden* (Eastern European Jews) prevailed; he criticized Zionist ideas and the literary creations of East European Jewry.

* * *

Despite the naive optimism of the Jewish professors the situation of the Jews in the Second Republic worsened every day. In those gloomy days it was heartening to me to come from the hatred outside into the atmosphere of human decency at the university. I was then in the final stages of completing my studies. My professors showed great understanding in helping me to win the race against time. There were persistent rumors about an impending exclusion of Jews from the Philosophy Faculty too, and I was worried. Who could tell how long they would be able to resist the strong pressure of the authorities?

Toward the end of February 1939 I was notified that my doctoral dissertation had been accepted and that the graduation ceremony was set for March 16. There is no need to describe the relief I felt. In my happiness I forgot the dismal reality and went about inviting friends to the graduation.

There was a curious incident in connection with this. I ran into Kubička, my former professor of Czech at the gymnasium. We were friends, and he was glad to see me after so long a time. He was known as a liberal and, in fact, was one of the few Germans in Brno who remained loyal to the principles of democracy throughout the Nazi occupation.

We chatted for a while, and before parting I invited him to the graduation. The expression on his face changed suddenly and he started glancing warily at the passersby in the street. "The 16th of March, you said? My God, that is after March 14. Can't you change it to an earlier date," he said in a whisper. His cryptic remark puzzled me, and I was about to ask him what he meant, but he hushed me quickly and was looking around in fright. "I have told you already more than is healthy for us," he whispered and left in a hurry.

I racked my brain to guess Kubička's riddle but could not come up with a sensible answer. The solution came about two weeks later. After the German invasion on March 15 it became known that Hitler had long ago set the date of occupation for

March 14. For months already the watchword among the local Germans was "March 14." But the organized Nazi terror was so great that even a friend like Kubička was scared to tell me about the impending occupation. The handwriting on the wall had been visible, but we Jews were too nearsighted to read it.

That Hitler did not keep his appointment with the Germans in Czechoslovakia on the planned date was due to a "minor technical delay." The day before, March 13, he had summoned Beneš's successor to the presidency, Hácha, to Berlin "for negotiations." The optimists among us were elated. "What do you say now?" Dr. Frost said triumphantly as soon as I entered his office. "Haven't I told you that he has no intentions of occupying us; he wants to negotiate."

In Berlin, however, an unexpected snag developed. Hácha refused to sign Hitler's prepared statement by which Czechoslovakia "asked" Germany for her "protection." Hitler became furious and threatened to turn Prague into ruins. The old feeble Hácha fainted and had to be given time to recover. Anyway, there was some delay in coercing Hácha into signing Hitler's sentence of death for Czechoslovakia, and the invasion had to be postponed until the next day.

*   *   *

During the night of March 15, the German panzers and armored vehicles kept rolling into Brno. The helmeted, fully-armed soldiers sat motionless in the trucks. Their taut, expressionless faces made them look to me rather like military statues being transported to some exhibition.

In the morning I went outside. A heavy pall of mourning descended on the city. In front of the houses stood groups of people, their pale faces expressing helpless rage and deep hatred of the Germans. Many were openly weeping for the tragic demise of Czechoslovakia. She existed no longer. Her western provinces were turned by Hitler into a German "Protectorate Bohemia-Moravia." The day before, Slovakia had seceded from the Republic and became a puppet state of Germany. The easternmost province of Carpathoruss, where I was born, was annexed by Hungary.

Despite all the rumors of the past weeks, the occupation came as a shock. But the naive optimism of some Jews even after the *fait accompli* was no less shocking. I passed the house of the Frosts. He stood there among a group of people. He whispered to me, "Don't worry. I have just spoken to a patient of mine higher up. He has it on good authority that the Germans are not going to stay here; they are on their way to Slovakia." I was not in the mood to argue with him.

Later in the morning I collected myself somewhat and went to the University. When I arrived there I was taken aback by the picture I beheld. On each side of the entrance stood a civilian in a brown shirt with a swastika armband and a gunbelt. The brown plague had reached the University.

I braced myself and walked in. The two brownshirts did not bother me, but I felt their hateful glances piercing my face. The one to the left measured me with a haughty smirk. His face seemed familiar to me, but I could not place it at first. Then I remembered: he was one of the German students at the University with whom I had attended the seminar on Goethe's Faust.

I was relieved to see no brownshirts inside. Professor Groh, who was to present me the next day for the bestowal of the Ph.D. degree, thought that the wisest thing to do would be to give me the Diploma without any academic fanfare. I could not have agreed with him more; the face of the Nazi Faust student at the entrance stood before my eyes. I was sure that his friends, without swastikas on their arms, were keeping a sharp eye on what was going on inside.

Arne Novák, the Rector of the University, was a famous scholar. His *History of Czech Literature* was a standard university textbook and used by faculty and students all over the country. Professor Groh decided to submit his proposal to the Rector. We went to see him. He categorically said, "No, the graduation will take place as scheduled; we won't let ourselves be intimidated by the Germans." He consented though to a compromise—to hold the graduation in his office instead of in the big auditorium as usual.

The Goethe student was not at the entrance the following morning; two other brownshirts stood there. It was an off-season graduation, only about a half-dozen doctoral graduates. I was the only Jew among them, one of the last Jews to receive that academic degree from the University. Soon afterwards the racial laws were enforced by the Germans.

There were few people present; who was in the mood then to attend graduations? The customary festive spirit of such occasions was subdued. But our spirits were lifted by the Rector's address. I still remember his words, "The enemy has conquered our land, but he can't take from us our will to remain faithful to the principles of truth, liberty and democracy as taught to us by our illustrious teacher Thomas Masaryk, whose name our University proudly bears."

Like their counterparts at the other Czech universities, the professors and students of Masaryk University remained loyal to democracy and resisted the Nazi spirit even after the invasion. Small wonder that the universities were a thorn in the flesh of the Germans. In 1941, upon the assassination in Prague of the German "Protector" Heydrich by the Czech underground, the universities were closed, thousands of teachers and students massacred, and many more thousands thrown into concentration camps.

I often think of that crucial graduation day and how my martyred professors helped me to get the degree which rewarded years of hard study. Now and then I take out my diploma and look at the signatures of Novák, Groh and Horák. They, like many others of my fine professors, were among those murdered by the Nazis after the Heydrich assassination. I commune with their memory, and my heart mourns their tragic deaths.

* * *

Walking out of the friendly atmosphere of the University, I re-entered the somber reality of the streets. I arrived home and fell into gloomy thoughts. True, I had finally achieved the long-coveted goal, but for its sake I had let slip by the chance to leave in time for America. Now we were suddenly inside the Nazi trap.

That night I left for Prague. There was already a very long line in front of the US Consulate when I arrived there in the morning. When I finally got inside the next day I was told that there was no telling now how long we would have to wait for our visa. But I was in for yet another disappointment. Some time before, we had asked relatives in Leeds, England, to get us a temporary sojourn permit to wait there for our American visa.

As far as we knew, the prospects were good. When I arrived at the British Consulate, I was told, "So sorry. But in view of the changed political conditions we can't grant you the permit without the American visa in your passport."

I returned home discouraged by the bad news in Prague. We realized that the only chance we had left was to go to Ida's parents in Latvia and wait there for the American visa.

There was in Brno an honorary Latvian Consul. In previous years, whenever we went to visit my in-laws, I used to go to him and get the visa right away as a matter of routine. Now, however, I was surprised to hear that he was no longer authorized to issue visas to "Protectorate" citizens. This could be done now, he said, only by the Latvian Foreign Ministry. This was one more setback in my attempts to get out from Hitler's claws. We immediately asked Ida's parents to get the visa from the Foreign Ministry. There was nothing we could do now but wait.

* * *

In the period of the Second Republic most Czech Jews still believed themselves relatively safe and did not seek to emigrate. Then the only ones in urgent need of finding a country to go to were the Jews expelled from the Sudetenland and several thousand Jews from Germany and Austria who, before Munich, had found a haven in democratic Czechoslovakia. But no country had been willing to admit these victims of Hitler.

The British Administration of Palestine had grudgingly issued 1,000 Certificates, a drop in the bucket for the more than 50,000 Jewish refugees whom the government of the Second Republic kept urging to leave as fast as possible. Now and then an international refugee committee would take a small group to Scandinavia—little indeed in view of the need. Thus far nobody had bothered about Czech Jews. In the eyes of the international rescue committees we were not as yet considered refugees.

The occupation, however, turned all of us into virtual refugees. We were suddenly all in the same plight, in need of a place of rescue, but the free countries closed their doors to us. Jews in the "Protectorate," even those who had never before thought of emigration, became overnight experts in world geography and began to study foreign languages. Remote countries, which hitherto had been mere irregularly shaped colored figures in the atlas, suddenly assumed a special importance and were studied as to their political, economic and climatic conditions. The lines at the various consulates grew. Soon a flourishing black market in foreign visas developed. Charlatans professing to have "good connections with the right persons" in consulates with exotic names bilked desperate Jews out of their savings. In most cases those visas turned out to be forgeries or worthless pieces of paper obtained from a consular employee.

A heroic chapter was written in that tragic time by the "illegal" emigration to Palestine. It had started immediately after Munich and continued after the invasion. It was initiated and carried out by men of the Jabotinsky Zionist movement. Brno served as the gathering and departure point of this rescue project, and I had an opportunity to observe it closely. Chartered trains with men, women and children would leave for the Rumanian Black Sea ports. There the refugees embarked on wretched ships, setting out on a journey fraught with hardships and dangers to the shores of the Promised Land. In the dark of the night the refugees were met by the *Irgun* underground and taken ashore secretly.

Thanks to these rescue activities thousands of Jews were saved from the German death camps and brought to safety in the Jewish Homeland. But many more thousands could have been saved if the other Zionist organizations had had the foresight and courage to lend a hand and develop it into a large-scale rescue operation.

*   *   *

The occupation had a paralyzing effect on the Czechs. Since Munich they had tried in vain to please the Germans. They defiled the memory of Masaryk and Beneš and renounced their democratic teachings. The invasion finally convinced them that Hitler's ultimate goal was the eradication of that small Slavic people that the Germans had always considered an obstacle in their traditional *Drang nach Osten*. The Czechs grew concerned over their sheer survival as a nation. The occupation became a personal tragedy to every Czech.

I had a chance to witness how deeply this tragedy affected some Czechs. Jara Mostecký, a promising scholar in his early thirties, was the assistant to the professor for whom I wrote my dissertation. We had become friends, and I got to like him very much; he was the typical product of Masaryk's humanism. Liberal-minded and idealistic, Jara had taken Munich very hard; I could see it in his eyes. But he tried to appear cheerful as before and used to tell me the latest anti-Hitler jokes. Shortly after the invasion he fell sick. When I came to visit him, he said that it was the flu. He displayed his usual cheerfulness, but his eyes betrayed a deep sadness.

The following week I heard that he was taken to the hospital and went to see him. It was not the same Jara. His face was drawn and his cheeks hollow. In the past it was he who used to cheer me up, now I was trying to encourage him. He reacted with a faint smile.

When I returned a week later I became worried about him. He reacted listlessly to my greeting and barely uttered a word. The physicians in the hospital made various tests but could not find anything physically wrong with him. They tried everything, but Jara was sinking gradually, and after a fortnight he died. The doctor shrugged his shoulders. "I simply cannot understand it. He showed no willpower to get well and went out quietly like a candle."

But I understood Jara. His heart was broken and he did not want to go on living; he died from the invasion.

* * *

Jara's death added sadness to my miserable mood. I waited impatiently for our Latvian visa, but the weeks passed and it did not come. Our relatives spared no efforts and in the beginning of May it arrived at last, to my great relief. All that was necessary now in order to begin the tortuous road of visits to the Czech authorities was the Polish transit visa. I had no particular difficulties in getting it.

The formalities required by the Czech officials of Jews who applied for emigration were complex and tedious. First I had to make out a meticulous list (in seven copies!) of all the things we were going to take with us. The number of pieces of each item permitted was extremely limited. During the rounds through the various offices an official—depending on his whim—would cross out some items, so that I had to redo the list several times until it was approved at last. The assessed export duty on each piece was so exorbitant that it practically amounted to rebuying our own personal belongings.

Then came a never-ending process of obtaining various papers and certifications from all sorts of institutions, some of which I had never heard of before. Everywhere I had to fill out long forms and questionnaires (in many copies each) with irrelevant questions. And when I thought that everything was finally in order, somebody somewhere would suddenly discover that I needed still one more paper or seal, and the running about started all over again.

One bureaucrat was horrified when he found out that his subordinate nearly let me get away without submitting receipts that I had paid fees due for hunting and dog licenses. I pleaded with him that I never owned a dog or went hunting, but it was of no avail. I had to waste a few days procuring an official statement that I was not "in arrears" for these licenses. Each office had a bureaucratic method all its own, and all of them together constituted a maze of red tape worthy of a Kafka.

It was distressing indeed to see that, instead of understanding our plight and—as we hoped—making it easier for us to save ourselves from the Nazis, the Czech authorities seemed bent on wearing us out with unnecessary entanglements. The Jewish emigrant was already a nervous wreck before he had to face the Gestapo, which would decide whether he would remain trapped in the Nazi jaws or be permitted to leave.

* * *

As the shock of the occupation wore off somewhat with the passing months, there grew beneath the surface of paralyzing desperation an undercurrent of new hope. The Czechs turned again to Eduard Beneš. The watchword, especially among the students and workers, was "Ed is working hard," meaning that Beneš was trying hard in the democratic West to achieve a new liberation and restoration of the old Republic.

But for us Jews there was no hope here. We were now between the hammer and the anvil. While the Germans "aryanized" our enterprises and stores, the Czech authorities barred us from the schools, prevented us from practicing our professions and eliminated us from cultural life. We were deprived of a living and ostracized from society. We were doomed, with no way out.

The reality was desperate. The Nazi oppression of the Jews progressed with German efficiency, and Gestapo arrests of Jewish leaders and prominent persons became widespread. Moreover, Hitler was already storming at Poland. Strangely enough, in that time of suffering and despair the Jews believed the most fantastic rumors.

One of those rumors, for instance, had it "on good authority" that Roosevelt had persuaded Hitler to withdraw from Czechoslovakia and that Beneš was about to return. It was pathetic to listen to some of my Jewish friends and to watch them clinging to every false hope. "There must come a change for the better," they persisted in order to exhort us to "persevere and stay at our posts." I did not know exactly what "posts" were still left for us or who cared for our staying here. But I did not have the heart to argue with them anymore. I arrived philosophically at the conclusion that living near the crater of a volcano, the best thing perhaps was to be an optimist.

* * *

About mid-June I finally finished the nerve-fraying formalities with the Czech authorities and began to prepare myself for the dreaded gauntlet of the Gestapo.

When I arrived early in the morning at the building in which the Gestapo was housed there was already a long line of people there. While at the Czech offices the waiting Jews still felt more or less at ease and were not afraid of talking to one another, here they stood in silence. It was not only the sight of Gestapo sentries at the entrance and the horror of what might await us inside that frightened us. Now and then local Gestapo informers would intermingle with the people in the lines to listen to what they talked about and to try to involve them in political conversations. Some Jews were arrested upon entering the building and were never seen again.

I had heard many stories told by refugees from Germany and Austria about their experiences with the Gestapo. Some of them were subjected to beatings. I am no hero and don't know how I would have endured physical torture. But the agony I experienced during my ordeal with the Gestapo was not less painful. I had sleepless nights and was often awakened by Ida from a Gestapo nightmare.

Only those who had the misfortune to enter one of the circles of the Gestapo hell—or, for that matter, the hell of its Soviet counterpart, the NKVD—will understand how I felt at the moment when I went inside that dreaded building. I was met by an outpouring of rudeness right away from the uniformed Gestapo man at the lobby desk. He then gave me a slip with the exact time of my arrival and yelled at me not to forget to have the slip signed when leaving the office to which he now sent me.

It is hard to describe the macabre atmosphere in the building. I walked uneasily through the long corridors, knocked on the indicated door, heard a roared "Come in" and entered. A civilian with a military haircut and a freckled, wrinkled face did not bother to answer my greeting; he only cast a hateful glance at me.

I gave him the bundle of papers, and he began leafing through them. Then he set out on a protracted interrogation. From his knowledge of Czech and familiarity with conditions in the town it was obvious that he was a local German who had been groomed long ago for his job as a Nazi commissar for Jewish affairs in his native city. He appeared to be thoroughly acquainted with the nature of all Jewish organizations and institutions and all phases of Jewish life.

There existed in those days an underground railroad which helped people sought by the Gestapo to escape abroad. Many did indeed succeed in going to Poland, especially through the maze of coal mines on the Polish border. During that "interview," as well as the others that followed in the coming weeks, my fellow-townsman grilled me, demanding that I tell him where this or that "Jewish traitor" was hiding. Among the papers I gave him there was a list of organizations and societies I belonged to. He wanted to know about my past political activities, and particularly whether I had held some offices in the student organizations at the University. He used coarse language, richly interspersed with open threats.

He professed great "expertise" in matters of Judaism and

seemed to have read the infamous anti-Semitic pamphlet, *The Protocols of the Elders of Zion*. Seeing that I was a Hebrew teacher, he went into a lengthy discourse about the blood libel, asking me to tell him how we used the Christian blood on Passover. Listening to him was a gruesome experience.

At the end of the sessions he picked out a few documents and tossed them to me. "These damned Czech swine! No wonder. They don't even know how to make out a paper properly." Then he stamped my slip and dimissed me. My "Thank you" and "Goodbye" remained unanswered.

That small slip of paper was part of the sadistic Gestapo scheme and always caused me apprehension. In every office I went to, the exact time of my coming and going was put down on that slip. The Gestapo official at the lobby desk checked the time entries carefully. I had to account to him for the slightest discrepancy and explain where I had been for the extra few minutes, and only then was I permitted to leave.

One such incident happened to me a little later. I got lost in the labyrinth of corridors and could not find the office I was supposed to go to. Anxious about wasting a few minutes I would have a hard time accounting for, I asked information from a burgher passing by whose expression seemed to me peaceable enough. "You dirty Jew! How dare you address me? You had better not stick your crooked nose too much around here," he yelled and walked away. I then realized that I had violated a basic Gestapo rule—that a Jew was allowed to speak only if spoken to.

When I brought the documents to the Czech official in the Judicial Division, he was at a loss to find what was wrong with them. He read and reread them, shrugging his shoulders. The papers stated in simple language that I had never been arrested, tried for a violation of the law or in trouble with the police. He, like myself, knew that, in addition to tormenting a Jew, the Brno Nazi intended to demonstrate his contempt for the inferior Czechs. The official then called in an elderly clerk who, apparently, had started his career in the old Austrian era and asked him to redo the documents.

When I came back for the papers a few days later, I hardly could understand them. They were drawn in a heavy Hapsburg officialese richly embellished with nebulous phraseology that The Good Soldier Schweik would have enjoyed immensely.

I then returned the rewritten documents to the Brno Gestapo official, but he barely glanced at them before putting them into my file. Another interrogation began. The same questions were rehashed. He wanted to know more and more names of my friends and about their "subversive activities against the Reich." A favorite refrain of his was, "Where have you stashed away your money?" When I dared to turn his attention to the receipt in my file confirming that I had handed over to the Reichsbank our valuables and jewelry, including our wedding rings, he burst into cynical laughter. "Don't give me that baloney! All you Brno Jews are wealthy." I became alarmed. Maybe it was only my imagination, but I thought I perceived in his words a concealed hint that a satisfactory bribe would make things easier for me. What would happen, I asked myself with horror, if he became more specific, and then found out that I had no money?

Each of the Gestapo officials had his own method of approach, but all of them pursued the same sadistic cat-and-mouse game. They shouted at you, humiliated you and frayed your soul into shreds until you felt lower than dirt. Their purpose was to knock you off balance and keep you in continuous suspense. My biggest fear during those grillings was that I might succumb to some provocation, lose control and say something that would get me in trouble (I knew that my tormentors were just waiting for such an occasion). I prayed for the spiritual fortitude to remain calm and endure until I received permission to leave the country.

One never could guess whether the "interviewer" intended to conclude the interrogations. The idea was to keep the subject in the dark and turn him into a nervous wreck. Since I never dared to ask even the most innocent indirect question, I did not have the slightest inkling of my prospects. One day when I came to my fellow-townsman, to my surprise he picked up my file and took me to a new interrogator. I felt great relief. In the course of my ordeal with the Gestapo I had gone through the hands of various officials. My German linguistic knowledge helped me before long to judge by the accent from what part of the Reich my tormentor came. There was a large variety, from arrogant

Prussians to moon-faced grandfatherly-looking Austrians (the latter usually proved to be the cruelest), but all had the same goal in mind—to humiliate and torment.

The successor of my fellow-townsman this day was a haughty, monocled Prussian. His approach was cynical and concise. He did not tolerate elaborate explanations and would interrupt me with a brutal command to "get to the point."

The weeks dragged on in agony. July was already coming to an end. My next interrogator was a barrel-chested Bavarian. The pupils of his chilling, ice-gray eyes pierced through me like two spear points. He was always poised like a bird of prey, hoping to trick his victim into an entanglement. My ordeal with the Gestapo was compounded now by my worries over the worsening political situation. Hitler's ranting at Poland increased, and his threats intensified. There was widespread talk of massive German troop movements toward the Polish borders.

The Czechs did not try to conceal their malicious joy at the troubles of the Poles. The memory of the treacherous conduct of the "Slav Brothers" during the Munich crisis and their annexation of the Czech Těšín province was fresh. Apart from this, they were stirred by the prospects that a German military attack on Poland would most likely involve the great powers in a larger war, which would lead in the end to the liberation of their own country.

About that time I visited Dr. Frost. Even this unflinching optimist was now in a gloomy mood. He asked me what we were going to do. I had no answer. "And what are your plans?" I asked. "Oh, we are not worried; my husband is a foreign citizen," his wife said. I was glad for our good friends. I thought that by some stroke of luck Dr. Frost had become a British or U.S. citizen. But Mrs. Frost caught my curious look and elaborated. "Don't you know that my husband was born in Slovakia? We are making preparations to go there shortly.

Slovakia had become a puppet state of the Reich. The situation of the Jews there was actually not much better than in the "Protectorate." The Slovaks were backward Catholics with a long tradition of anti-Semitism. Monsignor Tiso, who headed the government, enthusiastically collaborated with Hitler. In fact, since the "independence" of Slovakia there had already been anti-Jewish riots and pogroms there. Nonetheless, there was not as yet the physical presence of the German Gestapo in Slovakia. The "Protectorate" Jews who were born in Slovakia returned therefore to their places of birth.

Not long after that, the Frosts sold their furniture and office equipment and left for Slovakia. But the Slovaks did not want to admit them, and the Germans refused to let them come back. For about two weeks the Frosts, with their three small children, remained in the no-man's-land on the border until they succeeded somehow in returning to Brno a few days before our departure.

After the war I learned with sadness that the entire family perished in Auschwitz.

*   *   *

One day in the beginning of August I came to the Bavarian sadist for another of his interrogations. When he finished, he tossed a small green card to me and shouted, "Show this to the guard at the entrance and you'll not have to wait in line. Be here on August 14 at 10 A.M. sharp!"

I had never before been given a green card and was puzzled by it. Why should he be suddenly concerned about my waiting in line for hours, I wondered. The suspense became unbearable.

On August 14, when I entered his office with trepidation, the grim Nazi to my great surprise lifted his bulky frame from the chair and thundered, "Come with me!" I walked behind him down the corridor and then up the staircase to the third floor. There the echo of his heavy steps was muffled by a thick rug. He stopped at a leather-panelled door and cleared his throat. I took a glance at the shiny sign on the door—Johann Kesselmann, Head of the Division for Jewish Emigration.

When we entered the office, my companion saluted with a roaring "Heil Hitler," walked up to the desk and placed my file on it. Then he clicked his heels again and marched out of the office.

I remained standing at the door. My heart was beating fast, and I tried hard to compose myself. An athletic-looking man with a swarthy, eagle-nosed face and shiny, thinning hair combed back was busy at the desk. After a while he began leafing through my papers, completely ignoring my presence in the room. By now my heart was pounding wildly, and I felt cold sweat trickling down my spine.

Then—whether after hours or mere minutes I could not tell; time stood still for me—I heard his voice. "Ah, you are going to Riga?" He glanced at me for the first time and beckoned me to come to the desk.

And now something incredible happened. The dreaded Gestapo chief, the mere mention of whose name drove terror into Jewish hearts, motioned me to sit down. For a few moments I was at a loss and hesitated. None of my interrogators had ever before offered me a chair during the long interrogations. But I sat down.

In a voice that sounded quite human he said, "When you arrive in Riga, go to the brothers Eric and Jacob Kitow and give them my regards." Then he began telling me that he went to school with the two Jews and that they were good friends. They were neighbors, and his father was an accountant in the Kitow furniture factory in Berlin. After 1933 he had helped them to leave the Reich with most of their assets.

Kesselmann's stern features softened, and I even thought I saw a tiny smile on his face. While talking about the Kitows, he began stamping and signing my papers. As he came to our passport he stopped for a moment and said, "I see you have a Polish transit visa. I'm afraid you won't be able to take that route anymore. Your only chance to get to Riga is through Germany and Lithuania."

But there was no longer a Lithuanian Consulate in the "Protectorate." He thought for a moment and then stamped into our passport a one-week sojourn permit in the Reich and told me to get the Lithuanian transit visa in Berlin. "Tell Eric and Jacob not to worry about their folks in Berlin; they are being well taken care of," he said. When I thanked him and said goodbye, he remarked in passing, "Try to leave as soon as you can."

* * *

Upon leaving Kesselmann's office my thoughts were confused. When I was outside the dreaded building, I took out the passport and examined it for a long while, pinching myself to make sure I was not dreaming. It all seemed unreal. But there was no time to lose pondering what had happened. I had to get new train tickets. A routine thing once, this too was in these days a difficult matter for a Jew.

I phoned Ida to tell her the good news. First she did not want to believe me, saying not to make such jokes at a time like this. However, when I asked her to start packing right away by herself because I had to hurry to the ČEDOK, the official Czech Travel Bureau, she became nearly hysterical with joy, "It is a miracle! In answer to my fervent prayers." I did not argue with her; maybe she was right, I thought.

In order to purchase foreign tickets, a special permit from the Finance Ministry was necessary. Mr. Wertheim in the ČEDOK helped me to obtain that permit. He was a cultured, fine man, about my age, who came from an assimilated Jewish family with deep roots in the Czech culture, and he was therefore very disappointed with the behavior of the Czechs toward the Jews. He used to like to chat with me about Jewish matters, and we had became friends.

When I came to see him that day, I noticed that he was in a subdued mood. He then confided his worries to me. The other day his boss had told him that he was under pressure to dismiss him. Realizing the urgency of my problem, Wertheim managed to cut the red tape and change the Polish route to one through Germany and Lithuania.

I recall with sadness his last words as we parted that day, "You know, I have been married for over two years. Both my wife and I love children, but we have decided that the best way to solve the 'Jewish Problem' is to stop having children." I was taken aback by his desperate attitude. But in that troubled time nothing could shock me anymore. Some Jews sought refuge in conversion to Christianity (which did not save them, however, from the German death camps). Suicides among Jews grew alarmingly. A period of untold suffering descended on Czech Jewry.

I do not know whether the Wertheims became victims of Hitler's Final Solution of the Jewish Question or survived the Holocaust, or if, for that matter, they carried out their strange private solution to the Jewish Problem.

I hurried home from the ČEDOK. Leaving many important

matters undone and without having a chance to say goodbye to any of our good friends, I hailed a *droshky* and we rushed to the station. I urged the driver to hurry, and by the skin of our teeth we made the evening train to Berlin. As the train pulled out from the terminal and the houses of Brno slid by, I asked myself whether we would ever come back. And the monotonous clatter of the wheels echoed my question until it gradually lulled me to sleep.

THREE

I awoke as we approached the border with the Reich. The Czech customs official hardly looked at the list of belongings and chalked our suitcases without opening any of them. I smiled sadly recalling how much money, worry, paperwork and running about it had cost me to have that list approved. The Gestapo official who checked our passport took a longer than usual look at our faces (or perhaps it only seemed so to me) to discern in them non-Aryan features. But he did not molest us and gave me back the passport without a word.

As sleepy and exhausted as I was, I could not doze off again all through the journey to Berlin. Involuntarily I relived the scene in Kesselmann's office. I was too excited and bewildered to think about it clearly. Maybe Ida was right after all, I told myself, but I was too skeptical to acknowledge the miracle. As our sages say, "He upon whom a miracle is wrought does not realize it."

Later I would reflect a great deal about it. It was, of course, the strange coincidence of Kesselmann's friendship with the Kitows that brought it about. (At that time I did not know the whole story as told to me later in Riga by Eric and Jacob. As Latvian citizens they had managed to get some compensation for their factory, but the money was deposited in a frozen account in a Berlin bank. Through sinister manipulations Kesselmann and his father, who was the Nazi-appointed manager of the Aryanized factory, systematically withdrew substantial sums from the account and pocketed them, occasionally throwing a pittance to the Kitows' in-laws in Berlin. Fearing lest the two Nazis harm their helpless relatives if the withdrawals were blocked, they let Kesselmann go on with his blackmailing.)

In retrospect I have often tried to fathom the deep recesses of the black soul of that Gestapo chief. But to this day I have not quite been able to explain in a rational way why he behaved in a human manner and went out of his way to help me. Only God knows the strange ways of a man's soul. To me, Kesselmann's soul has remained a riddle.

During the night the Gestapo, in uniforms and in plainclothes, walked through the car asking for identity papers. Everything went off without a mishap, and we arrived safely in Berlin that morning.

* * *

It was our first visit to that city. In the unexpected hurry of leaving Brno, it had not occurred to me to find out from friends the name of an acquaintance or place where we could go, so we checked our luggage at the station and decided that Ida should wait for me there until I came back with the visa from the Lithuanian Consulate.

I anticipated that getting the transit visa would be a matter of routine and that we would continue our trip from Berlin the same day. When I came to the consulate, however, I was in for a shock. The secretary told me that our visa application must be sent for approval to the Foreign Ministry in Kaunas. He did not have to draw me a picture. I understood that he was trying to tell me in diplomatic language that his country had now closed its doors tight to Jewish refugees, barring them from even traveling through its territory.

After much begging he agreed to take me to the consul. I appealed to his humanitarian feelings to appreciate our terrible predicament. We were not permitted to return home anymore, and we could stay in Germany only for one week. If he did not help us to get out of the Reich by that time, we would be arrested by the Berlin Gestapo. "By denying us the visa you deprive us of our last chance to save ourselves, and it is tantamount to putting us in a concentration camp. Can your conscience be peaceful knowing that you have failed to help two innocent people escape such a tragic fate?" I concluded in desperation.

The two officials exchanged looks. The consul asked me to wait in his anteroom. I probably did not wait more than 20 minutes, but to me it seemed like an eternity before the secretary opened the door and called me in. The consul told me that he had phoned the Foreign Ministry and was promised that our visa would be cabled as soon as possible. I felt relieved and waited impatiently in the consulate for the arrival of the visa. But by closing time there was no word as yet from Kaunas.

I returned to the station empty-handed and in low spirits. My expectation of getting the visa and leaving Berlin that day had not come true. Moreover, a fear that we might not get the visa at all began gnawing at my heart. What would happen to us then here in the capital of the Third Reich?

For the moment, however, I was faced with an unforeseen and immediate problem—where to sleep. To stay in the station was not safe. The terminal was crowded with soldiers, and from time to time there were checks of identity papers; we might arouse suspicion. For a while I considered going to some hotel. The giant-size letter J (Jew) in glaring red was not as yet stamped inside and outside our passport; nor were "Israel" and "Sarah" inserted before our first names. We could probably pass off as regular Protectorate citizens, I thought. But then I realized that it would be foolhardy to push our luck too far. We finally decided that it would be less dangerous to spend the night riding the subways or sitting in some park.

The August evening was warm and pleasant, and we strolled through the streets. In one of the side streets we noticed an elderly woman with the Star of David on her sleeve passing by on the other sidewalk. At first I was shocked; it was the first time that I had seen a Jewish person in the flesh wearing that medieval yellow badge of humiliation, invented by the Catholic Church. I collected myself quickly, and we crossed the street to catch up with the woman.

First she was wary and afraid to talk to us. When I told her who we were and what our problem was, she gave us the address of a restaurant in a Jewish neighborhood where they might be able to help us. Before I had time to ask her how to get there, she hurried off and soon disappeared in the lengthening shadows cast by the setting sun.

After a long subway ride and a walk through streets of shabby tenements we found the small kosher restaurant, which was located in the basement of an old house. We were in luck; the old couple who owned the place agreed to accommodate us for the night.

As tired as I was, I stayed up very late. The couple told me many saddening stories about the plight of the German Jews since Hitler's seizure of power. They also showed me pictures of their only daughter, who had left for Palestine in 1934. She married there and had two lovely children. With tears in their eyes the old parents kept kissing the snapshots of their *sabra* grandchildren and praying to be united soon with their beloved ones in the Jewish Homeland.

The next morning I went to the consulate long before it opened, in the hope that the cable had arrived during the night—it had not. I waited with growing impatience all day. The secretary kept asssuring me that the cable would arrive any moment. When the consulate doors closed, however, I left again empty-handed and disappointed. I hardly closed an eye that night.

When I heard the following morning that the cable had not arrived, my hope of getting the visa faded. To my chagrin, the consul came very late that morning. When he arrived, he assuaged my fears that some higher official in the Foreign Ministry could have changed his mind and told me that he was positive that everything was in order. Nonetheless, he agreed to call Kaunas again. He was told that the cable was on its way.

There are no words to describe my relief when the cable was finally delivered in the afternoon. I got the visa right away and was overjoyed that the unexpected hurdle on our road to rescue was surmounted. I called Ida immediately to have her meet me at the station as fast as possible.

I had already lived for about half a year under the shadow of the Hakenkreuz and the Gestapo, but the sight of the Führer's face glaring at me from the large posters all around and the swastikas flying from the buildings gave me an eerie feeling. The entire atmosphere in the capital of the Third Reich was tense with war fever. I was anxious to get away from it as soon as possible.

*   *   *

The train that we had to take left from a terminal about two miles away. After many futile attempts I managed to find a taxi, but as the driver began loading our luggage, a Prussian officer showed up and got inside with a stern frown on his face. The cabman shrugged his shoulders and drove off. I gave up looking for a taxi and with difficulty finally found a porter with a hand carriage who was willing to transport our luggage to the train.

On the way to the terminal, however, I had an experience that left a bitter memory.

The porter, a middle-aged man, turned out to be a very talkative fellow. First he asked me where we came from, where we were traveling to and other personal questions. Then he began telling me that he had once worked in a factory, but because of his previous socialist activities the Nazis had fired him and later kept him in a concentration camp for a year. Since then he had to eke out a living as a porter.

I did not know how much truth there was in his hardship stories, but I was afraid to get involved in political talk and changed the subject. Suddenly he stopped the carriage and began sighing that he did not know the load would be so heavy and that I did not pay him enough. Although the agreed upon sum was very exorbitant as it was, I did not want to have trouble with him and promised him to double that sum.

After some time, however, he halted again and scratched his head. "You Jews are very rich but don't show your gratitude to reward those who are helping you to get away from the Nazis." Realizing that he was up to further extortion I did a very foolhardy thing—"If you don't stop your foul play immediately, I'm going to fetch the policeman at the corner!" He began grumbling some filthy insults, but to my surprise he resumed the trip and brought our baggage to the train without any more complaint.

* * *

We were practically the first passengers in the Berlin-Riga car, so we were able to select two facing corner seats at a window. Gradually the car filled up. I felt great relief when the train pulled out from the terminal and, after winding its way through the maze of the Nazi capital, finally reached the countryside and began racing toward the northeast.

The car was crowded by then. Many were sitting on their valises or leaning out from the windows in the corridor. I had hoped to get away from the war atmosphere in Berlin, but here too the topic of conversation was the Polish crisis. There were many soldiers in the car, apparently going to the Polish borders. It was noisy, everyone trying to outdo his neighbors in hurrah-patriotism and clamoring for the command of the Führer "to teach those insolent Polish swine a thorough lesson."

Some Hitler Youth fellows began singing Nazi songs. The atmosphere grew saturated with hatred and lust for war. It became increasingly hard to breathe the poisonous air. We tried to make ourselves as inconspicuous as possible in our corners and decided that the best thing to do was to doze off.

The train made many stops. Most of the military men eventually got off. Toward dusk the bustle and crowdedness ebbed and the agitated talk began to peter out. At one of the stations an elderly couple got in and sat down next to us. They were silent and took no part in the political conversation. It did not escape my notice that from time to time they looked at us sympathetically, and after some time the man began to talk to us. They were returning to Königsberg from a visit with their daughter. He asked me where we came from. "Czech citizens going to visit relatives in Latvia," I said. But I suspected that they knew we were Jewish.

Once during an innocent chat he whispered to me, "It is not good to let one's fear be shown; the more nonchalantly one behaves, the better the chances that nothing is going to happen." These kind people were very helpful to us all through the journey. It was heartening for us to have found two just Germans in the Nazi Sodom. I wondered, however, if I would ever be able to discover the other eight.

As night fell it became quieter in the car. The passengers set about making preparations for sleep. I too dozed off. Later in the night I was awakened by excited voices—"The Danzig Corridor!" There was a bustle; people hurried to shut the windows. The Germans apparently loathed to breathe the Polish air. It was pitch-black outside, but the faces clung to the window panes and the eyes tried to penetrate the darkness of the night.

I sadly recalled the joke I had heard lately that Hitler could not sleep nights because he heard the Poles scurrying about in the Danzig Corridor. Now it did not strike me any longer as a quip; it was bloody real. I felt the hovering of Mars, the ancient Roman god of war, overhead.

The mood in the car had changed as if by the touch of an invisible hand. Gone was the boisterous chatter. The people looked somber and grim. There were only hushed whispers. Our two neighbors were silent, emitting deep sighs from time to time. They probably thought about the suffering in World War I and remembered a fallen father or brother.

The lights of the passing train momentarily reflected on the bayonets and steel helmets of the soldiers on both sides of the Corridor borders. More than any other sight, the eerie glint of weapons in the night convinced me of the reality of imminent war.

As we reentered German territory, the people came to life anew and reopened the windows. The subdued mood vanished, and there was again lively chatter all around. Ida slept throughout the night and woke up only in the morning when the train was already racing across East Prussia.

* * *

In Königsberg most of the passengers, including our two neighbors, got off. By and by new passengers came in. Two middle-aged men with stern Prussian faces sat down next to us. Before long the train continued its route toward the Lithuanian border.

The closer we came to the border, the more intense became my trepidation. Are we going to surmount safely the last German hurdle to freedom, I kept asking myself. When we approached the border, two uniformed Gestapo men and a customs official entered the car and set about checking the passengers' documents and luggage. As one Gestapo officer was examining our passport and papers, he exclaimed to the other two busying themselves opening our suitcases and rummaging in them, "Hey fellows, we seem to have got two Jewish birds here. Do a thorough job!"

He took us to his office in the station where he subjected us to a brutal treatment of which the Brno Gestapo men would have been proud. First we had to empty on his desk the contents of our purses and pockets. The 70-odd marks still left from the amount allowed us for the journey he put immediately into his pocket. Then he searched us in a rough, humiliating manner and shouted, "Where are your gems and foreign currency? You'd better give them to me if you don't want to rot here in jail."

All my explanations were to no avail. He went on shouting and hitting his fist on the desk. Then his colleague came back from the train, and we were ordered to wait outside. Indescribably agonizing minutes passed. The door opened. Our tormentor tossed our passport and documents on the floor and roared, "Go back to your car!"

When we returned to our car, I thought I was going to faint. All our things lay strewn around on the benches and floor. The lining of the clothes was ripped open and the bottoms of the suitcases cut. Even the salami and loaf of bread that we had bought in Berlin for the trip were sliced into small pieces and tossed on the floor so that it all had to be thrown away.

We were just starting to repack our things when the train began moving. Soon it was rolling over a bridge, and before long it halted again. I looked through the window and did not believe my eyes—a Lithuanian flag was flying from the station! I thought I was dreaming. Could it be true?! No more swastikas? No Gestapo?

When the Lithuanian border officials came aboard, I felt like embracing them from happiness. Everything went off politely and smoothly. The customs official looked at the mess our things were in and shrugged his shoulders. He understood without words that it was the "farewell" given to us by the Germans.

The first thing we did after repacking was to look for other seats. When the Gestapo man had made his remark about two Jewish birds, our two Prussian neighbors had joined the laughter of the officials. Anticipating that we were going to be arrested, they'd moved over to our corner seats. When we returned, they looked surprised, but did not move back. I could not stand any longer to see their arrogant faces; they personified to me the German brutality.

* * *

We found seats at the other end of the car. It took me some time to recover from the traumatic experience on the German border. After so many months of fear and humiliation it would take time to get used to the feeling of equality among human beings again and to look people straight in the eye without fear.

For the first time in many days I read a newspaper and chatted freely with the people around me. I made the acquaintance of several Jews who boarded the car at one of the stations. The news I heard was not very encouraging. Lithuania had had its own experience with Hitler in April, when he annexed the Klaipeda region by force. The Polish crisis had gotten worse during the past days, and there was deep concern over possible German aggression against Lithuania.

We were hungry, but all of our food had been ruined by the Nazi brutes on the border. Fortunately I recalled that I had some money in my overcoat pocket, which had remained hanging in the car, and was thus saved from the piracy of the Gestapo man in his station office. I scraped together the single bills and loose change and calculated that we could afford to have a light bite in the dining car of the train.

It was a marvelous feeling to be able to walk into a public place, unhindered by the infamous sign *Juden verboten!* (Jews prohibited) on the door, and to sit down at a table and be served like all other people.

I had not slept in many nights and, feeling extremely tired, I dozed off as soon as night fell and soon sank into a deep, restless sleep. Before long I had a strange dream—first I was in Kesselmann's office, then in the office of my Gestapo tormentor on the border. After a while, bursting into laughter, they began hurling me to one another through the air. Then the two somehow fused into one diabolic monster who suddenly grabbed me and started flying with me after the train. He went on tossing me against the car roofs, and I bounced back to him like a rubber ball until my body was aching all over. Suddenly he dug his claws deep into my flesh. I felt a sharp pain and began begging him to let me go. He shook me violently and shouted, "Ah, you thought you could get away from me!"

I opened my eyes and looked around in bewilderment. Over me stood an elderly man in a strange uniform shaking my shoulder, "Wake up. Your tickets please; I'm the new conductor." My heart pounded heavily, and I was bathed in cold sweat. "You must have had a terrible nightmare, you just went on moaning and whimpering," he said. It was only about midnight. I closed my eyes in the hope of dozing off again, but sleep did not come back for a very long time.

When I woke in the morning and looked through the window at the colorful scenery sliding by, I was surprised at the beauty of God's world. The sun was shining brightly, and everything around looked so peaceful and friendly. The fat Lithuanian cows grazing in the meadows lifted their heads and flicked their tails as if in greeting.

The speed of the train appeared not to be fast enough to carry us to our destination. About noontime we finally reached the Latvian border. All formalities passed smoothly.

I felt very happy; Ida, however, was absolutely transformed. Like the ancient Greek earth goddess Gaia, she too gained new strength and vitality by contact with her native earth. I marveled at her lifted spirits. She would get out of the train at the stations and inquire about friends and relatives she knew who lived there. From time to time she strolled through the cars to look for familiar faces.

Once she returned with a happy smile; she had run into a former classmate at Riga University, who promised to call Ida's parents about our arrival as soon as he got off at the next station. Smelling the scent of home, she was in her element again and kept complaining to me, "It is just to spite me that the train has begun to creep like a lazy snail."

* * *

The air outside was balmy and pleasant, and the azure of the sky was barely marred by sparse patches of white cloud floating high above. In a word, it was a gorgeous Baltic summer afternoon when we finally got off the train at the small station of Skriveri.

The fact of rescue ought to have been ten times over a reason for elation. But standing now on the station platform I suddenly had a strange sensation, as if some tightly wound spring inside me had snapped and the long pent up inner tension was starting to escape. Soon I felt as flaccid as that punctured balloon dropped by a boy from the train, which, after being whirled around for a while by the draft, had come limply to rest between the tracks as a useless piece of rubber.

I was jolted out of my gloomy thoughts by the joyous welcome of Ida's family, who had came to meet us, and I cheerfully participated in the happy exchange of greetings. Old Zalman Mikhalovich loaded our luggage onto his *droshky,* and we set out on the long drive to Jaunjelgava.

During the ride I tried to take part in the animated exchange of news but was not quite successful and remained a peripheral participant, leaving the briefing to Ida. We learned only now how difficult it had been to get our visa. My father-in-law was a respected rabbi and a leader in Jewish affairs. He also took an active part in communal life and for a time had served as vice-mayor of his town. But it took his petitioning the President of the Republic and the intercession of a Jewish Member of Parliament with the Foreign Ministry to obtain a visa for his daughter and her husband. Latvia had shut her doors tight to Jewish refugees.

The road was familiar to me from previous visits. I always liked to ride with Reb Zalman, who reminded me of the East European Jewish coachmen in the stories of Scholem Aleichem and Mendele Mocher Seforim. However, unlike Mendele's talkative coachman, he sat on the coach-box withdrawn and taciturn, hardly uttering a word.

The *droshky* looked even more time-worn now, there were a few more patches on its leather upholstery and the horse appeared older and flabbier. But Reb Zalman himself was as solid and sturdy as when I had seen him last. Only now some additional silver threads were woven into his trimmed beard, and his shoulders seemed a trifle rounder. I stared at his back, but after a while it was the back of the Czech coachman in Brno hurrying with us to the station. Soon it changed into the sturdy back of the extortionist German porter in Berlin.

I was drawn away from my brooding as we entered the forest that held my favorite stretch of the road. There was a mysterious semi-darkness inside. The glaring sun struggled to conquer the shaded shelter, but only here and there did single rays manage to penetrate the leafy maze and spray the ground with golden spots. The refreshing coolness and the abounding beauty of the woods soothed my heart, and for a while I forgot all my troubles. When we came out of the forest, my eyes were dazzled anew by the glaring sun, which poured its gold on the green of the meadows and fields.

After some time the glistening, winding ribbon of the Dvina River came in sight. As we approached the river, the ferry was just departing for the other shore, and we had to wait for its return. I glanced at the evening paper and noticed its date— August 19, 1939. Today was my birthday, and I smiled sadly.

Under normal circumstances the 30th birthday is a milestone in a man's life, pointing the way to a hopeful future. But what was there for me to celebrate? My becoming an uprooted refugee? On that milestone day I saw only the question mark of an unknown future. My gaze wandered to the swimming place on the other shore. The miniature figures of bathers reminded me of the carefree summer days when Ida and I used to swim there.

Once there had been a bridge across the river, but it was destroyed in World War I and never rebuilt. The crossing was done by a creaky wooden pram. I remember the strange impression it made on me when I first saw it in action.

A heavy rope of twisted wires spanned the river. The ends of the pram were fastened by chains to metal rings hanging loosely around the rope. As soon as the *droshky* drove onto the ferry, I used to jump out and walk over to the ferrymen to watch them make the crossing. Their tools were handmade, boomerang-shaped pieces of wood with deep notches on the inside. I marveled at the dexterity with which the teeth of the boomerangs grasped the rope and pulled the pram forward. The clicking of the boomerangs against the steel rope and the clanking of the chains and rings mingled with the creaking of the pram, which groaned under the heavy load of people and vehicles on its back. The wide, majestic Dvina resented the disturbance and lashed out with its waves at the pram, pushing it downstream.

This day, however, I remained sitting in the *droshky,* indifferent to the operations of the ferrymen. I was reliving the painful experiences of the past months and brooding about what the future had in store. I was torn from my thoughts only as the *droshky* stopped in front of my in-laws' house. We walked inside, where a new round of happy welcoming awaited us.

2
Interlude in Latvia

ONE

O UR ARRIVAL CAUSED a sensation in town; people kept dropping in to say hello. Against my will I felt myself back a few
generations to the time when it was the custom in well-to-do East
European Jewish families to marry a daughter to a poor Talmudic scholar. The young couple with their newborn children
would then live for several years with the wife's parents until the
learned son-in-law became a rabbi. The Torah he studied during
that time was the most cherished treasure that his in-laws could
present before the Heavenly Throne.

But my father-in-law, a rabbi himself, hardly needed my recommendation in heaven. Besides, as a tolerant person he did not
mind my studying Kant in addition to the Talmud.

My leisure was soon over. A week after our arrival the Stalin-
Hitler pact was concluded, and on September 1, 1939, Germany
attacked Poland. World War II was on. I was forbidden to seek
gainful employment in Latvia, but through the turn of events
the government itself provided me with work, though not exactly in my field or to my liking. When the war broke out, an
edict was issued that refugees from Hitler must work on farms.

I went first to work for a Jewish farmer near Jaunjelgava. But
apart from the long distance I had to walk, it turned out that
there was practically no work for me on the small dairy farm. I
then went to work in the fields of the local Baptist Church. I was
not used to hard work but made every effort to keep abreast of
the seasoned laborers.

The minister was a kind and modest man, so different from

44

the magisterial Catholic priests and the stern Lutheran pastors I had seen. He worked with us in the fields and helped me in every way to overcome the hardships of the exacting labor. I spoke no Latvian as yet, but my gymnasium English enabled me to converse with him about religious and philosophical questions. He had been trained for the ministry somewhere in Indiana and told me a great deal about life in America.

I had known this town somewhat from my previous visits, but during the months I now spent there, I got to know the people and their town well. I gained many fascinating impressions of life in an East European town, a colorful Jewish world later wiped out forever by Hitler. Some of the characteristic figures among the intelligentsia and common people have remained in my memory.

There was Dr. Herzberg; a mischievous fire lit the eyes of the dignified octogenarian when he told his favorite story. Being barred as a Jew from studying medicine in Czarist Russia, he went to the University of Leipzig. Later he became very sick. His mother came to Leipzig, and a famous heart specialist at the university told her that her son had an organic heart disease and could not endure the strain of the study of medicine. He advised her to take him home and give him all possible care if she wanted him to live. He refused to listen and went on with his studies.

"And you know what happened?" he concluded his story with a boyish wink. "Months later the famous professor died in his sleep from a heart attack, but I am still alive and kicking."

Dr. Herzberg was already hard of hearing and spoke to people in a loud voice. At first I was embarrassed. After getting to know him, however, I saw that he was a kind and gentle man. In dealing with a patient the doctor's word was law, not to be questioned. Nonetheless, he was the favorite physician in town, and his waiting room was full. Quiet reigned there, as in a church. Even the children spoke in whispers.

Between 12 and 2 P.M. passersby tiptoed past his windows, and even the young boys moved their noisy games to the farthest end of the street knowing the old doctor was napping.

Dr. Herzberg's closest friend was his old classmate Herr Hartmann (nobody ever omitted the "Herr" even in his absence), a

German who was a very popular and respected figure in the Jewish community as well. He belonged to one of the oldest families in town. In the Czarist era he had been the principal of the Jewish school. The Latvian regime pensioned him, but he continued to teach German at the Hebrew school.

He used to drop in for a chat at my in-laws', and I enjoyed talking with him. He was versatile in world literature and could recite by heart the poems of Goethe, Heine and Schiller. His hatred of the Nazis was ferocious. When the Baltic Germans were repatriated by Hitler to the Reich, the Hartmann family refused to leave.

Each time I saw Dr. Herzberg and Herr Hartmann on their daily walk, I was inadvertently reminded of Chekhov's delightful stories. The two old gentlemen seemed like two characters just stepping out of the pages of his books, Dr. Herzberg walking slowly and pointing somewhere with his silver-knobbed cane, sprightly Herr Hartmann at his side.

* * *

A figure of a different type was Martin Luther, a Latvianized German who was the principal of a Latvian school. He was in the habit of dropping in at any time of the day or evening. Literature did not interest him; his favorite topic of conversation was politics. He was a tall, fat man with chronic asthma. He drank like a fish but could hold his liquor. As soon as he came in, my folks would put a bottle of brandy on the table, to which he helped himself often and generously. `

Luther was a troubled person. He was a great admirer of Churchill and loathed Hitler. It was a time of anguish; the Western powers were watching as Hitler and Stalin dismembered Poland. "What is Churchill doing?! The democratic world lets the Nazis and Bolsheviks take over all Europe." Luther was close to tears.

Whenever he stormed in, panting heavily with excitement, I knew that a new international calamity had occurred. On November 30, 1939, when the USSR attacked Finland, he came in late in the evening. He looked desperate. "What are you Westerners doing?" His bitter reproach was, of course, directed to me, the "Westerner," as if I were too lazy to use my influence with Churchill to stay Stalin's hand.

(Later, in 1941, Luther and the Hartmanns were among the many intellectuals and prominent persons of all nationalities in town to be shipped off by the NKVD to Siberian labor camps.)

* * *

Fräulein Ehrlich was supposedly descended from an impoverished Teutonic Baronial family that had founded the town a few centuries before (the Germans called it Friedrichstadt). She was in her seventies and lived alone in a dilapidated stone house. On our previous visits Ida never forgot to go to see her; she had been Ida's music teacher. She drew a tiny pension as a former schoolteacher and was practically starving. But she indignantly refused to accept public welfare or support from friends. In order to direct some help her way, my mother-in-law and other kindhearted Jewish women made their daughters take piano lessons from her.

Several days after our arrival there was suddenly an uproar in our house. "Fräulein Ehrlich is coming!" I looked through the window and saw a tall, slender, feminine figure approaching the house. It was hot outside, but her face was covered with a black gauze veil descending from a wide-brimmed hat. One hand adroitly held the train of the barrel-shaped dress, while in the other hand there was a multicolored parasol. She walked in gayly, shaking her black-gloved finger at Ida. "It is not nice of the favorite pupil not to come to visit her old teacher."

Upon exchanging embraces with the womenfolk she sat down and tea was served from a boiling samovar standing on the table. Everything about her had an aura of the old noblesse oblige. She poured the steaming liquid from her glass into the saucer and sipped it quietly through a piece of hard sugar. Occasionally she helped herself to jam and cake.

* * *

Before World War I Jaunjelgava had been a prosperous town with a large Jewish community. With the outbreak of that war, however, the town's Jews, like the entire Jewish population from all the border regions, were deported by the Czarist government to the interior of Russia. Many of the deported Jews perished in exile from starvation and cold, and only some of the survivors returned home after the war. The others preferred to settle down in the larger cities.

The town itself had been nearly destroyed in the battles between the Czarist and German armies. Even in my time the streets bore the scars of burned-out buildings and rubble-filled lots. The Jewish community was a skeleton, a shadow of its past. Most of the indigenous families were gone. The decline of the material and spiritual qualities in the life of East European Jewry since World War I was quite apparent to me in Jaunjelgava, or Neiri (short for New Riga), as the Jews called it.

I remember the early mornings when I used to go with my father-in-law to the synagogue. From the open windows of the houses we passed, the melodious chants of morning prayers and Psalms floated out. I used to halt and listen with fascination to the homage these hard-working Jews paid to their Creator before hurrying off to their daily tasks.

But there were also a few rotten apples in the barrel. Reading Isaac Babel's stories about the Jewish underworld characters of Odessa, I thought they were mere fiction. I simply could not believe that Jewish hoodlums or gangsters existed. During my stay in Neiri, however, I was shocked to learn that there really were Jewish hoodlums.

There was a clandestine Robin Hood-like brotherhood of all nationalities in the vicinity. Its brains were Meiremke and Motke. From time to time the gang carried out a burglary or holdup. The victims were warned not to contact the police, and, strangely enough, they seldom did. If they paid the ransom money, which usually was reasonable, everything would be returned to them in order. Occasionally some gang members were arrested, but they would soon be released; the gang leaders had proper connections with the police. After each successful feat, the gang celebrated with feasting and drinking.

The trouble in town began when Motke and Meiremke, who got rich by their booty, eventually tried to take over the leadership in the Jewish community. Used to bribing and arm twisting, they organized an opposition group. The sad thing was that the

tiny Bund organization joined hands with them. In their fanat-
ical hatred of religion and Hebrew, the Bundists strove to
change the Hebrew school into a socialist secular Yiddishist one.

Meiremke and Motke with their Bundist friends resorted to
the meanest intrigues and calumnies in order to embitter the life
of my father-in-law, who was the principal of the Hebrew school.
The overwhelming majority of the parents, however, were honest people and loathed the leftist Yiddishist gang. They wanted
to give their children a proper Jewish education and stood by my
father-in-law.

* * *

Living in the house of the rabbi of the town, I had a good
opportunity to observe the pulsation in the life of the community and the various problems of the people. One such problem
that has remained in my memory was Kusielke, the sexton and
reader of the Torah in the Big Synagogue, and his wife Nekhe.

Both of them were pathetic figures, right out of a Sholem
Aleichem story. He was short and slender, with a few tufts of hair
growing on his chin and cheeks, each hair shooting wildly in a
different direction, as if to prove its independence from the
weak Kusielke. He read the Torah with a thin, androgynous-
sounding voice. Nekhe was nearly two heads taller than he,
broad-shouldered and moon-faced, with a strong double chin.
In her wide, ankle-length dress, which looked out of fashion
even in that East European town, she looked even more substantial than she really was.

There were constant quarrels between the couple. They were
childless and went on blaming one another for their misfortune.
Occasionally the quarreling reached a climax. Kusielke would
come running all excited to ask my father-in-law to get him a
divorce. Soon the subdued Nekhe would appear and join her
husband in my father-in-law's study.

One could hear the whining Kusielke telling for the nth time
the story that was so similar to Laban's swapping daughters on
Jacob. "Her father promised me her younger beautiful sister,
but gave me instead this barren virago." Nekhe would break out
in bitter crying, swearing by the sacred memory of her parents
that she was the most beautiful of all her sisters.

The rabbi usually succeeded in composing the quarrel and before long the couple came out from the study. Their heads lowered, they walked together—he shuffling one foot after the other, and she wobbling alongside him like a fattened goose. With my inner eye I see that unhappy couple walking in the same manner to their tragic deaths in the Holocaust at the hands of the bestial German or Latvian murderers.

TWO

In October 1939 Soviet troops were stationed in Latvia. To be sure, Moscow solemnly promised that it would not interfere in the internal affairs of the country. But it was clear from the outset that it augured basic political changes in government and in the entire life of Latvia.

For me personally, though, that event brought immediate changes. The edict of compulsory agricultural work for refugees was rescinded, and I stopped working on the Baptist farm. What is more, the employment prohibition for refugees was practically abolished. But there was no chance to find work in my field in this small town, and so we moved to Riga, the capital of Latvia.

Before parting, however, with my Jaunjelgava period, I would like to relate in brief one more episode which is connected both with that town and with Riga.

Before World War I there lived in Jaunjelgava a prominent family by the name of Malish. The youngest son, Leib, however, did not follow the traditional way of life of his parents and was considered the black sheep of the family. One day Leib ran away to Riga where he became a coachman.

During the war he made the acquintance of high Czarist army officers who used his services as cabman. Being an energetic young man he won their confidence and eventually became a large-scale supplier of grain and forage provisions for the Russian Army. He made a fabulous fortune, and after the First World War he wound up owning a few factories and whole blocks of tenements in Riga.

But he never forgot his humble beginnings. His cabman's cap and whip hung on the wall over his bed. Getting up in the morning, he would put on the cap and walk around in the bedroom, lashing noisily with the whip. "Hey Leib, don't you forget what you once were! Don't let your gold seal your heart to the poor!" He became a great philanthropist and never turned down anyone in need who came for help.

Leib came every year to Jaunjelgava to visit his parents' graves. He rebuilt the synagogue and Talmud Torah which had been destroyed in World War I and made generous contributions to charitable institutions. He died before I first came to Latvia, but on one of our visits to Riga my mother-in-law took Ida and me to the Malish family house. Leib's whip and cap were still hanging in their place in the bedroom.

* * *

In Riga we took a small room and I began to look around for work. Ida's family had connections in the area of Jewish education, but there were no prospects of finding work there. Rapid changes in the Hebrew school system had taken place since the arrival of the Soviet troops, and its entire future was uncertain. All I managed to get was a couple of private tutoring lessons—far from enough for our barest needs

One day as I was walking home disappointed and tired from looking for work, I passed a Trade Union Employment Office and decided to go in. I was in luck; they had a job for me at "Turiba." The next morning I reported for work.

Turiba, a state-owned company exporting fodder, grain and other agricultural products, was located at the railroad freight station. My work consisted of loading and unloading freight cars. The work was back breaking. After a few hours my body was aching all over and the skin on my shoulders was bruised. But I watched my seasoned colleagues putting a couple of empty sacks under the heavy load and balancing it easily on their shoulders. I tried to do the same and found that it was now easier indeed to carry the heavy sacks.

After work the manager called me to his office and filled out my papers. To his question where I had worked before, I answered on a farm. I actually told him the truth. Only, fearing lest it might affect my labor qualifications, I neglected to volunteer that I was by profession a teacher with a Ph.D. degree. He gave me a Labor Union card, and I was proud of my dazzling career in Riga. In Jaunjelgava I was a plain farmhand, but here I became a member of the elite proletarian class, now in the ascendancy with the rising dawn of the new order in Latvia.

I adjusted gradually to the work and was accepted by my fellow workers and learned to speak Latvian from them. Listening to their talk, I realized how deep their hatred of the Russians was. Hatred of the oppressors had begun in the Czarist era, but the great stimulus was Soviet cynicism.

Formerly the firm's exports had gone to Western countries; now it was diverted entirely to the Soviet Union. On the empty freight cars returning to Riga from Russia was still legible in the chalked giant Cyrillic lettering—"For the Starving Working Masses in Latvia." This perverted propaganda trick, meant for use in Russia to stimulate the workers to tighten their belts in order to feed the "starving" proletariat in Latvia, deprived Stalin of the sympathies of those Latvian workers who might have appreciated his freeing them from the semifascist Ulmanis dictatorship.

This and similar cynical Soviet lies added insult to the injury of the people; they were not deceived by them. The emaciated faces of the Soviet soldiers and civilians (to be sent on a *komandirovka*, or an official business trip, to Latvia was a privilege for deserving Party members only), who descended like locusts on stores and bought up everything in sight, told us about conditions in Russia more eloquently than all Stalinist propaganda.

* * *

One day an accident happened. My left hand was caught in the heavy sliding door of the freight car we were loading. My fingers were mauled badly and bled profusely. I was taken immediately to a clinic. The doctor examined my hand; I was lucky—no bones were broken. He bandaged the hand and sent me home.

Seeing me walk in during working hours with a bandaged hand hanging in a sling, Ida became panicky and burst out crying. She did not know the nature of my work at Turiba; I had told her that it was office work. But now the truth came out, and she cried even more.

I stayed home for about two weeks. Every other day I went to the clinic for treatment. The rest of the time I could look around again for work in my field, but the prospects now were even gloomier than ever.

Since the founding of Latvia after World War I, the Jews, like the other national minorities, had a certain cultural autonomy and their own schools, which were financed by the government. An extensive net of schools with Hebrew as the language of instruction was administered by a Jewish School Department at the Ministry of Education. During the past weeks, however, that Department had been taken over by the *Yevsektsia*, a handful of fanatic Jewish Communists. The Hebrew schools were to be converted into Yiddishist ones and "unreliable" teachers dismissed. It became clear to me that I did not have a ghost of a chance to get a position there now and gave up trying. I was soon to meet two such hard-boiled *Yevsektsia* characters unexpectedly. Wolf was the son of my mother-in-law's sister. Once a bashful Yeshiva student, he later became a communist. His parents were pious people, and his brothers and sisters were active in Jewish organizations. Only the younger sister, Eva, had been converted by Wolf to communism.

One day Wolf had been caught red-handed while distributing Communist leaflets among the soldiers at the military fortress in Dvinsk. The charge was treason and subverting the army, which could have entailed a death sentence. My father-in-law's efforts greatly contributed to Wolf's getting off with a prison term of several years. Typical of Wolf's ideological fanaticism, however, was the fact that when my father-in-law had attended the trial, Wolf refused to talk to him and only cast a contemptuous look at him.

He came out of prison an even more hardened communist. He married, and when the first girl was born, named her Biro-Bidjan, after the Far Eastern Siberian region allotted by the Soviets as a "Jewish Autonomous Republic."

I had never before met Wolf; he kept aloof from my relatives. Eva, on the other hand, remained friendly with Ida's family, and I had seen her on earlier visits to Latvia. Shortly after our moving to Riga she asked me to give her German lessons. One evening during the lesson, Wolf and another man came in unexpectedly. Eva introduced me to them. Wolf barely said hello to me and did not bother to ask how Ida and I were.

His friend, however, proved to be a very inquisitive fellow. Hearing who I was, he let loose in flowery Hebrew. "Shalom to you, Sir! I trust that the sun on your horizon is shining brightly." The sarcasm of his addressing me in Hebrew was obvious, but I controlled myself and answered him in Hebrew. He then asked me about my bandaged hand. When he heard how it happened, he remarked bitingly, "Well, it is about time for the rotten Zionist intelligentsia to toil in the sweat of their brow and help build socialism."

It turned out that he had once been a leader of the *Shomer Hatzair* movement in Latvia. Later he had gone to Palestine and lived on a kibbutz. But then he became a communist and returned to Latvia. Later he was arrested for illegal Communist activities and sat in prison together with Wolf. That unexpected meeting was a most unpleasant experience for me. It was also my last lesson with Eva. As badly as I needed the money, I was afraid lest I meet those two characters again.

Eva did not wear a leather jacket or high boots, the distinctive apparel of a communist Amazon. She dressed as elegantly as any other Riga bourgeois girl and had a good position as an accountant in a fur export firm. When the firm was later nationalized, she was appointed manager.

I never saw Eva or Wolf again. When the Germans occupied Riga, she was among the first to be massacred. Wolf escaped to Russia. (Interestingly enough, his daughter, Biro-Bidjan, emigrated recently from Russia to Israel.)

* * *

One day as I was walking home from the clinic, I ran into a man who seemed familiar. He too turned around, and we looked at each other for a moment. Then I recognized him—it was Pelzer, who had studied years ago in Prague, where we belonged to the same Zionist student organization. We stopped to chat. He told me that upon returning to Latvia he could not, as a Jew, get work in his profession and had to work in his father's store. Only recently had he found a position as an engineer in a factory. He asked me what happened to my hand. I told him about my work in Turiba and that I had looked around in vain for work in my own field. "Wait a moment," he said, "I have a friend who might be able to help you." He then told me that a classmate of his from the gymnasium was now the Head of the Department of Higher Education at the Ministry of Education and that he would talk to him and get in touch with me.

My hand was not healed as yet, but I needed the money very badly and went back to work in Turiba. The manager was hesitant at first to let me resume work too soon, but I promised to stay away from the freight car doors. He assigned me to lighter work.

One evening in January 1940 Pelzer dropped in unexpectedly to tell me that he had made an appointment for me with his friend Macis. When I met Macis I was pleasantly surprised. I knew from Pelzer that during the Ulmanis regime Macis spent several years in prison because of his Communist activities. But unlike the embittered Jewish *Yevseks,* he turned out to be a friendly human being. He was a recognized Latvian poet, and our meeting turned into a leisurely literary chat. He was familiar with contemporary Czech literature. In particular, however, he admired the tender lyricism of Ottokar Fischer and was delighted to hear that I had been a student of that remarkable poet at Prague University.

Meeting Macis was a great experience for me. He was warm, and showed deep understanding of my situation. "I hope to have good news for you soon," he said as I left. (Macis made a brilliant political career. Before long he became Minister of Education, and during the war he headed the Latvian Government in exile in the USSR.)

I continued my work in Turiba. About one week later the manager called me to his office; there was a telephone call for me from the Ministry of Education. It was Macis's secretary, who asked me to come to see him at once.

On the way to the Ministry some disquieting thoughts came into my mind. Maybe I was pushing my luck too much. After all, I was a Hitler refugee, with an "undesirable" political past, added to which I was the son-in-law of a rabbi and Zionist leader, hardly recommendations for a sensitive job in the Ministry of

Education of a Communist regime. An even darker thought assailed me: maybe they were aware of all that, and it was a trap to get me to the Ministry to arrest me. I decided to phone Ida so that in case I did not come home on time, she would know where to look for me.

My anxiety, however, was dissipated as soon as I came to Macis's secretary. He was very friendly and took me in to Macis, who gave me a letter to the Director of the Institute of Foreign Languages and told me to go there right away.

*   *   *

The Institute of Foreign Languages was affiliated with Riga University. When the secretary took me to the Director's office, she said "Comrade Director, this is the German teacher about whom Comrade Macis spoke to you." I gave Macis's letter to the Director, Zoya Weiss. She was a good-looking woman, about 40. The delicate tint of her alabaster skin, her raven-black hair and hazel eyes lent her the grace of a Grecian goddess. We talked for a long time about my professional training and experience, but she asked me no questions about my political background. Then she said, "The spring semester is beginning soon. Do you want to start teaching right away?"

Do I want?! My heart was bursting with happiness. It sounded too good to be true—to be able to work again in my profession. When I began teaching there I felt born anew. My dignity was restored.

The new administration of the Institute had purged the pro-fascist elements, and new teachers were hired. The classes were expanded, and tuition was suspended in order to admit those who, during the previous regime, had been deprived of a higher education for political or racial reasons.

I studied Latvian diligently and did my best to adjust to the atmosphere of the Institute. Zoya Weiss, new there herself, was always considerate and very helpful to me. The pay was good, and my financial situation improved greatly.

Not long after starting work at the Institute, Zoya sent me to teach two evenings a week at the DKA (Red Army House). I liked teaching there very much. My students were officers of high rank and *politruks* (political army instructors). The Red Army had ordered its officers to study German intensively, and my students were eager to learn. I enjoyed chatting with them; they were the first Soviet people I had met, and it was an interesting experience. I was pleasantly surprised by their friendliness and simple behavior, so refreshingly different from the rigid caste consciousness and rank pulling among the officer corps of other armies, not to speak of the haughty arrogance of the German officers.

In addition to this class, I also had at the DKA a very important and interesting student, General Lubchenko, the Advocate General of the Soviet forces in Latvia. His high rank entitled him to private tutoring, and I went to his home twice a week. In the beginning I felt uneasy with him, but before long I found that he was a warm person, and eventually we became friends. He was in his fifties and, apparently, had received his education in the Czarist era, so he appreciated my European background.

(Later General Lubchenko helped me a great deal in times of trouble. Toward the end of the war I read with great satisfaction that my former student was the prosecutor in the first trials of the Nazi war criminals in the liberated Soviet territories.)

I made many friends among the officers at the DKA. One of them was Major Logunov, the academic dean of the Military College, which had been moved to Riga from Pskov, Russia. (For practical purposes, I'll henceforth use its Russian initials, VU, from *Voyennoye Uchilishche*.) One evening, shortly after I started to teach at the DKA, he asked me if I was interested in organizing German classes at his school. I gladly accepted his proposition and went there next morning. Logunov took me to the commander, Colonel Ryabov, and I was hired immediately.

I set to work right away at that school, and it eventually became my principal job. The salary was fabulous, commensurate with the high pay scale for teachers of higher education in the Soviet Union. From the very outset I struck up a close friendship with both Logunov and Ryabov, who proved to be loyal friends in time of need.

I worked very hard now. Classes at the VU began at 7 A.M. so that I had to get up very early to take the long bus ride to the suburb where the school was located. After finishing work there I would hurry to the Institute and then in the evening to the DKA or to Lubchenko. My working hours usually lasted till 10 P.M., but I felt very happy. Looking back to that period, I consider it one of the most rewarding and fruitful times in my teaching career.

* * *

Despite Soviet promises that the occupation troops would not interfere in the internal affairs of Latvia, it was clear that a Communist takeover was bound to come sooner or later. The press, radio and public life in general gradually switched to a pro-Soviet orientation. There were extensive purges among the ruling hierarchy and officers' corps. Many of them were arrested and quietly deported to Siberia.

The ordinary citizen, however, was not much affected by the changes. True, food and all other commodities became scarcer, and prices skyrocketed. Nonetheless, life in the beautiful city of Riga, called the Baltic Paris, continued to be bearable and even pleasant. In view of Hitler's conquests all over Europe and the bitter suffering of the Jews in the Nazi-occupied countries, one felt safe under the protective wings of the Red Army.

I earned a good salary and indulged again in my passionate hobby of acquiring books. There was then good opportunity for this, for when the Baltic Germans were repatriated to the Reich, entire households, and their livestock and farm equipment, were loaded on German freighters. But Heine, Schiller, Lessing and other German classics were not welcome in the Third Reich. I bought whole sets of these classics and gave them hospitality in my home.

The formal Red *Anschluss* came, to nobody's surprise, in July 1940, when the puppet government "asked" Moscow to accept Latvia as one of the republics of the Soviet Union. An intensive process of sovietization of the economic, social and cultural life began. Overnight, former owners became employees—in some cases, temporary managers—of their expropriated enterprises. The proletarization of the declassed middle class was a difficult social transition, and for many the adjustment was painful.

* * *

During this period I had a tormenting experience. All of a sudden we received a notification from the Reich Consulate to come there with our passport. I became worried and had sleepless nights. There were rumors then about a secret Soviet-German deal to exchange jailed communists in Germany for refugees from Hitler in whom the Gestapo was interested.

It is hard to describe my feeling when I entered the German Consulate and saw the swastikas and pictures of Hitler. They took away our Czech passport and gave us separate Reich passports with a large J stamped in red conspicuously inside and outside. Sarah and Israel, respectively, were added before our first names. It drove the terror of God into my heart. I had hoped to have gotten out of the shadow of the swastika; now, however, I had the feeling that it was creeping after me.

I stopped going to the American Consulate. Even if we had, by some stroke of luck, been given the visa, it would have been of no use to us. After the incorporation of Latvia into the USSR the borders were hermetically closed. I had to resign myself to the new situation and await whatever was in store.

There was talk now of impending arrests of former political leaders, clergy and other "unreliable bourgeois elements." In Jaunjelgava Meiremke and Motke with their Bundist friends were put in charge of community affairs. The Hebrew school was turned into a Yiddishist one, and my father-in-law was removed as principal. He was warned by Latvian friends that he was earmarked for arrest by the Jewish *Yevsektsia,* so they left everything, moved to Riga and took an apartment near us.

* * *

One day shortly after the annexation we got a new Director at the Institute of Foreign Languages. From his outward appearance it was clear that Paltis had just arrived from the Soviet Union. He was lean, with a drawn, stern face. Though no more than 50, his thin hair was as white as snow. He was taciturn and aloof. Zoya, who now became Paltis's assistant, told me that he had fought in the Red Guards during the short-lived Bolshevik Latvian Republic in 1918. Upon its defeat, he fled to Russia, where he had lived since. He had never before worked in the field of education.

In order to assuage the fears of the Latvians about an enforced Russification and to give them the feeling that they were still governed by their own people, the Russians sent back from the Soviet Union reliable Latvians—some of them born there and totally Russianized—to help the handful of Communists at home carry out the sovietization process. A student of mine, the wife of the new Rector of Riga University, with whom she had recently arrived from Russia, told me that her husband hardly spoke a word of Latvian.

Arriving from Russia with Paltis was Zagorsky, the new teacher of the History of Communism and Dialectical Materialism. These fields now became the most important subjects of instruction at the Institute. Zagorsky organized a special course for the teachers and took great pains in "reeducating" us.

Unlike Paltis, he was talkative and outgoing and liked to chat with us in order to sound out our way of political thinking. Once I nearly got into trouble. It was because of the Marr theory. During a private talk Zagorsky asked my opinion about that linguistic theory. In brief, according to Marr, the Semitic and Indo-European groups of languages are only a later stage in the development of Caucasian languages. I told him that, as far as I knew, Marrism was considered by Western linguists as lacking any scientific basis.

He became enraged and interrupted me. "This is not what Comrade Stalin thinks about it! I see that you have still a lot to learn about Marxism." Zagorsky's menacing tone scared me. I went to the University Library to read up on Marrism in Soviet sources. I found out that Marr had been elevated by his fellow Georgian Stalin to a very high pedestal. His theory was proclaimed by Stalin as an "extension of Marxism into the field of linguistics." (In 1950 Stalin suddenly denounced Marrism, and since then it has become an official taboo in the Soviet Union.)

I became very concerned about my "political blunder" and worried about its repercussions. I considered resigning from the Institute and spoke to Zoya about it. She smiled. "You naive Western fool! Don't you know that in the Soviet Union one cannot quit; one can only be fired." She told me not to worry about the incident, that she would speak to Zagorsky. But she advised me to be careful in the future when talking to Soviet comrades.

The first thing I did was to study diligently the Soviet Bible, Stalin's *Short History of the Communist Party,* in order to be prepared for Zagorsky's next private chat. But he never broached the subject of Marrism again. In fact, we eventually became friends and talked often about various topics. Despite all the bragging about the wonderful life in Russia, the newly arrived Soviet people could not help being dazzled by the tremendous difference in the standard of living in Latvia and at home. Even the vociferous *politruk,* Zagorsky, I suspect, must have been asking himself many a vexing question. He was very interested to know about life in the West.

* * *

The VU eventually became my main place of work. I made many friends there. Nobody was curious about my background, nor was I bothered about political theories. But I had an unpleasant experience there concerning a more prosaic matter—money. In the end of July, when I came to the bookkeeper of the VU for my monthly pay, he asked me how much I wanted to subscribe for the *Narodny Zayom* (National Loan). I had never before heard of it. But to show my gratitude to the school I gave him 200 rubles. I was very proud of my contribution.

The next morning Captain Popov, the political commissar of the school, came to see me. We knew each other well. He began to explain the great political and educational significance of the Loan, that it was customary for every Soviet teacher to subscribe annually one month's salary. I became pale and Popov must have noticed it. "Don't worry," he said. "I know your devotion to the school and that you did not know about this custom. Give me the balance of the amount and I'll correct the figure in the list; nobody will know about it." I had to learn the Soviet "customs" the hard way; often it was like skating on thin ice.

My work at the VU was most rewarding. I got the German program rolling. Before long another teacher was hired, Vera Pashkewicz, who came from the German Volga Republic. Her German was poor, but she had the strongest recommendation—her husband was a senior officer at the school. The number of students kept growing, and after some time a third teacher had to be added.

* * *

On August 8, 1940, a joyous event happened in the family—our first son, Raphael, arrived. We nicknamed him Raphi. He became the center of our whole life and brought us endless joy and bliss. He was born in the Jewish Linas Hatzedek Hospital, under the care of Professor Joseph, himself a refugee from Germany.

I remember an amusing incident. The morning after the birth Ida's sister Nechama, who was a nurse at the hospital, brought the baby to Ida. She untied the diapers and said to her, "I know what you are curious about; here you have what you want to look at. . . ."

(After the War we learned that on November 29, 1941, Latvian henchmen under the command of SS men surrounded that hospital and set it afire. Those who attempted to escape were cut down by machine-gun bullets, including pregnant women and newborn babies. All patients and staff were massacred. Among them was Nechama. Her husband, whom she had married a few months before, perished during the war in a German death camp.)

THREE

Toward the end of 1940 strange rumors began to circulate. People whispered that something had gone sour in Soviet-German relations. A teacher at the Institute told me that Hitler demanded the cession of the Baltic countries. I shrugged it off as mere rumor. I had gone through it all in post-Munich Czechoslovakia. Before long, however, I noticed an air of nervousness among the officers at the VU, which began to disquiet me. I did not, however, dare to ask one of the officers for the reason. Once I mentioned it in passing to Logunov. "Oh, it is nothing serious. The Germans are carrying on some foul play. Keep it under your hat," he said.

Soon something did happen—the VU left for field maneuvers. It had never happened before. For an entire week I had to get up before dawn and take a long train ride to the camping place. These outings began to occur more and more frequently. Later the teachers had to live with the cadets in the field. The winter months passed in growing tension.

Sometime in March 1941, while traveling home together with Vera from the military camp, she told me about her native village on the Volga. Then she said, "I can hardly wait for the school year to end and to go with the children to my parents."

"Don't you like it here?" I asked her. "The Baltic summers are wonderful."

"Oh yes, they are marvelous indeed; but my husband insists that we leave as soon as possible," she sighed. I looked at her inquiringly, but she changed the subject quickly.

Vera's puzzling remark worried me. Before long I was able to put two and two together. There was talk about the capture of subversive Latvian bands, supposedly headed by German agents, who carried out acts of sabotage on Soviet military installations and also perpetrated attacks on Russian soldiers in various parts of the country.

Secret arrests took place. Not only supporters of the former dictatorial regime but also many previous leaders of democratic and socialist parties were deported to Siberia. In the beginning of June 1941, however, mass arrests of "unreliable elements" started. For some reason they began in the provinces; Riga was left for later.

The arrests were carried out at night. In the hours between midnight and dawn the NKVD knocked on doors. Families were given 20 minutes to pack some warm clothes and then put on a truck. The arrested were taken to the freight station, loaded into cattle trains and shipped off to Siberia.

The NKVD seemed to be nervous and worked in a hurry, for the arrests were rather haphazard. There was no yardstick by which to guess who would be rounded up, so most families packed and waited in agony and fear for the ominous knock on the door. During the daytime one was safe and went to work as usual.

The Jews made up only about 5 percent of the general population, but thanks to the zeal of the fanatic *Yevsketsia,* about half of the estimated 50,000 deportees in June 1941 were Jewish. Every Jewish owner of a small store was labeled a "dangerous bourgeois" and was deported. My father-in-law's two brothers in Dvinsk had a paint store. They were hard-working men, but they too were sent to Siberia.

(The youngest son of one of these two families did not happen to be at home on the night of the arrest. After the outbreak of the war he escaped to Russia where he joined a partisan group and fought behind the German lines. He fell shortly, giving his life for those who had sent his parents to their deaths in Siberia. The two brothers of Ida's father and their wives perished in a Siberian forced-labor camp, one of them in a very tragic way. Sleeping at night in the open in the forests, where they were felling trees, the starved and exhausted prisoners would build a bonfire and huddle close to it. One night, numbed by cold and exhaustion, he fell asleep and tumbled into the bonfire and was burned to death. After Stalin's death their children were allowed to return to Latvia, and later they succeeded in going to Israel.)

*   *   *

The mass arrests in Riga began during the night of June 10. In the morning I heard that many refugees from Hitler also were taken away. I became very worried and spoke to Ryabov and Logunov. "In case the NKVD comes for you, ask them to call us and we'll get you out," they said. That afternoon I had a lesson with General Lubchenko. He too promised me his help in case of trouble.

Nonetheless, I lived in constant fear. We packed our valises. "Just in case," I said to myself. The arrests of the NKVD were unpredictable and their methods cruel. How heartless they were I had a chance to witness. Ida's sister, her husband and their two small girls were refugees from Czechoslovakia and lived in Riga. Two nights after the arrests started, the NKVD came for them. Our brother-in-law, who was a physician, was on duty in the hospital that night. When he came home in the morning he hurried immediately to the station and pleaded with the NKVD commandant of the train to allow him to join his family. But all his begging was in vain. The heartless NKVD soldiers chased him away, yelling at him cynically, "Go home and wait for your turn. There'll be time enough for you and your family to spend together in Siberia." With a broken heart he watched the long cattle train with its unfortunate human cargo pull out of the station and carry off his family to an unknown fate in Siberia.

During the day I went to work as usual, but my nerves were on edge and I hardly closed an eye at night. Every noise of a motor vehicle driving past in the street made me jump out of bed and rush to the window to see if it stopped at our house. My tension became unbearable, but the NKVD kept me in suspense till the night of June 22.

About 1 A.M. I heard a truck halt at our house. Through the window I saw the milk-white light of the Baltic night reflecting in the rifle bayonets of the soldiers standing in the corners inside the truck and guarding some dark figures squatting on the floor. NKVD soldiers got out and headed for the house door. I woke up Ida. After a while I heard the elevator stop at our floor.

There was a loud knock on our door. I went to open it. An NKVD officer with a drawn gun pushed me inside. "Give me your gun!" he shouted (I had heard of cases when former Latvian officers shot at the NKVD men who came to arrest them). "I never had a gun," I answered. While the soldier and a civilian went to search the other rooms, the officer asked me for our papers.

Seeing the swastika emblem on our passports, he exclaimed, "Ah, spies whom Hitler has sent to us! You are under arrest, get packed and come with us!"

"We are packed," I said.

Looking at our suitcases in the corner, he remarked sarcastically, "I see you have been prepared to run back to the Nazis!"

The search of the apartment seemed to be very thorough. The other two NKVD men were looking for weapons even in the baby's crib and woke him up. Ida wanted to go to the crying child, but the officer rudely stopped her. Strangely enough, in a way I felt relieved that the suspense was finally over and resigned myself to the inevitable fate. But the crying of the baby somehow tore me out of my apathy. I imagined him crying hungry and parched in the overcrowded freight car on the way to Siberia.

I mustered up courage to take out my military ID cards from the VU, General Lubchenko's office and the DKA and showed them to the officer. "If I were an unreliable person, they would have hardly engaged me to teach in these institutions. You can call them and ask their opinion about me," I said.

The officer examined the ID cards carefully. Then he put

away his gun and called in the other two men. After a whispered consultation with the civilian (he was a Latvian NKVD man who usually accompanied each arresting party), he made a phone call to Colonel Ryabov. Then he made a second call, to his own chief. It lasted only several minutes, but to me it seemed like an eternity. At the end of the call I heard the officer saying, "Yes, Comrade Commander, I understand; we'll leave them."

After replacing the receiver he was a changed person. His tone was now calm. He told Ida to go and take care of the crying child. He took with him our passports and most of my military ID cards and told me to come in the morning to NKVD Headquarters where I would be issued a paper in order to be safe in the future.

The NKVD men spent only about half an hour in our apartment, but after they left I felt as if I had aged by years. I walked up to my son, who was now sleeping again like a little angel. For a long while I stood bent over his crib and watched his calm, happy sleep. Then I suddenly felt two warm rivulets trickling down my cheeks.

*　*　*

Hurrying early in the morning to NKVD Headquarters I met my father-in-law coming from the synagogue on his way to us. He looked very upset and asked me if I had heard that war had broken out. I had no time to stop to talk to him, thinking that he meant a new Hitler campaign somewhere in Europe or Africa.

When I asked the NKVD officer on duty for the office I was supposed to go to, he said that nobody was there now and told me to come back in the afternoon. I saw there was a bustle in the corridors, but knowing where I was, I did not want to show curiosity, and I left the building at once.

On the way home I saw groups of people standing on the street corners talking excitedly. I stopped at one of the groups to find out what had happened. At dawn the Germans had launched a sudden attack on the Soviet Union; heavy battles were going on at the border, and many cities near the frontier had already been bombed by the Luftwaffe. I realized that this was the war my father-in-law had wanted to tell me about.

I hurried home and turned on the radio. There was terse news about the successes of the Red Army in repulsing the fascist hordes and throwing them back across the border. Then came an address of a Communist leader, exhorting the Latvian people to stand united behind the Party and to be alert to the external and internal enemies.

I switched to the Moscow station and listened to Molotov's speech. His tone was meek and somber; he appealed to Hitler, saying that Russia had carried out loyally all points of the Agreement and was willing to negotiate any further justified German demands. Molotov's words left me in a depressed mood. Realizing that one of those demands was the cession of the Baltic states, I preferred the war.

I went to the VU. There were no classes anymore. Everything was on full alert. The cadets busied themselves putting up flak emplacements. I thanked Ryabov for bailing me out from the NKVD. "We like you here; besides, it would be too cold for you in Siberia," he said jokingly. He told me that in case the school should be evacuated to Russia, they would take me and my family along.

When I went back to the NKVD, I was told that they were busy, that I should try again next morning. There was even more running about than in the morning. One could feel the nervousness in the air. I had to leave empty-handed again.

There was a nervous atmosphere in the city too. In front of the bakeries and food stores stood long lines. Military patrols and civilian Red Guardists with bayoneted rifles on their shoulders walked around in the streets. Between the trees in the park I saw flak positions.

Walking through the streets of Riga during those days one could distinguish two sorts of people. Some were somber and worried. Others, especially the Lettish, had haughty smirks on their faces and pierced one through with hateful looks. They could hardly wait for the arrival of the Germans.

On the way home I dropped in at the Institute of Foreign Languages. Paltis and Zagorsky and other staff members walked around outside before the building with brand new rifles on the shoulder. Zagorsky asked me jokingly if I wanted a rifle also.

"What for?" quipped Paltis. "A scholar like him would not know what to do with it." I knew that what he really meant was "we do not trust him that much."

I went in to Zoya and told her about my experience with the NKVD and Ryabov's promise to take me along. She urged me not to miss that chance. She looked very worried. It was the last time that I saw that kind woman. I do not know whether she survived the Holocaust.

* * *

There were no more arrests, either that night or the following nights. Instead, that night we had several air raids and flak fire from all directions. The Germans attempted to bomb the Riga harbor and various military installations.

When I came in the morning to the NKVD, I beheld a strange picture. There were no sentries at the entrance. I walked inside. Red Guardists carried cartons with papers to the yard. From the open side door came the smell of burning paper. After a while a Red Guardist asked me what I wanted there. I told him. "There is nobody in the offices here any longer," he said and ordered me to leave.

I was stunned and walked out. I began thinking what to do. I was now in real difficulty; no passports, no military ID cards. I phoned Logunov. "Don't hang around in the streets," he said. "It is war, and you know what they do with a person without papers." He told me to come to him right away, and he would give me a new identity card. On the way to the VU I stopped at the DKA. It was closed. The sentry at the entrance did not know when the office would open. I then went to Lubchenko and told him about the NKVD. He replaced my ID card.

There was a big bustle on the VU campus when I arrived there. Feverish preparations were going on all around. The senior-class cadets had new uniforms and were very proud of the lieutenant insignia, which they had unexpectedly received that morning. Logunov told me that they were waiting for evacuation orders and an available train. "Go home to pack and come here with your family early in the morning," he said. Little did I suspect as I said to him, "I'll see you in the morning," that I was never to see that loyal friend again.

There were more air raids and runs to the shelter at night. I went out early in the morning to get a taxi or *droshky* but could not get one. We took the tramway. When we arrived at the last stop in the suburb I went to look for the bus going to the VU. To my consternation I found out that there were no buses running there any longer. I tried to phone the school but could get no connection. I consoled myself that it was probably because of the damage done to the electric power lines 'during the night by Latvian fifth-column bands. But I was apprehensive nonetheless.

I walked around in the neighborhood streets to find some vehicle, but nobody wanted to take us to the VU. First I considered somehow carrying the four suitcases, but then I realized that I would never make the two-mile walk there. I became desperate.

As I was passing one of the small houses, I noticed a pushcart in the yard. I knocked on the door. An elderly man came out and asked me in Russian what I wanted. "Oh no, not there. There was shooting in the woods there all night," he said, "people say that German parachutists were dropped in that vicinity."

"Sell me your pushcart for 200 rubles," I said. "You'll buy a new one for less than 100." Dazzled by the sight of that much money, he scratched his head and said, "Add 100 rubles and I'll take your luggage to the school."

We set out on our way; Ida with the sleeping baby in her arms and I helping to push the wagon. Our porter took us on narrow paths through fields and meadows to the rear side of the school campus. The sentry let me in and I walked to the administration building. I was puzzled by the strange calm on the campus. Gone was the bustle of yesterday. There were only a few cadets walking around.

The lieutenant in the office had terrible news for me; the VU had been evacuated during the night. He was left in charge of a company of cadets and was awaiting orders. The lieutenant knew me and had sympathy with my misery. As I was leaving in a desperate mood, he said, "Why don't you try to get on the train that is being prepared at the station to evacuate the families of Soviet military personnel?"

Our porter did not look happy about having to wheel our

baggage back, but there was no choice, and we started on our way. After about ten minutes we suddenly heard shots and shouting in Russian and Latvian. We made for the nearest corn field and hid there. We lay low for some time until it became quiet and then crawled out. But our porter absolutely refused to go back for the pushcart. As I was about to go fetch it, he stopped me, saying that he was not going to risk his life because of our belongings.

He led us through fields until we came to a heath. We dashed across it, then we heard more shots. But this time they came from far away, in the forest somewhere. We walked through tortuous byways. Raphi began to cry, but the porter urged us to hurry. Finally we reached a suburban street. All exhausted from the running and crawling, we came at last to our porter's house. After paying him off and resting a little we left.

When we came to the tram stop we found out that the streetcars to the city were not running anymore. We began walking home. The sight of the streets was distressing. Many power lines were cut and dangling dangerously overhead. Here and there lay overturned streetcars and buses, their wheels pointing into the air like the legs of dead horses. We decided to turn off the thoroughfare and walk through the side streets. After some time we came to a tram stop from which there were still some streetcars going to the city.

*   *   *

It was nearly dark when we returned home. Our people were surprised but very glad to see us. My mother-in-law grabbed Raphi and began crying, "Now I'll have my little angel near me."

Ida put Raphi to bed and then she too fell asleep at once. Exhausted as I was, I did not feel like sleeping. I was distressed about missing the departure of the VU and reproached myself for not having gone there with my family yesterday. I slumped on a chair and began pondering the day's adventure. I realized now what a close brush we had had with mortal danger. Seeing how peacefully Raphi was sleeping in his crib and looking at our cozy apartment and at my books, I began having second thoughts about leaving at all. "What is going to happen to other Jews will happen to us too," I thought.

But then I recalled my experience with the Gestapo. Because of my work in Soviet military institutions I was bound to be one of the first victims, and I decided to spare no effort to escape to Russia. I stretched out in my clothes on the bed and dozed off. Before long I was on the train with the school. Ryabov was surprised to see me. His mild friendly eyes smiled. "The Germans are driving us to Siberia. But how will you be there without warm clothing?" he said. The rest of his words, however, were muffled in the clatter of the wheels and the whistling of the locomotive. I opened my eyes—through the open window came the howling of sirens and rapid thuds of flak fire. I was too numb to run to the shelter.

I could not fall asleep again. Before long the first rays of the sun tried to penetrate the room. Raphi started to stir, and I sneaked up to lull him back to sleep. As soon as he noticed me, however, he turned his head and stretched out his arms. I picked him up. How wonderful it was to feel his tiny warm body curling up against my chest. Before long he was fast asleep.

My father-in-law came early that morning. The news he brought from the synagogue was alarming. The Germans had penetrated deep into Soviet territory and were not far from the Latvian border. The Soviet front communiqués were cryptic; they spoke only about stubborn battles. Reading between the lines one could deduce that the situation was bad.

Before long Ida awoke and her mother arrived. Over breakfast the pros and cons of staying or leaving were rehashed. My father-in-law picked up Raphi and began pacing the room with him. I watched his intelligent face framed in his black Herzl beard. His wise eyes were gazing into the distance, and he hummed the Hebrew lullaby my son loved. But I noticed that he was listening attentively to my efforts to persuade the two women that we must leave.

Then my father-in-law suddenly halted and said to Ida, "My daughter, I think that your husband is right. We will muddle through somehow. The Jews in Poland and in other countries manage after all to live with the Germans. But your husband has held important positions with the Soviets, and you can imagine what will happen to him if Hitler comes here. You must all go at once."

I got up and said to Ida, "Come let us go!"

We had no suitcases, so we took a few blanket covers and stuffed into them what was still left of our clothes. We took a last sad look around the apartment and walked out. My in-laws and Ida's brother Zavel with his wife, whom he had married several months before, walked us to the next street corner.

Little did we suspect as we turned around to wave our last goodbye to our dear ones from a distance that we were never to see them again. My in-laws were murdered in the Riga ghetto in December 1941. Zavel's wife also perished there. He himself, a journalist and co-author of a Jewish history book for Hebrew high schools, died of hunger in Dachau shortly before its liberation. To his last day, we were later told he shared his meager camp rations with the sick and weak.

The husband of Ida's deported sister joined us, in the hope of being reunited with his family in Russia. The trams were not running anymore. Clinging closely to the walls of the buildings (there were rumors about fifth-column snipers on roofs) we made our way to the station.

The train was standing on a sidetrack near the freight station. The cars were crowded already. But my military I.D. cards, as so often in the future, proved reliable talismans. The train commandant admitted us and gave us seats.

3

Escape to Russia

ONE

THUS, ON JUNE 25, 1941, less than two years since my first escape from the Nazis, I set out for the second time on my flight from Hitler, facing an unknown future.

The hours passed in impatient waiting. Nobody knew when the train would leave. To all questions the commandant had the same answer—"Very soon." After some time there was a big commotion; shots were fired at the train from a nearby street. The passengers were ordered to stay away from the windows and sit on the floor. After a few minutes some more shots were heard and then a loud explosion. By a freak accident a grenade carried by one of the soldiers was hit by a sniper's bullet and blew him to pieces. There were hysterical cries from women and children. In the car next to ours the windows were shattered, and people were wounded, some of them seriously. Panic ensued. Some passengers got off the train and went home. Later we heard that the snipers were captured and shot on the spot.

When dusk fell, the train pulled out at last. We got up from the floor and returned to our seats. I had no idea in what direction we were traveling, but what difference did it make? The main thing was that we were not standing at the same spot in the station any longer.

The Soviet returnees kept asking how far we were from the old Soviet border. Nobody knew. The expression "The old border" was pronounced by the Soviet people with pride, as some mysterious formula that would bring safety. I must admit that I too waited anxiously to cross that border. There had been so

73

much talk about the impregnable fortifications on the border that I believed the Germans would be stopped there. For some reason I thought that Hitler's intention was to annex the rest of the Polish territory and the Baltic states. I could not imagine that he wanted to get entangled in a protracted war with Russia.

Little by little the excitement subsided, and the passengers began to doze off. There was a salty whiff in the air; apparently we were traveling along the sea coast. It was dark all around us. The train stopped often, but nobody knew where we were. After midnight someone said that we were in Estonia. I dozed off but was awakened by a sudden commotion and noise. I opened my eyes and saw that it was already dawn. Green-capped NKVD frontier guards walked through the car and checked papers. The Soviet returnees were all excited, asking the soldiers for information about train connections to their native towns.

I became apprehensive about the examination of documents, but everything passed without a mishap. To the question of the young NKVD soldier where we were traveling, I took out my ID card from the VU and told him that I was on my way to rejoin the school. Anticipating that the VU had returned to Pskov, I asked him how to get there. "You are very far from there," he answered and mentioned the name of some station where I could get information.

* * *

The NKVD screening at the border station lasted several hours. Some of the passengers were taken off the train. When the train finally pulled out of the station, I felt very relieved at being already in safety beyond the "magic wall." The train turned off to a secondary branch and began zigzagging through the countryside in a southeasterly direction. Later we stopped at a rural station. On the platform stood old men and women, offering food and produce for sale. "A kolkhoz bazaar!" the Soviet returnees exclaimed excitedly and hurried out of the car.

I too got off to buy some food but was surprised by the prohibitive prices. I bought only a bottle of milk for Raphi and a few *lepyoshkas* (flat cakes of rough, dark wheatmeal). The patched shabby clothes of the people depressed me. Thus I made my first acquaintance with the kolkhoz market, the only place of free trade in the USSR, which was to be the most vital source for survival during our sojourn in Russia.

The locomotive whistle summoned the passengers back to the train. But the Soviet returnees paid no attention to it, buying up all the food they could get (a very prudent foresight, as I was to find out before long, that is acquired only through experience in the bitter Soviet reality). Only as the train began pulling out of the station did the shoppers run back to the cars.

The train seemed to be in no hurry. It stopped very often at some small stations to wait for military trains to pass in the opposite direction. Now and then we also halted for some time in the middle of nowhere.

That day we experienced our first air attack. Out of the blue two German planes appeared and began circling overhead. In a matter of seconds they dived and sprayed the train with a hail of machine-gun bullets. They were so close that some passengers said they saw the grinning faces of the pilots. Then the planes swung around and repeated their attack.

The train began racing to the wooded area ahead of us and halted. There were some dead and many wounded. The soldiers chased us out of the train and ordered us to lie down among the trees, but the planes did not appear again.

Besides my brother-in-law there were a few other physicians and also some nurses on the train, and they began to attend to the wounded. The luggage car was improvised into a ward. The medical personnel did their best to help the wounded, but though there were some bandages, there were no medications available. Many suffered nervous breakdowns. One woman, whose baby was killed, went out of her mind. There was crying and wailing, and the tragic scenes broke the heart.

To me that air attack was a terrible shock. It had shattered my illusions of safety inside Russia. I realized with horror that Hitler's murderous arm was reaching out after us here too.

The train picked up speed and went for several hours without stopping. Before midnight we halted at a large station. Many Soviet returnees got off to take trains to their home towns. But we had nowhere to go. The train became our home. We had no choice but to wait until we were told to leave it. But what was our destination and when would we arrive there? Nobody knew, not even the commandant.

In the morning we stopped at a rural station. "Come let us go for *kipyatok!*" the Soviet returnees exclaimed enthusiastically. I went too and was introduced to this old Russian national drink.

In larger stations there is a kettle with boiling water in the wall from which one can tap freely around the clock. I do not know who was the first to establish it, but he certainly deserves a monument for his humanitarian invention. My family and I are indebted to him. The *kipyatok* literally kept us alive. For many days it became the only warm intake we had. First it felt strange to drink plain hot water without tea or sugar, and I had a hard time swallowing it. I used to watch with amusement the old Russian women patting their chests and sighing with relish, "Oh what delicious *kipyatok* we are having this morning!" But eventually I got used to the *kipyatok* and even appreciated it.

The *kipyatok* was beneficial in another way too. It was hot outside. Whenever the train stopped people would rush to find a drink of water. Before long there was diarrhea and also dysentery, which became a scourge. Then we learned from the Russian returnees to stay away from unboiled water.

An empty bottle became a treasured possession. But it is not so easy as you might think to tap boiling water into a narrow bottle neck. In the beginning I used to scald my hands badly. Then an old Russian woman, who stood behind me in line, had pity on me. "You poor foreigner! You don't even know how to tap *kipyatok* properly," she sighed and showed me how to do it. In time I became pretty adept at it.

After breakfast that morning the passengers were told to get out of the train. The commandant instructed us how to behave in case of an air attack. He placed lookouts on the roofs of the cars and organized squads in each car to help us get out of the cars quickly.

We drove on. Before too long there was another air raid. The train halted and we hurried out of the cars and spread out in the adjacent fields. A single plane appeared and sprayed us with machine-gun fire. At first I smiled to see our sentries firing their rifles at the swiftly circling plane. Nonetheless, it deterred the plane from diving lower. As a result, only a few were wounded that time.

Three hours later we were not so lucky. This time there were many casualties. And the meadow in which we took cover turned out to be swampland. I threw myself to the ground with Raphi in my arms. When I saw that we were lying in water I tried to hold him above the surface, but he had already swallowed some swampy water. That night he had a high temperature and got an acute case of diarrhea, which lasted for many days and caused him great pain. We became very worried.

Before dusk we stopped at a bombed out station. There was a destroyed train there with damaged cars loaded with military provisions. The train was guarded by soldiers, but some experienced Soviet returnees on our train sneaked up to the cars and helped themselves to the various goodies. They ran away only when the guards began shooting in the air. They came back with pockets stuffed with sardine cans and a mixture of sugar, raisins and dried food. Soon there was lively trading and bartering all over the train.

The next day there was another air raid and more on the following days, with new casualties each time, but we got used to it and took it in our stride. The Germans were trying to disrupt the railroad lines, and we civilians were caught in the middle.

Nobody knew where the train was traveling. Sometimes we had the impression that we were going in circles. In the morning of the fifth day after leaving Riga we arrived in Staraya Russa. Our locomotive left the train, and so did our commandant. A sentry said that he went to the station for new instructions.

We got out of the train and strolled around chatting. It felt good to stretch our legs. Before long a freight train pulled in on the track next to ours. It was loaded with heavy machinery, and there were many passengers. We went over to talk to them. They had been evacuated several days ago from Minsk with their factory and were on the way to Central Asia. The news we heard was sad. Minsk and many other cities were nearly destroyed. The Jews among them told us that the Germans had massacred the Jewish population in the territories they captured. My heart was filled with horror; I was thinking of our people in Riga.

Our commandant returned before dusk. Ignoring our questions as to our destination, he said laconically, "All aboard! We still have a very long trip ahead of us." While in the past days the train did not seem to be in a particular hurry, zigzagging and stopping frequently, it now picked up speed and was going in an easterly direction. We stopped rarely.

On the morning of July 3 we arrived at a rural station named Palkino. We had traveled through the night and were glad for an opportunity to fetch *kipyatok* and to buy something to eat. But as we began to get out of the car, we were stopped by our sentries and ordered to stay inside. All the passengers were told to take their belongings and leave the train. We were led to a large meadow across the tracks and told to sit down.

After sitting for nine days on the hard wooden bench in the train and breathing the stuffy air, it felt marvelous to stretch out on the soft green grass. The July morning was beautiful. The sun was young and bright. The azure sky was limpid and serene; no enemy planes, only the larks were circling above. The war seemed far away.

Then I was torn from my leisurely musing. Blue-capped NKVD soldiers were approaching the meadow. I became alarmed and sat up. An NKVD officer announced that the Soviet returnees could go right away to the station and take trains to their home towns. The rest of us, Latvian evacuees, were told that we would be sent to kolkhozes (collective farms) and then later given work in our professions.

The NKVD set out to check papers and to register us. When the officer came to us and examined our documents, he exclaimed in surise, "Foreigners?!" He listened to my explanations, but then he told a soldier to take my brother-in-law and me with the family to a separate corner of the meadow.

We stretched out again on the grass. How strange, I thought. We had gotten away from the NKVD in Riga only to fall into their clutches here. A soldier was leading an outlandishly dressed man to our corner. As miserable as I felt, I could not help laughing. The man carried in one hand a valise and in the other a violin case. His violin contrasted so much with the sad reality. The man sat down next to us. He was a Jewish refugee from Vienna where he had once played in a philharmonic orchestra. He had escaped to Latvia and now had come with his violin to this remote Russian village.

After some time kolkhoz wagons arrived at the station. Many of the evacuees were put in the vehicles, which drove off shortly. A little while later a soldier came and told us to follow him. A glimmer of hope lit up in my heart; maybe we too were to be sent to a kolkhoz. But the soldier did not stop at the station; he led us toward the village.

The procession of a European-dressed woman with a baby and three men aroused the curiosity of the villagers. But the sight of the NKVD soldier accompanying us prompted them to hurry into their houses. It did not escape my notice that many eyes were watching us from behind drawn curtains.

* * *

We finally arrived at the militia (police) station and were led inside. We were not actually under arrest; we could move around freely. When the NKVD officer returned from the railroad station, he interrogated the other two men. Then my family and I were taken to his office. He was not at all familiar with geopolitical conditions in Europe. I had a hard time explaining to him that Hitler was not a born Czech and that the Czechs were Slavs and not a Germanic tribe; that we were not Hitlerites but unfortunate Jewish refugees escaping for the second time from Hitler. He examined my ID cards again and again and nodded his head. But at the end of the long interrogation I had no idea what he intended to do with us.

We slept on bare wooden bunks with no mattress, pillow or blanket. As the heavy door was locked from the outside, it dawned on me that we were prisoners after all. Maybe it would have been better if the Riga NKVD had arrested us that night, I thought. At least we would have known where we were going.

We were awakened at dawn. As we walked outside, I saw a kolkhoz cart waiting in front of the house. My hopes rose. "They are sending us to a kolkhoz," I whispered to Ida. An elderly woman sat in the driver's seat. We got into the cart and settled in the straw. The wagon did not move. "What are we waiting for, auntie, we are all set," I said. But the woman did not answer. At that moment a soldier came out and sat down next to her. My hopes were dashed.

We drove through the village. The people in the yards looked at us but quickly turned their heads away. Soon we came to a very dusty dirt road. To the question where he was taking us, the soldier answered, "*Nye skazhu,*" which in the Russian idiom can mean both "I don't know" and "I won't say." He told us to talk neither to him nor to the woman nor among ourselves. Before too long we were covered with dust. Raphi began to sneeze and cried loudly. Later we arrived at a hill and the cart halted. The old, emaciated horse hung its head in shame for being unable to show Soviet hospitality to the capitalist enemies. But in its mute equine language it was telling us, "You do understand that it is not my fault but rather because of the miserable food I get in the kolkhoz."

While we men, including the soldier, took a shortcut across the meadow, the woman in the cart began to chat with Ida. She quickly gave her a piece of bread and a bottle of milk and whispered, "Poor woman! My heart cries for your sick baby that he has to go with you where you are going."

In the afternoon we reached the outskirts of a large city. From the signs on factories and institutions I gathered that we were in Yaroslavl. After some time the wagon stopped at a huge, many-storied stone building with grated windows. We drove into the yard. The soldier handed us over to the NKVD officer on duty who signed for the duly delivered human cargo. As the cart was driving out of the yard gate, I looked after it with sadness as our last link with freedom.

*   *   *

A sentry took us to a room in the basement. After a long while Ida and I were taken to an office for interrogation. Behind the desk sat a stocky man in his thirties, with energetic features and a shock of black curly hair. Realizing that he was Jewish, I was apprehensive. I recalled Wolf and his friend and the other *Yevseks* in Riga.

The lengthy interrogation began. Then suddenly came the question that I had heard from the NKVD officer in Riga and also yesterday in Palkino but did not expect to hear from this shrewd-looking NKVD official—why had we come to the USSR and for what purpose? I knew that any further explanations would be useless. Pointing at Ida with the sick baby I said, "These are hardly suitable companions for a spy and saboteur." There was a faint smile in his shrewd eyes. Then I asked him to call the VU in Pskov to get information about me. He did not answer. My hopes of getting in touch with the school were dashed again.

We were taken back to the room in the basement. My brother-in-law and the musician were not there. We never saw them there again. Later the sentry brought us some gruel with unsweetened tea and we went to sleep. Turning from side to side on the bare wooden bench I thought with sadness about our fate.

Early in the morning we were again taken to the NKVD official. To my surprise there was no further interrogation. He took us to a car in the yard. We drove through the streets of Yaroslavl. I had no notion of where we were going. Then we arrived at the station. He handed Ida a parcel and said, "There is some food from my mother for your child." He gave me a letter and said, "Show this to the NKVD in case they check you again on the way." Then he took us to a freight train. "The train is going to Kazan. Don't get off before," he said. "It is better for you to be as far away from the front as possible."

I asked him where our brother-in-law was, that we wanted to be together. "Don't worry," he said laconically. "He will come after you and you'll see him soon." (That "soon" turned out to be several years later. But it was not entirely the fault of the NKVD official. My brother-in-law had asked to be sent to his family. As a "favor" they sent him with the violinist to a Siberian labor camp. It took my brother-in-law a few years to find his family.)

TWO

The cattle train we boarded was crowded with refugees, mostly Jews from the Lithuanian border towns who fled in the first days of the war. But there were also some Latvian and Estonian Jews who had escaped on foot and boarded the train later at various stations. Unlike our previous train, this was a civilian one, without a military commandant. The conductor was in charge, but one hardly ever saw him. Each car was a separate island, left to take care of itself.

Our car was overcrowded. With great difficulty we finally found a place and sat down on the floor. The hygienic conditions were terrible. The straw on the floor was filthy and smelly. Before long we began scratching ourselves—lice. Our neighbors were Dr. Bronstein from Estonia with his wife and a ten-year-old girl. Eventually we struck up a close friendship with them which lasted all through the years we spent in Russia.

There were sick people in the car. Dr. Bronstein did his best to help them, but apart from giving them an occasional aspirin he could do little. The most serious case was an elderly Lithuanian Jew. He had a high temperature and lay listlessly in a corner. Dr. Bronstein suspected typhus and tried in vain to have him taken off the train.

When night came, we could not sleep; the lice tormented us. Raphi did not feel well and cried. Dr. Bronstein gave us some alcohol to rub his body. He quieted down and fell asleep undressed. During the night more people became ill. The condition of the Lithuanian Jew got worse. The suspicion of typhus leaked out somehow, and the people became panicky. When the train stopped at a station, many got off with the intention of staying there, but they were put back on the train.

The next morning we arrived in Ivanovo, the textile center of the country. Dr. Bronstein went with the conductor to the station. Later they returned with a woman physician. She examined the sick man and her face became somber. She left and before long she came back with two sanitary orderlies and a stretcher and the old man was taken to a hospital. It was a sad picture to watch the wife and the two teenage children walk behind the stretcher. She also examined the other sick persons and some of them she likewise took along for hospitalization.

We remained sitting in the car in a gloomy mood. After a while medical officers came and ordered all passengers to take their belongings and to get out of the train. People became excited and said that we were going to stay in Ivanovo. We were led out of the station and walked through the streets. The people turned around to look at this strange procession of foreigners.

They took us to a city *banya* (public baths), the indispensible institution in every Soviet town.

While we were taking hot showers, our clothes were disinfected. I had not taken a shower or bath since leaving Riga. When we looked at one another in our disinfected clothes, we burst out laughing. The sleeves and trousers of our suits were shorter. To be sure the width too had shrunk, but there was no trouble on that score. Only then did I realize how much weight I had lost. Nonetheless, everybody was happy to be clean and refreshed—and especially to have gotten rid of the lice.

Our hopes of remaining in Ivanovo soon evaporated. We were lined up and taken back to the train. When we came to our car, we hardly recognized it. The filth and straw were gone. The floor was washed, and there was a strong smell of carbolic acid. We were lucky in another respect—Dr. Bronstein had been given a supply of various medications.

There was a better mood all around now. The men shaved and the women fixed their hair and put on lipstick; everybody looked years younger. We left Ivanovo late in the afternoon and traveled again through the countryside, with numerous stops and endless waiting. But hygienic conditions were better now, and we were not so tormented by lice. On the third day, in the morning of July 8, we finally arrived in Kazan. The train stopped in the freight yards, far away from the station. Two militiamen met the train and told the passengers to take their things and walk to the station to register with the *Evakpunkt* (Evacuation Center), which would take care of them.

* * *

Kazan, the capital of the Tatar Autonomous Republic, is a very large railroad junction with several lines connecting the western parts of the country with Central Asia. It also lies on the main Trans-Siberian Moscow-Valdivostok railroad. I was amazed by the mass of men, women and children who filled not only the station but also the square and park nearby, waiting for trains.

We finally managed to check in our belongings and find a place in the park. Later I went with Dr. Bronstein to the *Evakpunkt*. There was a large crowd of refugees from the western parts of the country, including the Baltic states and Poland.

Many had been separated from their families and were trying to find them through the Information Office.

To our dismay we learned that nobody was allowed to stay in Kazan. All refugees were sent to kolkhozes or to lumber work in the vast forests of the region. Still, we went to the Tatar Commissariat of Education and Health. There would be no problem finding jobs for us, the official said, but the city was already overcrowded with refugees from Moscow and Leningrad who had been evacuated here with their offices and institutions. He sent us to try our luck in Cheboksary, about 85 miles from Kazan.

We returned to the station empty-handed. With the evening came the problem of where to sleep. The weather was warm, and we decided to stay in the park. But later it got chilly, and we went to the waiting room. It was terribly crowded. People were lying or sitting on the floor so that it was impossible to walk. Finally we managed to squeeze into a corner and sit on the floor. But it was very hard to sleep. As soon as a train arrived many picked up their bundles and rushed to the platform to try once more to board. Most of them returned even more morose than before, only to find their places on the floor taken by others. Arguments broke out; children woke and began crying. Militiamen came in to restore order.

Early in the morning I took a bus with Dr. Bronstein to Cheboksary, the capital of the Chuvash Autonomous Republic. The Chuvash official in the Commissariat was not too polite to us. "The big shots in Kazan have sent us another couple of *intelligentchiki* (bespectacled intellectuals)," he snapped. He could send us to work in a kolkhoz or in a sawmill, he said.

We were not sorry to leave that sordid, Asiatic-looking town. We went to the koklhoz market there to buy something to eat. A young Chuvash woman became interested in Dr. Bronstein's summer shoes and offered him a plate with *lepyoshkas* for them. My net gain from that visit was the loss of my Czech stainless steel pen knife. On the bus ride back I took it out to slice the bread. I saw that the eyes of the Chuvash kolkhoznik sitting near us lit up at the sight of the shiny knife. When I returned to Kazan I discovered that it was gone. I missed it very much; it had a can opener, scissors, etc. It took me some days to find in a Kazan bazaar a homemade pocket knife with a primitive wooden handle.

* * *

When we came back to Kazan I found Raphi in bad condition. He had a temperature and acute diarrhea; he also vomited a lot. We took him to a clinic. The physician examined him and sent us at once to the hospital. Those were typhoid symptoms, the doctor said, and put him in the ward for infectious diseases. Ida had to stay there to help take care of him.

This was the worst blow that could hit us in this strange city. I returned to the station in a desperate mood. The next morning the Bronsteins went to the *Evakpunkt* and wanted me to come along. But I was not interested in anything now. I hurried to the hospital. Raphi's condition had worsened during the night. They were waiting for the ward physician to make the necessary tests.

Walking back from the hospital I passed a *laryok* (small stall) on a street corner where bread was sold. There was a long line. I joined it, but long before my turn came, the manager announced that there was no more bread. The people grumbled and began to disperse. I lingered on for a while to watch a column of mobilized men marching to the station, a sight I had seen so often during the past days and nights.

Meanwhile the manager came out and set about locking up the *laryok*. I noticed that he was looking at me; my European apparel probably drew his attention. After some hesitation he said, "A refugee from the liberated places?"

"Yes," I answered. "I wanted to buy some bread but had no luck." He went inside and brought me a piece of bread. We began to chat. I told him where I was from and that I was just on my way from the hospital. Leonid Berman told me to come every morning for a piece of bread.

I went to the *Evakpunkt* to look for the Bronsteins. They were not there. After some time they came with beaming faces. They had succeeded in getting a place to sleep in a school that had been converted into a dormitory for evacuees. We hurried there, but there were no more vacancies. All the director could do for me was to give me some coupons for soup in the school *stolovaya* (public kitchen).

* * *

Some acquaintances at the *Evakpunkt* told me that many refugees were staying at the river station of the Kazan Volga Port where, so they said, one could, for the proper price under the table, get on a boat going south. I went there. The harbor was crowded with refugees dreaming about Central Asia where the weather was warm in the winter and food was also more readily available. Most of them had waited there for many days, but so far very few had been lucky enough to get on a boat.

That was the first time I saw the Volga. I was overwhelmed by the majestic flow of the Mother of Russian rivers. One could hardly see the other shore. The Volga was the hunting ground of Maxim Gorky's heroes, and watching the boatmen on the barges, I imagined that they had just stepped out of the pages of a Gorky story.

As I was walking along the quay I noticed a young woman leaning on the railing and gazing with nostalgic eyes into the distance. Her profile and auburn hair seemed somehow familiar, but I could not place her at first. I stepped over closer. It was Miss Scher, an English teacher from the Institute of Foreign Languages in Riga. She turned around; it took her many seconds to recognize me. I realized how much I too must have changed since we saw one another last in Riga.

She told me about some mutual friends who likewise managed to escape and reached Kazan. They were sent to work in the forests of the region. She was dreaming about the balmy south. When later I left Kazan, she was still there.

I went to the hospital in the afternoon. Ida had bad news; the tests confirmed the doctor's suspicions of typhus. Raphi had a very high temperature and dysentery. I went to the Bronsteins in the dormitory. Dr. Bronstein meanwhile had seen the official in the Commissariat, who sent him to Yoshkar-Ola to look for a position there, and he wanted me to go with them. "You must find a place to live when your child is discharged from the hospital," the Bronsteins urged. They were certainly right. But how could I leave Raphi in such a condition even for one day?

We went to the school *stolovaya*, and I was introduced to the important Soviet institution which was to play such a significant role in my struggle for survival during our sojourn in Russia. The cashier at the door gave you a spoon and asked for a ten-ruble deposit, which she gave back upon the return of the spoon. This was not so bad. Later I found out that some *stolovayas* asked a deposit for the plate also, or worse, you were required to bring your own spoon and plate, because the customers would steal everything they could lay their hands on.

The vegetable soup cost only a few kopecks, but it was very thin and watery; only a few slices of potato or cabbage floated around in it. To me, however, it tasted delicious; it was the first warm food I had had since Yarolsavl.

I went back to the station and found a place on the floor in the waiting room. About midnight I had a frightening experience. The NKVD came and rounded up the younger men. At the last moment I sneaked out with several other men through the door to the platform. The rest of the night I spent walking the streets.

I learned the art of survival in Russia the hard way. I now stayed away from the station and went there only for *kipyatok* to wash down the piece of bread that I bought from Berman. The most important thing was to watch out for the NKVD. There were thousands of refugees everywhere. NKVD men in uniforms and in plainclothes went around checking papers. I witnessed many heart-breaking scenes. Men were picked up and crying women and children tried to block the way, but they were pushed aside rudely by the NKVD men, who led the men to the nearest military point and sent them to the front.

In the evening I sat down in the park. Next to me sat a middle-aged man. After a while we began to chat. Vasya was from Vitebsk and had waited many days already for a train. "Where are you going to sleep," he asked me. "Right here if nobody comes to disturb me," I said.

"Don't worry. I'll show you where to sleep," he winked.

When it got chilly, he took me to the Telephone and Telegraph Office a few blocks away. There were many people there, sending telegrams or making long-distance calls. We sat down on a bench. Vasya told me that he was going to take a nap and asked me to wake him up as soon as a militiaman came in. "Then I'll watch and you'll sleep," he said. Remembering what happened the past night in the station, I was afraid to sleep when it was my turn. But I was very tired and eventually dozed off. Suddenly I felt a sharp nudge in the ribs. Let us hurry to the park," Vasya whispered. We rushed out through the side door before the militiaman came to our corner.

When I came to the hospital in the morning, Ida did not come to the window through which we usually spoke. I waited for a long time, walking around the building in the hope she might be at another window, but she was nowhere. I became worried and went to Dr. Irina Harkavy, who was in charge of the ward. She told me that Ida had become ill during the night and that there was suspicion that she too had caught typhoid fever. Since this was a children's hospital, she had been taken to a regular hospital. Seeing my misery, she assured me that Ida was going to be well in several days. The condition of Raphi was unchanged. She took me to the glass door of the ward to see him. I hardly recognized him. His face was drawn and pale and his beautiful eyes large and sad; his curly black hair was clipped.

I felt miserable as I walked to the tram to go to the other hospital. My world seemed to have collapsed. The doctor did not let me see Ida. I began reproaching myself for taking my family along only to have them wind up in hospitals in this remote city. If they had stayed at home, they would not have become sick, I thought in desperation.

From the hospital I went to the dormitory to see if the Bronsteins had come back. They had not. I went to the *stolovaya* for soup. As I was walking to the *Evakpunkt,* an NKVD plainclothesman suddenly stopped me and asked for my papers. He took me to the NKVD where I was locked up in a room. I was overcome by despair and resignation to whatever fate might have in store and thought in agony that neither Ida nor anybody else would know to where I had disappeared.

After many hours I was taken to a young NKVD officer who began a lengthy interrogation. I told him in detail how I had missed being evaucated with the VU and about our escape from Riga. He looked again and again at my military ID cards and asked me the questions I had heard so many times before. How come the Nazis let me leave Czechoslovakia? For what purpose had I come to Kazan? Here the paper from the Yaroslavl NKVD proved to be of great help. It stated that I was cleared and allowed to go to Kazan to find out where the VU was.

I told the officer that my wife and child were sick in the hospital and would perish without me. He called the hospitals to verify it. Then I was taken back to my cell. After a long, agonizing time a sentry led me again to the office. To my great surprise, the officer gave me my documents and told me to find work and a place to stay.

An attempt at achieving these two objectives, however, meant moving in a vicious circle. When you asked for work, they wanted to see your permit to live in the city, and if you looked for a place to live, you could not be registered with the militia without confirmation from your place of work. But how to square that circle the NKVD officer did not bother to tell me. Anyway, I was too happy to ask him. I could not believe that I was free to go.

It was already late in the evening when I returned to the station. When Vasya heard what had happened to me, he shook his head, "Oh brother! You still have a very long way to go before you'll know how to cope with life here." We again spent the night in the Telegraph Office.

THREE

When I came in the morning to the station for *kipyatok*, I was pleasantly surprised to find Dr. Bronstein there. He had accepted a position at the Yoshkar-Ola hospital and had come to pick up the family's belongings. When he heard my adventures during the past days, he insisted that I go with him.

The miniature train drove slowly through thick forests. The branches of the trees hung so low overhead that I could stretch out my arm and reach them. But I was in no mood to indulge in admiring the beauties of nature; my thoughts were with my dear ones in the hospital.

Yoshkar-Ola, the capital of the Mari Autonomous Republic, was a fair-sized town about 80 miles from Kazan. What struck me was that all the houses, including the large government buildings, were made of wood. Even the sidewalks were paved with logs. I was in the Central Russian forest heartland where lumber was plentiful.

The Director of the Teachers' Institute was willing to give me a position in September and also promised to help me find a room. The salary was small, but I hoped that somehow I would be able to make ends meet. This town too was full of refugees, but living conditions seemed bearable, and I was happy to have found a place to settle.

Early next morning I returned to Kazan. One detail from that visit has remained in my memory. Walking to the station I met a kolkhoz woman who carried a basket of strawberries to the market. I stopped her. For five rubles she poured me some berries into a newspaper. They tasted so delicious—it was the only time I ate strawberries in Russia—that to this day whenever I eat strawberries they call forth Yoshkar-Ola in my memory.

*   *   *

The condition of my two patients was the same. I could not see Ida but left her a message with the good news about Yoshkar-Ola. When I came to Berman that morning, he was worried that for two days I had not come for bread. I told him about my trip to Yoshkar-Ola. When he heard about my experience with the NKVD, he whispered, "I was afraid that something like this was going to happen to you. We can't talk here; come to my home in the evening."

Berman lived alone in a tiny room. When I came in, he was preparing his supper on a kerosene cooker. I looked at his furrowed face and white hair. He was only about 50 but looked 70. At first he talked haltingly and as if in riddles. I saw that something was on his mind and that he was pondering how to get it off his chest. We ate in silence, each of us submerged in gloomy thoughts.

He began slowly. "The war will end and you'll return home. But you are totally unfamiliar with life here and are bound to get in trouble. Don't tell anybody that you are from Czechoslovakia. Say that you come from Latvia and have lost your documents." Then he gave me an old suit and, pointing at my European clothes, said "Put those away for better times; you are conspicuous in them as a foreigner a mile away."

He paused and then started thoughtfully, "I want to tell you something which I'd like you to retell to the free world." What I heard from him made my hair stand on end.

Berman was born in Kazan. In World War I he moved to Vladivostok in Siberia, where he eventually became a well-to-do merchant. In 1922, after the Bolshevik takeover of that region, he fled to Kharbin, Manchuria. He opened an export business there and everything went well—until the trouble came. Their only son became a Communist and wanted to return to Russia to help build socialism there. All efforts to talk him out of it were in vain. In 1927 he left for Vladivostok. He wrote enthusiastic letters, exhorting his parents to join him. The mother pined for her son and begged her husband to move there. When the first grandson was born, he could no longer withstand her insistence. "If we don't like it there, we can always come back," she said.

To make a long story short, in 1930 they returned to Vladivostok. Berman got a position as a store manager and everything seemed to be alright. Their son, an active member in the regional Party leadership, had a great career and eventually became the director of a large plant. One night in 1934 the NKVD suddenly arrested him.

All efforts to find the reason for his arrest remained futile. "You had better not ask," was the answer of the NKVD. Many months later they learned that he had been sentenced as a "Japanese spy" to an indefinite term in a labor camp with no right of correspondence, which in the NKVD parlance was tantamount to a death sentence.

Not long after their son's arrest his wife too was sent to a labor camp. The two small children were taken away by the NKVD and placed in a children's home, and to this day Berman could not find out where they were. Some time afterward he and his wife were exiled to a remote Siberian village. His wife died there from grief, and he became ill. After many appeals he was at last allowed, about three years before I met him, to go to live with his sister in Kazan.

I listened to Berman in silence and was shaken to the depth of my soul by his tragic tale. During the years in Russia I was to hear countless such stories. I came to realize that it was no exaggeration that ". . . there was not a house where there was not one dead" (Exodus XII:30). For in that tragic time of the Stalin purges there was hardly a single Jewish family that did not have someone murdered or languishing in a labor camp. The only difference from Egypt was that there was no "great cry in the land." Those who were stricken cried only in secret and at night wet the pillows with their tears.

* * *

It was already past midnight when I returned to the station. I looked everywhere for Vasya but could not find him. He had probably managed to get on a train and continue his trip to Central Asia; I never saw him again. I did not feel safe enough without him in the Telegraph Office and went to the park. Very tired, I sat down on a bench, but could not doze off; I kept thinking about what I had heard from Berman; it haunted me like a nightmare.

Toward dawn I had a frightful experience. On a bench across from me lay a woman with a knapsack on her back. Suddenly I saw a man sneaking up behind her. He looked around and tried first to open the knapsack. Then he took out a knife and began to cut through the strings. I was petrified and closed my eyes quickly. I knew that if he noticed that I was awake he would not hesitate to use the knife on my throat.

After a long while I dared to peek from the corner of an eye. The thief was gone and so was the knapsack, but the woman went on sleeping peacefully. I left the park in a hurry and walked around the streets; I did not want to witness the scene when the poor woman woke up and discovered the theft. Besides, I could easily have gotten involved in some trouble.

Coming from Czechoslovakia, where you could practically leave your doors unlocked, I was shocked upon my arrival in Russia by the number of thefts and robberies. I recall the strange feeling I had the first night at the station in Kazan when I saw people tying their bundles to their bodies with strings before going to sleep. Nevertheless, this precaution did not deter thieves from ripping bundles open with a knife or from stealing a whole bundle. In the middle of the night we used to be awakened by the sudden cry of a victim who had just discovered that he had been robbed.

But the culprits were usually never found. People were scared and nobody "saw" anything. I witnessed countless similar scenes at other stations, in trains, in the streets and in market places throughout my sojourn in Russia.

* * *

Tosya, the *stolovaya* waitress, had usually seen me in the company of the Bronsteins. Now that I came alone there, she apparently assumed that I was unattached. Once after serving me the soup she sat down next to me and asked where my friends were. I told her and we began to chat. She wanted to know who I was, where I came from and what I intended to do. Then she asked where I was staying.

"For the time being at the station," I answered. She blushed and began hesitantly "My husband left for the front after the outbreak of the war. I have a large room and could take in somebody. There will be plenty to eat for both of us, and we won't have to worry about anything."

I looked at the young beautiful woman and pitied her, thinking in that moment of all the Tosyas, Carolyns and Gretchens whose husbands go off to slaughter one another and leave their young wives alone at home. It serves them right, I said to myself. The women too are, after all, only flesh and blood and need someone to alleviate their loneliness.

I did not react to Tosya's remark and went on chatting amiably about various things, as though I had not taken the hint. After a while I glanced at my watch and said delicately that I must be off to visit my sick wife and my sick child in the hospital. Her eyes became sad, and she fell silent. I must give her credit for not holding it against me; whenever I came to the *stolovaya* she was friendly and usually treated me to a second soup. I do hope she found somebody to share the burden of her loneliness.

The problem of where to spend the night and how to avoid the curious eyes of the militia and NKVD became more and more excruciating. I practiced Vasya's pattern of alternating between the park, Telegraph Office, station and walking around in the streets. Lacking, however, his experience and sharp sense of timing to evade an unexpected checking of documents, I often had close brushes with danger.

Fearing to stay too long in the Telegraph Office, I once had a foolhardy notion—to place a long-distance call to our number in Riga. I knew that Riga was already captured by the Germans; but since there was no official communiqué about it, I ventured to play the fool. After about four hours of trying, the operator told me nonchalantly that she could not get the number. Waiting for my "call," I could spend the night there without fear. I used that gimmick a few more times later. But then I was at my wits' end and lived in constant trepidation.

*   *   *

July dragged on in deep anguish. The condition of Raphi continued to be serious and at times even critical. I went through a frightful time. In the first days Ida too was very ill, but she got better gradually and was discharged on July 26. She was still weak when I took her back to the children's hospital, but the thought of being together again with her son gave her new strength.

One morning Berman told me that his sister's son was about to leave any day for the army. Since his room would be requisitioned for some evacuee family anyway, his sister would rather let us have it, he said, and added, "For money we can get you a permit to live in Kazan and then you'll be able to find some position." So on August 6 I moved in to Mrs. Kassierer's apartment. The first thing I did was to go to a city *banya*. After hours of waiting I finally managed to get in. The steam bath was a great treat, and it felt wonderful to be rid of the lice and the sweat and dirt accumulated since my shower in Ivanovo. For the first time since leaving Riga I slept in a bed that night.

Mrs. Kassierer was a wonderful woman and helped me greatly to settle down. She too had a sad tale to tell. Her husband had been killed in the civil war, and the husband of her older daughter had been sent to a Siberian labor camp several years earlier. Recently though they had received word from him that he had been freed and sent to the front. She also told me a great deal about the suffering of the Jews in Kazan from the Stalin terror.

I felt encouraged by finding a place to live. Even though in

Yoshkar-Ola food was cheaper and living conditions in general easier, I nonetheless would have preferred to live in Kazan. It was a large city and one of the important Russian cultural centers. It had an old university and many other educational institutions. Before the Revolution it had been considered the intellectual capital of eastern Russia.

I spoke to Dr. Harkavy to find out if she could discharge Raphi. Her beautiful dark eyes smiled sadly. "That is out of the question. His condition has improved somewhat, but he is still far from being out of danger." I had no choice but to wait and postpone all plans for the time being.

*   *   *

So often in the course of the difficult struggle for survival in Russia, and also later in life, I have convinced myself that it was futile to make plans for the future. You rack your brains to plan, and then something totally unexpected happens and changes everything. Call it blind coincidence or Providence—man proposes and God disposes.

Anyway, the next day after my conversation with Dr. Harkavy, as I was standing in line for *kipyatok* on the station platform, I felt a slap on the shoulder and a friendly voice exclaimed "What in the world are you doing here?!" I turned around and stared at the man, trying hard to remember who he was. "Don't you recognize me? I'm Ivanov, the bookkeeper from the VU in Riga," he said. I was so startled that it indeed took me a while to recognize him in his military uniform.

He told me that the VU had returned to Pskov, but shortly after its arrival there had been ordered to move to Tamak, in the Urals. Now the train with the school was standing at the station in Kazan.

We went to the train. Colonel Ryabov was surprised but very glad to see me. I told him what I had gone through since seeing him last in Riga. "Your troubles are over now. Go and get your family from the hospital and come with us," he said.

I was dizzy from happiness, it was all unreal, like a dream. I hurried to the hospital. But all my pleading with Dr. Harkavy was useless. She adamantly said, "I won't let you kill your child. He is too ill to travel and would not survive the long trip." I returned to Ryabov with a heavy heart. He told me to cable him as soon as the child was well enough to travel, whereupon he would send me an official request to resume work at school. In the meantime he gave me a letter asking the authorities to assist me in my efforts to get to Tamak.

I walked around in the train to say hello to friends. I missed my close friend Logunov very much. I learned that he, like many other officers and most of the cadets, had gone to the front straight from Riga. When dusk fell, I watched sadly as the train pulled out of the station and disappeared in the distance. For the second time unfortunate circumstances had prevented me from traveling with the VU.

FOUR

August 8 was Rafi's first birthday. I talked with Ida through the hospital window about how we would have celebrated that happy day under normal circumstances in Riga; what fuss his grandparents would have made about it. But he was fighting for his life instead, and I could not even see him.

During those days there was a kind of tug-of-war between Dr. Harkavy and me. I tried to persuade her that unless we left soon for Tamak, the school would engage another teacher, and she constantly refused to discharge Raphi.

I vividly remember the afternoon that I was sitting in her office and arguing with her. By that time we had become rather friendly. In the course of our talk I asked her in passing if she was not related to the renowned Jewish scholar Harkavy. She became pale and whispered to me to change the subject. In my ignorance of the facts of Soviet life I did not notice that a nurse was within earshot.

On a later occasion when we were alone she said, "How terribly naive you are to ask such questions in the presence of other people. You seem to forget where you are." It turned out that she was a niece of the famous professor. Then she began to unburden the heavy pain from her heart.

In 1937 her husband, a high government official, was suddenly arrested and had not been heard of since. All attempts to find out what the charge was and what had happened to him were without result. The NKVD gave her a cynical, laconic answer—to forget him and remarry. It sounded like a nightmare. I looked at the beautiful woman. She was hardly 40, but her raven-black hair was woven through with gray.

* * *

On August 14 I finally telegraphed Ryabov. The coming days passed in suspenseful waiting. Several times a day I ran to the General Delivery window in the post office to inquire if there was a telegram for me. On the fifth day it arrived at last.

The military commandant of the station issued me train tickets. Moreover, since it was a trip officially requested by a military institution, I also received "dry provisions" for four days. Raphi was still very weak. He looked pale and emaciated, only skin and bones. Dr. Harkavy gave us medications for the trip and impressed on us that if his condition became worse, we must interrupt the journey and take him immediately to a hospital.

We left Kazan on August 20, at 10 P.M. Berman came to see us off. "Let us still talk for a while; God knows if we'll see one another again," he said. I had come to like that kind, heartbroken man very much. We exchanged letters from time to time until the winter of 1943, when he stopped writing. Then I received the sad news from his sister that he had died suddenly a few months before.

By traveling on the Trans-Siberian Express we could have been in Ufa, 80 miles north of Tamak, in about 24 hours. But such luxury was out of the question for simple mortals. It was reserved for Party and government officials only. Every time the Express, with the prerevolutionary French inscriptions on the sleek cars, pulled into the station, it was cordoned off by militiamen to fend off the people who would run to each arriving train, trying to get on its steps or to climb in through the windows or onto the roof.

As soon as the regular passenger train arrived, there began a stampede to the cars. The conductors locked the doors and admitted only people with tickets. Crying women holding up infants wrapped in shawls pushed forward. The scene broke the heart. With great difficulty we finally succeeded in getting into the car.

Millions of refugees got stranded in those days at the stations. Eventually the authorities realized the seriousness of the problem and little by little made efforts to transport them to the east.

I left Kazan with mixed feelings. Despite the suffering I experienced there I had come to like that city, and upon leaving I felt that I was parting with my last link to European civilization as I approached the unknown of the distant Urals.

I noticed that the train turned off from the main eastbound line to a branch leading south along the Volga. The principal railroad artery had to be kept free for the trains that, day and night, evacuated government offices and institutions from Moscow to Kuybyshev. The foreign embassies also were moving there. The Germans came closer to Moscow, and only Stalin with the *Stavka* (War Council) and the Commissariat of Defense remained. Kuybyshev was now practically the capital of the country.

The car was crowded and noisy. Now and then a quarrel broke out about a seat on the wooden bench or a place on the floor. Children cried. It was impossible to sleep. The train stopped at a station and people tried to get on. I wanted to go for *kipyatok,* but the conductress told me to stay in the car unless I wanted to be left.

Before long it was dawn and people began to awaken. They were a colorful mixture of nationalities from all western regions of the country. It seemed as if the entire nation was on the move, one part escaping east and the other part going west day and night in long military trains to stop the Germans.

Soon there was lively talk all around. Total strangers befriended each other and told one another their troubles as if they had been old neighbors. Next to us sat an elderly woman in a patched army coat and worn boots. She had already been traveling more than a month to her daughter in Sverdlovsk. "Auntie, it won't be safe there from the Germans; you have to go farther east," said a burly Ukrainian with a cagey wink. The woman became bewildered and began crying.

Others discussed the respective merits of living conditions in the various towns to which they were going. But most passengers had no one to go to. They were looking for a place to stay and had no particular destination in mind. Our train was in no hurry and made many stops, but nobody minded. It was better to be on the train than stranded for days at some station.

The next morning we arrived in Penza, where we had to change trains. Our next train was to arrive in the afternoon. Ida sat down in the station, while I went with others from our car to the kolkhoz market to buy some milk for Raphi. On the way back we dropped into a store. The shelves were practically empty, except for flower seeds and some miniature clay busts of Lenin and Stalin. There were also beautifully painted wooden spoons and plates.

While my companions were making purchases, I walked around in the back aisles of the store. I noticed in a box on the shelf a pile of children's winter suits. The prices were amazingly low, and I bought all eight of them. They turned out to be too large for Raphi and I regretted having bought them. Later in Tamak, however, they proved to be of great value in bartering for food in the kolkhoz market to keep our child alive.

At that station I witnessed a tragic human event that has remained in my memory. While sitting in the waiting room we heard a heartrending scream. People ran to the platform. On the ground lay a woman tearing her hair and crying, "Oh my baby, my baby!" She was hysterical, and it was impossible to find out what had happened. It turned out later that she had gotten off the train to get some *kipyatok* at the station, and meanwhile the train had left with her baby. It was a horrible experience for me. After that I became very cautious when getting out of the train at a station lest something similar happen to me also.

Our train left Penza late in the evening, and we traveled all night. In the morning we came to a large station that looked somehow familiar. I looked at the name—Ulyanovsk—and remembered that we had passed through it once already after leaving Kazan.

After some time the train was rolling over a bridge across the Volga and began heading east. I felt enormous relief; at last we had reached the Ural region. The scenery of mountains and wooded valleys was breathtaking. Years later, reading Pasternak's *Dr. Zhivago* with its wonderful descriptions of Ural landscapes, I felt much at home, realizing with gratification that I had seen it with my own eyes.

We did not travel on the Trans-Siberian line but through the picturesque mountainous countryside. At the small stations where we stopped, Bashkir men and women in colorful oriental robes boarded the train. I felt suddenly the exotic breath of Asia. At night the air outside was chilly. At long last we arrived in Ufa, the capital of the Bashkir Autonomous Republic. We got off the train to change for another train on our last 80-mile leg to Tamak.

4

First Winter in Tamak

ONE

IT WAS ALREADY after midnight on August 26, 1941, when we at last arrived in Tamak. We got out of the train and stood bewildered on the platform. The darkness around us was only dimly lighted by a bare, dusty electric bulb over the entrance to the station. The air outside was much cooler here than in Kazan. People on the platform wore overcoats or cotton-padded jackets. I was told that the town was more than three miles away and that there was no transportation available. I would not have been able to find the VU in the dark of night anyway. The only thing left was to spend the night in the station.

When we entered the waiting room, I was surprised to see that the flood of war refugees had already reached this remote Ural area. With great difficulty we finally got a place on the floor to sit down. There was noise and bustle all night.

Early in the morning I set out on the long walk to town. The sun was coming up behind the wooded hills. As I walked along the dusty dirt road, I was puzzled by the strange reddish-brown color of the soil. I did not know as yet that I was in the Ishimbay oil region, one of the richest in the country.

On the outskirts of the town thin pillars of white smoke rose from the small, dingy huts. I envied the people inside who did not know the suffering of flight and wandering and were about to sit down to breakfast without the worry of finding a place to sleep. In sharp contrast to the rural look of the huts with their colorfully painted window shutters were the tenements and factory buildings farther off.

101

The town made a dismal impression on me. The houses were shabby, the streets and sidewalks unpaved and dirty. There was no sewage system. From the muddy rivulets in the shallow ditches along the road came an indefinable stench.

I finally came to the VU. It was housed in an old, spacious barracks surrounded by a high stone wall. The housing officer had a soldier with a horse-drawn wagon drive me to the station to fetch my family, then he took us to the living quarters that the VU had obtained for us from the *Gorsoviet* (City Administration).

*   *   *

Our living quarters consisted of a tiny, dark kitchen, nearly one third of which was taken up by an old Russian brick oven. From the kitchen a door led to a room in which a refugee woman with two children was already living.

When the officer left, we began to look around. The walls and ceiling were black from smoke; they had not seen a painter's brush in many years. The panes of the only window were broken. The room was entirely empty, without a single piece of furniture in it. We put Raphi to sleep on the oven and then sat down on our bundles on the floor to rest for a while. We were sitting in silence, as if to mourn for the past life that now seemed so far away and gone forever.

I had to go to the VU to make preparations for the coming school year, which was about to start that next week. I remained the only German teacher, and a heavy work load awaited me. The entire curriculum had to be adapted to war conditions. But I was very happy to get back to work. The end of the painful wandering and the reunion with the VU gave me the illusion that I was resuming work that had been interrupted by some unforeseen occurrence and that before long we would all raise anchor and leave for Riga to return to our previous life.

When I came back to the empty, dismal room I had, for the first time since Riga, the feeling of being home. Raphi welcomed me happily as if he had not seen me in weeks and rushed into my arms. We began to unpack and settle down in our new residence, trying to figure out a way that all three of us might sleep on the oven.

Later in the afternoon something happened that moved me to tears. There was a light knock on the door. I was surprised to see Colonel Ryabov. Behind him were two soldiers carrying an iron army cot with a mattress, blankets and linen. Ryabov looked around the room and sighed. When he was about to help the cadets put up the cot, I said in embarrassment, "Not you yourself, comrade colonel, let me do it." But he pushed me aside with his usual friendly smile, saying good-naturedly, "Never mind; for a nice man like you it is an honor even for a colonel to do it."

The cadets then went to the truck and brought in a small table with two chairs, some dishes and other kitchen utensils. "For the time being you have something to sleep on and these few things. Let me see what we can do for you later," Ryabov told us.

When he left, we remained silent for a long while, overwhelmed by what had happened. Ryabov was indeed one of the most wonderful persons I have ever met in my life. He represented to me the natural goodness of the plain, suffering Russian people, which I so often had an opportunity to observe.

One of the useful things Ryabov brought us was a pail. I took it and went for water. We boiled some *kipyatok,* soaked in it some of the *sukhari* (dried bread) that was still left from the trip and ate. Then we went to bed, Ida with Raphi on the cot and I on the bare oven. I lay awake for a long time, thinking about the cruel Nazi storm that had whirled us to this remote Ural town near the border between Europe and Asia and how we were going to manage to adjust to these dire conditions and survive.

* * *

The large wooden building at 11 Marx Street, where we lived, had belonged before the Revolution to a rich merchant. Now it was owned by the town. It was old and dilapidated and earmarked for demolition long ago, but thanks to the Soviet lack of efficiency this had not been done. Nobody had lived in the house for years. It was used now to accommodate war refugees, and the VU had obtained several rooms for its civilian employees. There was no gas, electricity or plumbing. Water had to be fetched from a pump in the street several blocks away, and the 18 refugee families living there had to use a primitive latrine about 50 yards back in the yard (which, especially in the winter, was an ordeal).

I had to learn the hard way to cope with the merciless realities of life in Tamak, and the process of adjustment was slow and painful. Early in the morning I had to go for water to the pump. There was always a line there. But this line was not so bad in comparison with the line for bread, which I had to face right after that.

I was already familiar with the long lines. At first I thought naively that it was only a war phenomenon. Gradually, however, I came to realize that the *ochered* (queue) had been a way of life from the start of the Soviet regime.

If I were asked to characterize the misery of daily life for the average Soviet citizen, I would express it in one single word: *ochered*. For nothing could describe more succinctly the failure and inefficiency of the entire economic system than the queue. You have to stand in line for everything you want to get—from bread to a needle to a shoddy pair of pants.

Everybody stands in various lines several hours a day. If multiplied on a national scale, it amounts to hundreds of millions of working hours wasted daily in lines.

No matter how early in the morning I came to the store for bread, there was already a long line outside. Those who had to leave early for work came at the crack of dawn and waited for hours in order to be first when the bread arrived from the bakery. Very often, however, the bread was delivered late, and we had to hurry to work. Ida then came with the child in her arms to take my place in the queue.

My daily bread ration was 600 grams, Ida's 400 and Raphi's 300; together, we shared a dark-brown, brick-shaped piece of a sticky heavy mass, whose taste was nondescript—a strange mixture of rye, barley and chaff (some claimed it also contained sawdust). As long as the bread was fresh it was somehow edible. The next day, however, it was like a tasteless piece of brick.

But our bread seldom remained till the next morning; it was the only food we had. We washed it down with *kipyatok* and, though of dubious nutritional value, it filled the stomach and stilled the nagging hunger for a while.

Now and then it happened that Ida came back from the line

with tearful eyes; she could not control her hunger and on the way home ate up piece by piece all our bread portions for the day. I knew myself too well the gnawing pain of hunger and understood her. Without a word I would take some salable item and go to the bazaar to sell it and buy some bread, at 25 to 30 rubles a pound (before long the prices soared much higher).

* * *

The *ochered* is an inseparable part of Soviet daily life and has its own unwritten ground rules that have to be abided by. I had to learn them fast in order to survive. The first thing you have to do when joining a line is to ask loudly, "Who is the last?" If someone answers "I am," you say to him "I am next." Only then are you considered a legitimate line member.

Some cynics continued this *ochered* ceremonial further as follows. You would ask the person ahead of you what was being sold. He'd answer "I don't know." But this is not merely a cynical joke; it rather expresses the sad Soviet reality. I soon found out that everybody carried in his pocket a cellular shopping net, called in Russian appropriately *avoska*, from the word "avos," or "perhaps," meaning that perhaps the net might come in handy if you happen to pass a line where they sell something.

What is being sold is quite unimportant. The rule is buy whatever they sell because later you won't be able to get it. And if you don't need that item or can't use it, you'll always be able to sell it in the bazaar at a high price or barter it to a kolkhoz farmer for food.

The state also issued ration coupons for meat, eggs, sugar, etc. But they were never honored, and people eventually stopped asking for those luxurious things. They were glad if they could get the daily bread ration.

Occasionally there was a sudden rumor in the bread line that in some other store in town that morning they were going to sell a few grams of margarine, jam or a slice of dried fish. A stampede began. In order to prevent quarrels, someone was put in charge of preserving the order of the line. He would walk along the line and write a number on your arm with a chemical pencil. Then you could run to the other line and try your luck there and then come back to the bread line.

But these rumors usually turned out to be false; and if your number was called before you returned empty-handed from the other line, you had to go to the end of the line and wait again for hours until your new turn came.

Despite my efforts to get familiar with the *ochered* rules I did get in trouble before long. One day there was no bread at all. The people grumbled and cursed but in the end dispersed and went home. The next morning I presented to Maria Yurievna, the store manager, both our unhonored coupons for that day and the day before. To my surprise she shouted for everybody to hear, "Just look at the nerve of this foreigner! He is not satisfied that the Soviet government is feeding him today but demands also the bread for yesterday!"

I found out that I had violated one of the basic *ochered* rules: "*Prozhil, tak prozhil!*"—if you survived the preceding day without your bread ration, then you were not entitled to it any longer. I became scared, and for some time Ida went for the bread, until one day a woman neighbor advised us to grease Maria Yurievna's palm. I took one of Ida's last Czech blouses and gave it to her. She gave me no trouble afterward.

TWO

Tamak was founded in 1766 as a Czarist military fort (the VU was housed in it now) in order to suppress the frequent rebellions of the conquered Bashkirs. After the fall of Czarism the Bashkirs, who are Moslems, established their own national state. In 1919, however, it was incorporated by force into the Soviet Union as the Bashkir Autonomous Republic, with Tamak as its capital until 1922, when Ufa became the capital.

When we came to Tamak it was already crowded with war refugees. The prewar population of about 30,000, mostly Bashkirs and other Mongolian nationalities but also many Russians, had more than doubled. But the refugees kept coming. The deeper the Germans penetrated into Soviet territory, the larger grew the stream of refugees into the Urals, Siberia and Central Asia.

There were two categories of refugees in Tamak. First there were those who had been evacuated with their factories, which were reestablished in Tamak and produced war materials. These evacuees were relatively fortunate in many respects. They could take on the trains which evacuated the plants a considerable part of their personal belongings, and they had priority in getting a place to live. Furthermore, each plant had a *stolovaya* where the workers got their daily bread rations and one warm meal a day.

But the bulk of refugees fell in the second category of people, those who had fled in a hurry before the advancing German armies and had very few of their personal belongings. They had to fend for themselves in the struggle for survival. If they were lucky, they got some dingy corner with a local family, for which they had to pay by providing food or firewood for the family.

The proportion of Jews among the refugees was very high. They came from all the western parts of the country; also from the Baltic states, the Polish provinces and Bessarabia, annexed by the Soviets after 1939. Each had a sad story of his own, and many of them perished during this time.

* * *

The only thing one could get in the stores was the daily bread ration. Fortunately, the state price of bread was very low. All other food had to be bought in the kolkhoz market, a vast open field on the edge of the town, where the collective farmers sold the produce from their small private plots, for which they were allowed to charge any price they wanted. In prewar years there had been a chronic shortage of food and indeed of everything else in the stores, so that people depended on the kolkhoz market, where they had to pay exorbitant prices. After the outbreak of the war, however, the prices began to soar sky-high.

Adjacent to the kolkhoz market was the bazaar. It was actually a rather shabby flea market called *tolchok*, from the Russian word for jolt, or push. A very fitting name indeed, for that is what went on in that fenced-in square. If you paid the half-ruble admission fee at the entrance, you could sell anything you wanted and ask any price you wished.

Along the fence inside the *tolchok* sat the native vendors, displaying on small stalls or on the ground a variety of wares, from a handful of rusty nails, a box of matches or a glass of salt, to an old pot or stove. The inner part of the *tolchok* was a cruising department store on human legs—refugee men and women walking around and offering for sale their garments, underwear, shoes, linen, etc., in order to buy some food later in the kolkhoz market. There was loud trading and dickering. Everything was in motion, like a humming beehive or a constantly changing kaleidoscope.

Besides used things, one could also buy there all sorts of new merchandise, pilfered by workers from the factories and sold at very high prices. If you could afford to pay a lot of money, you could get silk stockings, lingerie and other luxury items of foreign make. Only God knows how it all found its illicit way to the Tamak market.

The strange thing was that the authorities closed their eyes to this illegal trading. Since they did not sell you anything in the stores, they were hesitant to clamp down on the black market, which was the only place where people could buy what they needed.

Soon I realized that the market was not only a place for commerce but served also as a social meeting center, substituting for the missing café, restaurant, social club, church and mosque. It was the place where one could meet old friends and make new acquaintances.

I became familiar with the *tolchok* on the second day after our arrival. Besides the few household things that Ryabov brought us, we had nothing. But the item we needed immediately and most urgently was a primus. When I came to the *tolchok* I was shocked at the high prices they asked for even a junk kerosene cooker. It was more than my salary for a whole month. I stopped to ask an elderly Bashkir who had a small pushcart in a corner. He had none. But he told me, "Don't buy a primus from someone you don't know; it won't function, and you'll have to throw it out in the end. I'll bring you one in the evening, and you'll be able to try it out."

This old Bashkir, Akhmadulin, did bring us a kerosene cooker. But I did not have the cash to pay him. He asked us if we had something to sell. We showed him our scanty belongings. He took an experienced look at our clothes and remarked, "I see you are not Russian; the Russian evacuees have brought along lots of things." We told him who we were and under what circumstances we escaped from Riga. He put aside our personal clothing and said, "Don't sell any of these; you'll need each piece badly yourselves."

What caught his interest, however, were the children's suits which I had bought in Penza and considered a useless burden all the time. "For these you can get a very good price," he said.

There was something about Akhmadulin that set him apart from the other local trading sharpies who mercilessly skinned the inexperienced refugees; he was polite and dignified. Before long we became good friends. He proved to be an honest man, and we trusted one another. Only later, when he told me about his background, did I realize why he showed such understanding for my situation. All through the time of my sojourn in Tamak he was very helpful and gave me practical advice on how to cope with the daily struggle of survival. I also learned from him a great deal about the life of the Bashkirs and the town in general.

THREE

Our street was one of the thoroughfares to the kolkhoz market. From the early morning hours there was a stream of people going to or from the market. Little by little many faces of the passersby became familiar. One of them especially had drawn my attention in the first days after our arrival. I used to see him on my way to or from the water pump. He was an elderly man with soft, smiling eyes. His broad face was framed in a neatly trimmed gray beard. He wore a short coat with a caracul collar and a matching caracul hat. His boots were always shined and clean. He walked with a cane, but with a sprightly step.

In the beginning our eyes would meet for a short moment; my foreign appearance probably attracted his attention. Then we began nodding a good morning to one another. One morning I finally mustered up the courage to stop him and introduce myself. When he told me that his name was Menikhes, I recited in Hebrew the second verse of the 23rd Psalm in which one of the words sounds in the Ashkenazic pronunciation like his name. His eyes lit up and he remarked sadly, "A Soviet Jew your age does not even know what a psalm is, nor has he ever heard of King David."

During the years I spent in Russia I made the acquaintance of many Soviet Jews, including Party members. With some of them I became friends and we would talk freely. Nonetheless, even with them I always had the feeling that there was an invisible line of frankness beyond which they were unwilling to go. And I never tried to make them cross that line. It was amazing, however, how easily that dividing barrier fell between Mendel Menikhes and me even during our first talk. Very soon we struck up an intimate and lasting friendship. I felt entirely at ease with him and we talked about everything without a mask or fear, as if he were from my home town and I had known him all my life.

Before the Revolution he had been the spiritual leader of a congregation in Mozyr, White Russia. When his synagogue was closed by the Bolshevik regime he had gone to work in a furriers' cooperative. Since the death of his wife, several years before, he lived with his daughter. Upon the outbreak of the war, her husband, a chemical engineer, was evacuated to Tamak, where he was connected with the Ishimbay Petrochemical *Kombinat*.

Menikhes's fellow-townsmen in Tamak still considered him as their spiritual leader and called him Reb Mendel. He had a handwritten Jewish calendar that he had devised himself, and people would come to consult him as to when to observe a *yahrzeit* or a Jewish holiday as well as on other religious matters. I admired his untiring skill in soliciting money from acquaintances to help the sick and needy among the refugees. ("You would not believe how many Party members make contributions," he once told me.)

* * *

In the first couple of weeks after our arrival the weather was relatively fair. About mid-September, however, the rains began, and it poured day and night. Our topcoats, warm clothes and underwear, galoshes and umbrellas all remained in the luggage we had lost near the VU in Riga. Walking outside became a torment; the chill of the soaking-wet summer clothes penetrated to the marrow of our bones.

The incessant rain turned the ground into a sticky clay. The slimy mud of the roadway slid down onto the lower sidewalks. Very often I lost a shoe in the deep gluey slime and had a hard time fishing it out. Often, too, I was splashed all over with mud by the passing vehicles. The room became damp and chilly, and we had no firewood. To the misery of hunger was now added suffering from the rain and cold.

One morning I ran into Ryabov in the school yard. I was just coming from standing in the bread line for a few hours. My trousers were covered with slimy mud up to the knees, my summer jacket and shirt were soaked through by the rain. He looked at me and sighed; then he took me to his office and sent me with a note to the warehouse manager.

My miserable appearance must have moved even the tough elderly sergeant. "Oh my, what the *Fritzes* have done to us! I remember how you looked in Riga," he said. The old worn high boots, patched army coats and uniforms and underwear which he issued for Ida and me from discarded stock literally saved our lives. Without them I don't know how we would have survived the cruel Ural weather. I also asked the sergeant for a few discarded blankets and a mattress cover. From one of the blankets we made a footmuff for Raphi to sleep in and also to carry him in outside.

With the mattress cover I went to the horse stable of the VU and stuffed it with straw. Now at least I did not have to sleep on the bare oven. Several days later I bought some firewood in the kolkhoz market. In the evenings we lit the Russian brick oven and Ida with Raphi slept on top while I took their cot. Unfortunately, the wood did not last long.

After about two weeks the rains stopped as suddenly as they had started. When I went out in the morning, a pale sun tried to break through the overcast sky. The mud was covered with a thin frozen crust. The Ural frosts had set in; mornings the window was covered with the most fantastic flowery ice configurations, and the water in the pail was frozen. Before long the gluey mud outside became a solid, wrinkled mass, and when walking on it one's footsteps resounded with a hollow echo. The air was cold and crisp.

One morning in the beginning of October the brown bleakness disappeared and everything around was covered with a clean white blanket of powdery snow, which kept coming down from the sky. The approaches to the pump were slippery from the spilled, frozen water.

The appearance of the people changed too. They wore *valenkis* (felt boots) and cotton-padded jackets and pants. The women had heavy shawls around their heads and shoulders. All looked like jolly Santa Clauses. The mood in the *ochered* also improved. People were not as jumpy as during the rains when arguments burst out over every trifle.

The cold of the winter grew more cruel every day, and the promised load of firewood from the VU was still not delivered. The military personnel had priority, while we, the civilian employees, were left to freeze in our holes. All we could do was to sleep in our clothes.

The shortage of food supplies was incomprehensible. Tamak was situated in one of the richest agricultural regions in the country. Akhmadulin told me that many years ago when you showed the farmers in the market a five-ruble bill they would load you with produce. Collectivized agriculture, however, was unable to supply the urban population even with the daily portions of black bread. And the kolkhoz people themselves were not much better off either.

It was the same story with wood. Right outside the town began the rich Ural forests that stretched for hundreds of miles in all directions, yet the average citizen froze in his home. It was like parching in the middle of a lake for a drink of water. The state owned all the forests and sold wood only to factories and institutions, which in turn allotted it to their employees. But thanks to the chronic Soviet malaise in transportation and distribution, there were constant shortages and delays.

Despite the danger of lengthy prison terms, the kolkhozniks stole wood from the forests and sold it at a very high price in the black market. I too had no choice but to barter now and then part of our bread portions for a bundle of firewood. Wood now became as important as food.

FOUR

Toward the end of October Akhmadulin took me to one of his neighbors who was interested in exchanging some wood for one of our children's winter suits. As we were walking along Lenin Street, Akhmadulin pointed at a large house and said, "There, together with Feldman, I had a hardware store until the end of the NEP (Lenin's New Economic Policy) years in 1928." I was intrigued by the Jewish name he mentioned and remarked that I did not know there were Jews in Tamak.

"There are not any now; maybe one or two families still live here. But there were many Jews before the Revolution. Come, I'll show you where their 'church' used to be," he answered. He took me to a big wooden house in a side street. Over the entrance was a sign "Sverdlov Tailor Cooperative." There was no hint that this had once been a synagogue. For a long while I looked at the house in silence, wondering about the fate of those who once worshipped there. I asked Akhmadulin to find out whether the Jews he mentioned were still in Tamak and where they lived.

About a week later he brought me the address of the Plavniks. I told Menikhes about my discovery. He too was curious about the history of the extinguished Jewish community in town. The following Sunday we walked to a small, dilapidated house near the river. We knocked on the door. A woman in her thirties opened it and said curtly that they had no more living space for refugees. When we told her who we were and whom we came to see, she said in a more polite tone, "Oh, it is my mother you want," and let us in.

Sonya Plavnik, about 70, was sitting in an easy chair. Her legs, which rested on a foot stool, were wrapped in a warm blanket; one could see immediately that they were paralyzed. First she was wary and asked us many questions, but gradually her suspicions melted and she spoke more freely. What I heard from her then and on many other occasions revealed to me the sad story of the Tamak Jewish community and gave me a deeper insight into one of the tragic chapters in the history of Russian Jewry under the Czars.

Before the Revolution there were over 100 Jewish families in Tamak. Most of the Jews were *Kantonists*—those unfortunates who, in the 19th century, were kidnapped as young boys from their parents by the Czarist police and made to serve in the army for 25 years. Many of them were converted to Christianity by force.

Some of the *Kantonists* served in the local Czarist garrison. Those who survived the terrible ordeal of the long military service were allowed to settle in Tamak. The discharged *Kantonists* enjoyed certain privileges and were exempt from many of the Czarist restrictions against the Jews in the so-called Jewish Pale of the western provinces. They established themselves in trade and commerce and eventually founded a congregation and engaged a rabbi.

Sonya's late father had been a *Kantonist*. She told me many stories she had heard from him and from other *Kantonists* about their horrible suffering in the army as well as about the beginnings of the Jewish community in town.

After the fall of Czarism there were big disturbances in the region. The Bashkirs strove for national independence and fought against both the Reds and Whites. The Jews in Tamak suffered greatly, and many of them perished in the long civil war. Under the Bolshevik rule the Jews became totally impoverished and gradually moved away to the larger cities to find a livelihood. Because of Sonya's illness her family remained in town. Her husband had died several years before, and since then she lived with her daughter, whose husband was in the army.

*   *   *

The one who suffered most the first winter after our arrival in Tamak was Raphi. He had not fully recovered from his illness in Kazan. We did our best. But in order to regain his strength he needed nutritious food, which we could not give him. In the rainy weather he became sick with a high temperature. We were afraid of a relapse and took him to the clinic. Dr. Riva Or-shovsky, a pediatrician from Odessa, examined him and pre-scribed some medicine. But his condition became worse, and she told us to take him to the hospital.

And again, as in Kazan, Ida had to stay with him in the hospi-tal. Fortunately, after ten days he was out of danger and we could take him home. But he was very weak. Dr. Orshovsky prescribed for him a glass of milk for three weeks from the City Milk Center for Children, and this helped him to regain his strength. She used to drop by in the evening to check on his progress.

October was a trying time in another respect too. The military situation was deteriorating rapidly. The Germans were close to the outskirts of Moscow. The fate of the country seemed hang-ing in the balance. One could feel the suspense in the air even in Tamak. The most absurd rumors began to spread. Some natives even claimed to have "seen with their own eyes" German planes over the region. The Bashkirs, who hated the Russians and con-sidered the evacuees as intruders, were hinting that as soon as the Germans approached the Urals, they would know what to do with us. It reminded me so much of the hatred I had seen in the eyes of the Latvians in Riga after the outbreak of the war. How-ever, when the Germans were thrown back from Moscow, the agitation subsided and life in town returned to normal.

I remember the strange picture of the October Revolution parade in the yard of the VU. It was bitter cold outside and a snowstorm was raging. The lined up cadets and officers, with only their eyes visible from under the fur caps, kept stamping their feet and flapping their gloved hands against their thighs to prevent frostbite. And the feeling in the heart was not any war-mer either; there was a subdued mood all around.

* * *

As if our suffering were not as yet full, that winter of 1941–42 turned out to be very severe even by Ural standards. The natives said that they could not remember such bitter frosts and violent *purgas* (snowstorms) in decades. And a *purga* was a horrible ex-perience indeed. All of a sudden an icy north wind would begin to rage and whirl up thick clouds of snow so that it was nearly impossible to see yards ahead. If you stumbled and fell, you had to get up quickly lest you remained under a mound of snow. As a precaution, when a *purga* started, people would walk in groups and hold hands in order not to get lost and freeze to death.

The daily struggle for sheer physical survival became a nightmare. Less than half a year had passed since leaving Riga, but my life till then already seemed far, far in the past, almost unreal. Sometimes I had the feeling that it all had happened not to me but to someone else I knew.

Toward the end of November the VU finally delivered the long promised wood. It was not much, and we had to use it sparingly, but it was a great relief. We lit the oven only in the evening so that Ida and Raphi could sleep on a warm oven.

Sometime after mid-December Dr. Orshovsky suggested to Ida that she work as a nurse in the *Dyetdom* (City Children's Home) where she was the supervising physician. It came like help sent from heaven. Ida could take along Raphi and be in the warmth during the day. What is more, they also had soup at lunch time. If not for that unexpected stroke of luck, I don't know how we would have managed to survive.

* * *

The days without bread began to occur more and more frequently. Our coupons for such days were void. It was said that Maria Yurievna sold the bread in the black market. The people in the line grumbled and cursed, but there was not much they could do about it. Her husband was one of the powerful regional Party secretaries.

There were in the line many women with small children in their arms whose husbands were at the front, and they were not afraid to protest and to shout loudly. One breadless morning some of them became desperate and broke down the store door. The matter came to the attention of the NKVD. The scandal could not be squashed any longer, and an investigation was started.

One day at the end of December Maria Yurievna was not in the store anymore. There was a new manager, a war invalid with a wooden leg. There were no more days without bread, and the bread portions were not short-weighted either. To our great surprise, before New Year's day everybody got a small piece of margarine, some hard candy and a salted herring.

Nobody knew what happened to Maria Yurievna. Soon it was whispered that she had been sent to a labor camp for seven years. The rumors about her grew wilder every day. Some said that the NKVD had hauled off from her home a truck load of new clothes, fur coats and sundry other merchandise. A neighbor of hers said that money, jewelry and gold were found buried in her cellar.

* * *

That winter a new element of refugees began to arrive in Tamak—Polish Jews. After the Soviet annexation of part of Poland, in 1939, they were deported by the NKVD to Russian labor camps where many of them perished from hunger and cold. In accordance with the recent Polish-Soviet Agreement, they were now released from the camps. Some of those freed from the labor camps in the Ural forests came to Tamak. Their appearance was heartbreaking—emaciated figures dressed in sheer tatters. Most of them had no shoes; their feet were wrapped in rags over which they wore *laptyis* (homemade bast sandals) or pieces of tire rubber tied together with strings or wire. Looking at them, I no longer could complain about my own fate.

The local authorities were not willing to accommodate them in town, so they slept at the railroad station. Later they were housed in an unheated, dilapidated building that was once a flour mill. Some were sent to kolkhozes, where their plight was even worse, and they eventually returned to Tamak.

I became acquainted with many of these refugees. Two families in particular drew my attention from the start, and we gradually became friendly. Their tragic story epitomizes the suffering of the Polish refugees. The Gelbmans and Kutners came from Tarnow. The wives were sisters and all lived together as one family. The husbands, who both had long beards, wore a strange mixture of worn pieces of their old Hasidic apparel with labor camp clothes.

Both families had lost one child each in the camp. One of the remaining three Kutner children had died several weeks before in the Bashkir kolkhoz to which they had been sent.

At first the two families lived in the mill. Then the men got work in a chemical plant and managed to move in with a Bashkir family on the outskirts of town, where they lived in a dingy corner in terrible conditions. At the end of January 1942 misfortune struck again; the 14-year-old Kutner boy got typhus, and two weeks later he died. The religious family did not want to have him buried in a non-Jewish cemetery, but there was no Jewish burial place in Tamak.

Then I remembered Sonya Plavnik mentioning once the old community cemetery. Early next morning I went to her. She gave me the name of the former synagogue custodian who knew where the cemetery was. I hurried for help to Mendel Menikhes, the one-man Jewish charitable institution in Tamak.

When I came to him, I saw a *yahrzeit* light—a homemade cotton wick flickering in a small tin can with kerosene. It was not the same Reb Mendel with his usual smile. There was deep sadness in his eyes, and his thoughts seemed to be far away as he was sitting and reciting in a melodious voice portions from the Mishna.

He interrupted his reading and said, "Today my daughter went to the market to leave me alone with the memory of my wife. God was merciful to her but has kept me in this valley of tears with deep pain in my heart."

I was taken aback and puzzled by this Job-like language. Never before had I heard him talk like that. I remained silent, and he too went back to his gloomy thoughts. I decided not to disturb him and was about to leave. But he motioned me to stay and sighed, "Maybe it is God's finger that you have come on this day to hear the tragedy which has darkened my life."

Menikhes had a son, an engineer, who was considered a mathematical genius. He had occupied a high post at the Commissariat of Foreign Trade and used to travel abroad as an expert with trade missions. Often he had been sent for longer periods to various countries to supervise the construction of machinery under order. The parents had taken pride in their son's brilliant career, and everything went well until one night in

1935 when he was suddenly arrested along with other officials of the Commissariat. No reason for the arrest was given.

A few months later a show trial had been held. Their son was accused of being a German spy and was then sentenced to an indefinite term in a labor camp in Siberia, with no right of correspondence. "At that he was still considered lucky," Menikhes remarked. "Some of the arrested, including a Vice Commissar, were shot." Reb Mendel's wife died from grief shortly after the son's arrest.

"I have not heard from my son in many years. I go on believing that he is alive and will return one day," he sighed. "But looking at the *yahrzeit* flame a desperate fear keeps gnawing deep in my heart—is not my son's soul too flickering in it together with his mother's soul? I know that it is a sinful thought, but I hope that God will forgive a despondent old father."

I was deeply shaken and remained silent. All words of consolation that came to my mind would have sounded trite and banal in the light of his heavy grief. I did not have the heart to bother him about the funeral. As I was leaving, he asked me what I had come to see him about. I told him. "Why didn't you tell me sooner?" he said in a reproachful tone. I was amazed by the sudden change in Menikhes; he became agile again, and his look expressed the customary energy. He dressed in a hurry saying, "Let us go!"

Babayev, the old Bashkir caretaker, took us to a hill overlooking the river. The place was overgrown, but after rummaging around in the snow we found some overturned broken gravestones with barely legible Hebrew inscriptions.

The ground was frozen as solid as wrought iron, and it was impossible to dig it. Menikhes bought a can of gasoline in the *tolchok*. Babayev gathered some brushwood and twigs and lit a bonfire to thaw the soil a little. Nevertheless, he had a very hard time digging the grave, and it was already dark when he finally managed to finish it.

Several Polish Jewish refugees brought the body on a small hand-pulled sled. Reb Mendel performed the burial ritual. It was a very sad experience watching the heartbroken parents who were now burying their third child in Soviet exile. Each of us in attendance was probably thinking the same sad thoughts—

won't my fate too be to join these unknown *Kantonists* in their eternal rest on this hill?

Menikhes set about energetically to raise funds and had Babayev start to clean up the place. Unfortunately, Death had a rich harvest among the refugees, and before too long the Kutner boy had new neighbors. Eventually, some Soviet Jews also began to bury their dead there, and in time the hill became dotted with fresh graves.

FIVE

Not long after our arrival in Tamak I went to the post office to inquire whether it was permissible to write to relatives abroad. The manager said that I could and advised me to use postcards. I did so, merely notifying in a few lines our relatives in America, Palestine and England that we had succeeded in escaping from Latvia and were now in Tamak. The mail service was unreliable and chaotic. The young girl who brought the mail to our building would simply put the mail for all tenants on the floor near the entrance. I therefore used "General Delivery" as our permanent address.

I waited anxiously to hear from our relatives, and a few months later the first answer arrived—a letter from Ida's brother in Palestine. When the girl at the General Delivery window handed me the letter, she said that the censor wanted to see me. I thought that there was something wrong with the text of the letter and became apprehensive. Anticipating a rigorous interrogation by an NKVD official I left the letter unopened and went immediately to the given room. To my surprise I found there a gentle gray-haired lady, Ksenia Mironovna, who was not interested at all in the contents of the letter. She only asked me politely if I would let her have the stamps on the envelope. I felt so relieved that I promised her the stamps on any letters that I might receive from abroad in the future, and in time we became friends. She was an evacuee from Leningrad, where she had taught French and German at a high school.

Menikhes was worried about my foreign correspondence and asked me to be cautious with each word. The only other person in Tamak to whom I confided it was Dr. Riva Orshovsky. She was a very good friend, and I could rely on her in all respects. One evening when I walked her home, she asked me to come in and she introduced me to her family. Her brother, an engineer, had been evacuated with his Odessa factory to Tamak, and had brought with him, besides his own family, his widowed mother and Riva with her boy (her husband, a physician, was at the front).

Riva's mother, Esfir Solomonovna, impressed me the first moment I saw her. She had the appearance and manner of a dignified well-born lady—a vanishing species in Russia. Her wise eyes radiated human kindness, and there was an aura of warmth about her. She immediately made me feel at home. After our first meeting I used to drop in occasionally for a chat with her. As soon as I came in, she would treat me to a glass of tea sweetened with saccharin, a rare luxury in those days!

Shortly after I received the letter from Palestine, Riva told me that her mother wanted to talk to me. I went to see her. We began to chat as usual and then she said, "You know how afraid the people in this country are to trust friends and even relatives. But we consider you as one of the family, and I would like to ask you a big favor."

There was deep sadness in her eyes as she continued hesitantly. "You know my son, Misha. What nobody except our family knows is that I have another son in Haifa who is the real Misha. The 'Misha' here is in reality Volodya."

I was startled. At first I did not grasp what she meant and looked at her in puzzlement. She then went on with her story and what I heard stunned me.

The Orshovskys had originally lived in Nikolayevsk, the Ukraine, where Esfir's late husband was a respected leader of the Jewish community. Their older son, Volodya, had attended the university and became very active in the Zionist movement. The Revolution and the civil war years brought suffering and impoverishment to the family. After the Bolshevik seizure of power, they adapted themselves to the changed conditions and somehow made ends meet. Volodya became one of the leaders of the underground Halutz organization and prepared himself to go to Palestine.

One night in 1923 there was violent knocking on the door.

When they opened it, several GPU (secret police) men stormed into the apartment. The family did not have to ask for whom they were looking. For weeks mass arrests of Zionists had been going on. Volodya was in hiding in the countryside, where he waited with a group of Halutz youth for a chance to cross the border.

"It all happened so fast that I don't recall all details," sighed Esfir. "Without asking a single question they arrested Misha. I was about to exclaim that he was not the one they sought. But Misha cast an intent look at me and the words got stuck in my throat. Then his eyes rested for a brief moment on the young pregnant Zhenya, whom Volodya had married about a year before, and he went along without a word with the GPU men."

The shocked family had sat up all night, trying to figure out what had happened and discussing steps to help Misha. Esfir wanted to go right away in the morning to the GPU and clarify the mistake. But the father thought that this would make things worse for everybody. He theorized that as soon as they realized during the interrogations at headquarters that it was a case of mistaken identity, they would quietly release Misha.

"My husband was very proud of Misha who, though an active member of the *Komsomol* (Young Communist League) and wholeheartedly devoted to the Soviet regime, had not hesitated for a moment to risk his own freedom in order to save his Zionist brother from arrest and give him a chance to leave for Palestine," she continued.

The family waited, but the days passed and Misha was not freed. Volodya wanted to come out of hiding and give himself up but was dissuaded from doing so. It would have been too late anyway. In the meantime Misha and the other arrested Zionists had been shipped off to Siberia.

Neighbors and friends were curious to know where Misha had disappeared to, and some of them began asking suspicious questions. The Orshovskys had gone on inventing explanations, but in the end they became scared and moved away to Odessa. Volodya made repeated futile attempts to cross the Rumanian border. Eventually, however, he gave up all hope of leaving the country, and in his desperation he decided to do the most fantastic thing—he assumed Misha's identity. Using his papers, he joined a transport of people who signed up for construction work in Tomsk, in Siberia, where nobody knew him and where he could live in safety. His wife, with the little girl who was born in the meantime, went to live with her parents.

In the first months the family had received a few letters from Misha, who was in a labor camp in the Chita region near the Chinese border. But then he had stopped writing, and they could not find out what had happened to him. About two years later they got a cryptic notification from the police, stating tersely, "Your son Volodya drowned in the river by accident." All efforts to get more information were futile.

"You can imagine our deep shock and sorrow. Several months later my husband died; the grief and self-reproach that he might not have done enough to save Misha consumed his weak heart," she sighed and fell silent for a long while.

Then she went on. "One morning in May 1927, as I was walking home from the market, I noticed that a young man was following me all the way. When he caught up with me, he whispered, 'Your Misha is alive and well in Palestine. There is a note from him in your shopping bag. Don't look for it before you come home.' Before the mysterious messenger disappeared around the corner, he asked me not to mention it to anybody. I never saw him again. I felt like fainting and dragged myself home with difficulty."

While continuing her story, she began rummaging in a suitcase and pulled out a yellowed, crumpled piece of paper with Misha's Haifa address and gave it to me. "Since that day we have not heard from Misha. You'll understand why we have been afraid to write him all these years," she remarked. "Will you please let him know that we managed to escape from Odessa and are in Tamak?"

Only Esfir and Riva knew about my writing to Misha, and they waited impatiently for his answer. When it finally arrived, there was no end to Esfir's happiness. Mikhael (he now used the Hebrew name) sent regards from his wife Leah and their children Shmuel and Hilah. She embraced me and was beside herself with joy, "You have brought me also a daughter-in-law and two new grandchildren!"

One thing puzzled me though. In my postcard I deliberately

omitted mentioning the father, indicating thus to Mikhael that he was not alive anymore. Naming his boy after the father, however, showed that he had known it already. How had he found out?—I wondered.

Volodya learned about his brother's letter some time later, and Riva told me that he was furious at me. I therefore avoided visiting the Orshovskys for some time. After hearing the rest of his story from Riva, I understood his behavior. Later I befriended Volodya, and he told me much about his past, which gave deeper insight into his tormented soul.

Volodya worked very hard in Tomsk. As "Misha" the *Komsomol* member he was able to attend a *Rabfak* (Workers' University) evenings and became an engineer. When he deemed himself safe enough in Tomsk, his wife and child came to join him there. In this connection a bizarre event had taken place that adds rather a farcical note to the sad story. After receiving the news about his brother's death in the camp, he married his widow, marrying thus a second time his own wife and adopting his own daughter.

Volodya eventually became an active communist and a full-fledged Party member. In 1936 he considered himself sufficiently secure to move with his family to Odessa.

The puzzle of Mikhael's death and resurrection and the circumstances of his escape to Palestine intrigued me all through the years in Russia. I was able to solve this riddle only after the war when I met Mikhael in Israel. He told me in detail about his suffering since the night of his arrest. He was sentenced without any trial to a ten-year "reeducation" term in a camp.

However, the reeducation he had received in the Far Eastern labor camp turned out to be of a quite different character from that intended by his jailers. Many prisoners in the camp were Zionists, including some well-known former Zionist leaders. Under their influence Mikhael gradually had become a convinced Zionist.

To make a long story short, about a year later, while driving a barge with lumber from the camp, Mikhael and two other prisoners, after long preparation and careful planning, jumped unnoticed in the dark of night into the water and swam to the other shore, where they hid in the endless virgin forests. After wandering for weeks and facing untold dangers, they had finally crossed the border into Manchuria, and eventually they reached Kharbin, where the Jewish community helped them to make their way to Palestine.

What struck me most after getting to know both brothers was the fact that between the two took place not only a formal switch of names and identities but also an exchange of outlook and ideological persuasion—the former *Halutz* turned into a dogmatic Stalinist, while the dedicated *Komsomol* activist became an ardent Zionist.

* * *

As tempted as I am to dwell longer on this intriguing story, I must return to the gloomy reality in Tamak. I have briefly described already the sordid small kitchen in which we lived. Let me tell a little about Nusia Grigorievna and her two young girls, who lived in the adjacent room and had to pass through the kitchen. It goes without saying that we had no privacy at all, neither by day nor by night. But we had to take it in stride, and we tried very hard to establish neighborly relations with them.

Nusia, however, looked at us as intruders. She claimed that the kitchen had been allotted to her but was requisitioned later for us by the VU. We were friendly with the other neighbors, and we used to visit with some of them, but all through the years we lived practically together we never crossed the threshold of Nusia's room. That she never forgave us moving into "her" kitchen gave me a constant uneasy feeling.

Her husband, a Party official from some Ukrainian town, was in the army. Before leaving, however, he got her a job as a cook in a *stolovaya*, a position available only to Party members or to those who could afford to richly grease the proper palm.

She had a steady visitor, a tall Ukrainian about 15 years her junior. I never learned his name; the girls called him merely "Uncle." In the evening she would hop by with her heavy limp in the company of the "Uncle." Soon the smell of roasted meat would come from her room. The scent of meat, which we had not tasted for months, was tantalizing, and pulling the blankets over our heads did not help much. Early in the morning they would creep by again like two shadows. Sometime later "Uncle" moved in for good. Nusia grew angrier; we were now all the more in her way.

Comparing the abundance of food in Nusia's room with the starving family of the janitor was a good opportunity for a study in contrasts of the so-called classless Soviet society. I first saw Semyonov at the VU, where he took care of the garbage and the latrines. The emaciation of his body and the sickly pallor on his face were conspicuous even in the dire circumstances of Tamak. He was dressed in smelly tatters and made a pitiful impression.

Several days later I was surprised to see that he lived in our building. It turned out that he was the only son of a local merchant who had been exiled, after the Revolution, to Siberia. Semyonov's parents had perished there long ago. He suffered from advanced tuberculosis and shortly before the outbreak of the war had been allowed to return to Tamak. The City Housing Department permitted him to live in the damp, dark basement in return for his taking care of the house.

As soon as Nusia's older girl came home from school, she would take a pot and go to her mother's *stolovaya* for food. When she would return, the two little Semyonov boys would be waiting for her in front of the house. "Lenka, please only a spoonful of gruel," they would beg and run after her. Lenka would chase them away with curses, but they kept on begging and sometimes followed her into our room.

How does the saying go?—"people who are poor in summer are even poorer in winter." When the snow came, the barefoot boys stopped going outside. Passing by the low cellar window, you could see two pairs of sad eyes watching the legs of the passersby; the boys probably daydreamed about shoes. Their mother—a short, slender woman dressed in rags and with legs swollen from hunger—made the rounds of the neighbors, offering to do chores. Though hungry themselves, the refugee families did not have the heart to turn her down and would give her a piece of bread or some other food for her children. But not our Nusia. I remember the picture when the poor mother knocked on her door. She shouted at her, "It is a shame for a

Soviet person to go around begging! Only in the capitalist countries are there beggars." The frightened woman had burst out in
tears and run away. Never again did she try that door.

*   *   *

How true is the Biblical saying that not by bread alone does a
man live. I always admired the hunger for reading among the
Soviet people. In the park, bus or train I observed young and
old people immersed in books. What struck me was that very few
of the stereotyped socialist-realism works by Soviet authors attracted their interest. In their desire to escape the drab present,
they turned to classical literature, both prose and verse. In no
other country have I seen such widespread popularity of poetry
as in Russia.

The hunger for culture came to the fore even in the dire
conditions of Tamak. I was amazed to find what a number of
academicians, artists and other intellectuals had been blown to
that backwoods Ural town from the western cities. Now and then
an acquaintance would point out to me in the *tolchok*—"You see
that lady there with the dress for sale on her arm? She is a
famous pianist from Kharkov." Or, "The gray-haired man there
selling the cigarettes? He is a poet from Leningrad." So there
was no shortage of intellectual talent in Tamak. If the state had
decided to open a college, they could have recruited a first-rate
faculty right there in the market.

During the first winter we were in Tamak, an amateur theater
and ballet were formed. They used the auditorium of the VU, so
that I had a chance to watch. I admired the tenacity and capabil-
ity of the Soviet people to adjust to such hard conditions and
envied them for it. I felt inferior about my own soft bourgeois
background, realizing how much I lacked their experience and
initiative in tackling the problems of survival. It took me a long
time to learn.

The war had created a scarcity of men, and most of the per-
formers were women. Looking through the classroom window
at the amateur actresses wading through the deep snow and
raging storm to the auditorium for rehearsals, I marveled at
their dedication. Despite the hunger and cold, the standing for

hours in lines, the chores with children and household, they nonetheless found the time and stamina to perform in the theater.

At one of the performances in January 1942 I had an interesting experience. They presented Chekhov's "Cherry Orchard." In the unheated auditorium it was not much warmer than outside. The spectators sat bundled up in their overcoats and the players on stage had on overcoats or cotton-padded jackets over their dresses. I was there with Menikhes's daughter Anna and her husband.

In the middle of the play Anna whispered to me, "You see that young man dancing with the blond actress? He is from Palestine." I could hardly hide my surprise. "Anna, I'll never forgive you for this. How could you keep it from me for such a long time," I said.

"He does not want anybody to know it, and for good reason. But if you want I can introduce you to him," she replied.

I no longer had the patience to follow the show. Instead, I wondered by what strange fate that young man had gotten from Palestine to Tamak. After the performance Anna introduced me to David Langer, but he had no time to talk to us, so Anna invited him to her home on the following Sunday. I could hardly wait.

The 17-year-old David was reticent and suspicious when we met. I began speaking to him in Hebrew, but he was startled and said, "Please don't get me in trouble." I understood him. I tried very hard later to make him warm up a little and to win his confidence, but I never succeeded. He remained reserved and gave evasive answers. It took me a long time to piece together his story. Of great help were bits of information from the Menikheses.

David was born in Germany. In 1933 he left with his parents for Palestine. Several years later his father died. Early in 1939 his mother took him for a visit to her parents in Poland, and they did not get out before Hitler's attack on Poland. Upon the occupation of the town by the Soviets, they tried to return to Palestine, but the NKVD did not allow them to leave and took away their Palestinian passport.

In 1940 his mother was suddenly arrested and shipped off to

Siberia. David did not happen to be at home that night and was thus saved from deportation. After the outbreak of the German-Soviet war he fled to Russia. For many weeks he wandered on foot and went through a great deal of suffering. At one of the stations he managed to get on a train with evacuees from White Russia. On the trip he was befriended by the Nussbaum family. They treated him like their own son and took him along to Tamak. Anna's husband got David a job in the Ishimbay oil fields.

On the train one of the Nussbaum girls had fallen in love with David. The parents liked him and hoped that he would marry their daughter in time. Sometime later, however, he met a Leningrad actress—who was much older than he—and eventually moved in with her, leaving the Nussbaum girl heartbroken, to everybody's chagrin.

Like so many other refugees, David had no papers and passed himself off as a Polish citizen. I tried to persuade him to write to the British Consulate in the USSR or to Palestine. In the political climate of friendly gestures to the West then he stood a good chance of being permitted to return to Palestine. But he was a bewildered young man, hoping naively for the release of his mother from the labor camp.

About a year later David suddenly disappeared from Tamak. It turned out that he had volunteered for the Polish Army. He told his friends that he wanted in this way to help free his mother. But I had a strong suspicion that he desired to cut the entangled Gordian knot of his personal life in Tamak.

SIX

The pattern of instruction and life in general at the VU changed during the winter. Work was harder and more hectic. The Red Army had suffered tremendous losses, especially in officers. The cadets were being graduated in a hurry and sent to the front. More and more groups of recuperated wounded soldiers kept arriving from the hospitals. They were trained in accelerated courses as lieutenants and shipped back to the front.

Some of the officers whom I had known since the Riga days left for the front one by one and were replaced by newly arrived wounded officers. Little by little the school changed and became a less pleasant place to work, and this change for the worse added to the misery of the hunger and cold.

In Riga a number of Latvian officers taken from the disbanded Latvian Army had been at the VU. When the school was evacuated to Russia, some of these officers deserted and stayed in Latvia. Others, however, remained loyal and came along with the VU. One of them was Lieutenant Prusis. In Tamak he was put in charge of fuel supplies. From time to time he helped me out by selling me a little firewood, kerosene, etc.

In the beginning of March 1942 I went to his office to ask him for some wood. He was not there. I came the next morning, but his secretary told me that she did not know where he was. When I came the following day I was surprised to see an officer at Prusis's desk whom I had never seen before. I asked him where Prusis was. "He is not here any longer and will never be," he said laconically.

I was puzzled. After classes I went to Straus, a Latvian master sergeant who was the manager of the warehouse of textbooks and office supplies. We were good friends, and I asked him about Prusis. He said that Prusis had not been seen for days and nobody knew where he was. "If he had been sent away suddenly to the front," Straus reasoned, "he would certainly have said goodbye to his friends. There are rumors that he has been arrested by the NKVD."

Before long these rumors proved to be true. Two officers of the VU who were on duty the night before at the railroad station told Straus in confidence that they saw Prusis being escorted to the train by NKVD soldiers. He was dressed in prisoner's clothes. When he passed by he called to them, "Comrades, I'm innocent. It is a misunderstanding; I'll be back." The NKVD men shoved him quickly onto the car.

Prusis's arrest caused deep apprehension among the Latvian evacuees. He was known as an honest man with clean hands, so that an "economic crime" in connection with his work was out of the question. It was obvious that the arrest was for political reasons. But why we wondered. Did it signal the start of a purge? We were all seized with fear, but I had the more reason to tremble. Besides being a "Latvian," I was also a foreigner. For a very long time I spent sleepless nights. However, the weeks passed and none of the Latvians at the school were bothered. Gradually my fears calmed. Prusis's arrest remained a mystery and nobody dared talk about it. He was never heard of again.

As usual, Miss Lurie had a strange theory of her own. She knew "on good authority" that Prusis was connected with German intelligence, which planted him as a spy in Tamak. But she was known as a habitual gossip and nobody took her talk seriously. She worked as a bookkeeper at the VU, and in Riga I had hardly known her. A veteran communist, she had been one of the most enthusiastic activists in the "reeducation" of the Latvian civilian employees at the VU.

In Tamak, however, she—like so many other foreign communists who had the opportunity to see the "socialist paradise" with their own eyes—became disillusioned and turned into an embittered anticommunist. A spinster in her late forties, she felt very lonely in Tamak and was in the habit of dropping in on us unexpectedly. The trouble was that she had a loose tongue and liked to indulge in politically dangerous talk. In her bitter disappointment she now went to the other extreme and lost all rational proportions of objectivity in assessing the situation.

Miss Lurie went on lamenting that in the end the NKVD would arrest all of us and send us to a labor camp. I felt very uneasy with her visits, but somehow I did not have the heart to let her know that she was not welcome. I felt great relief when, tormented by her persecution fear, she moved to her sister in Semipalatinsk. She continued to write to us, but her letters were as incautious as her talk, so that we were afraid to answer her.

* * *

The long winter with cruel frosts and frequent snowstorms dragged on and wore us out. Our room was like an ice cave. The first delivery of wood by the VU was also the last one; after that the school notified its civilian employees that there would be no more wood allotments for them. We had to fend for ourselves.

From time to time, however, there were mild days. Then one could walk outside and marvel at the beauty of the Ural winter scenery without having to wrap one's ears and nose to prevent frostbite. On such days the kolkhoz market and the *tolchok* were crowded with refugees who crawled out from their ice caves to buy food or firewood. It was also an occasion for meeting friends.

I became acquainted with many Soviet Jewish evacuees in Tamak. In the beginning they were reticent and wary of speaking to a foreigner. Gradually they warmed up, and with some of them I became close.

The colorful mixture of the local Bashkir costumes with the European apparel of the evacuees and the varied features of the many nationalities fascinated me. Succumbing to my habitual curiosity, I often caught myself staring at people longer than I should have. On several occasions this habit nearly got me in trouble; I was often stared down by a suspicious hostile look of a stranger. In time I learned to stare unobtrusively.

One such case of staring led to my acquaintance with Sasha Levin. I noticed him the first time in the *tolchok* where he was shopping around for *makhorka* (rough, home-grown tobacco). His worn winter coat with fur collar and the tall fur hat, which he wore adroitly tilted to one side, had seen better days. What attracted my attention, however, was the energetic face, the rimless pince-nez and the well-taken-care-of goatee and moustache, all of which lent him the look of a typical prerevolutionary intellectual from a Chekhov story.

While cruising around in the *tolchok*, our looks met. He stopped and asked me who I was, and we began to chat. We then struck up a close friendship. He was one of the most interesting people I met in the Soviet Union, and we spent many an evening together in enjoyable conversation.

Sasha, in his fifties, was a lawyer from Moscow. His two sons were in the army, and he and his wife were evacuated to Tamak. He was intelligent and well informed about political developments. He never failed to make a correct evaluation of the military situation, and I learned a great deal from him.

He showed a great interest in Jewish matters. I remember his deep excitement when, in 1942, Stalin created the "Jewish Anti-Fascist Committee." As it turned out later, Stalin's real purpose was to organize Jewish material help abroad for his war effort. The tragic fate of all the Committee members, who were murdered by Stalin after the war, is well known, and I need not elaborate here. But at the time the creation of that Committee roused the hopes of Soviet Jews that Stalin had changed his policy toward them. They believed that the sending of an official Soviet Jewish delegation abroad signaled the start of free communication between Soviet Jewry and the Jewish communities in the other countries.

One evening Sasha dropped in unexpectedly. "Look at this, I received it today from a friend of mine in Moscow," he said with great emotion. It was the first edition of the *Einikeit,* the Yiddish semiweekly organ of the Committee. "Read what it says! It calls on the Jewish people the world over to unite in the struggle against Hitler," he exclaimed. "Never before was such language heard in the Soviet Union. Haven't I told you that there are going to be great changes for the better after the war? I can smell in the air the new spring of freedom." In his enthusiasm he took out of his pocket a package of business cards and said, "Take these along with you when you return home after the war. I'll be glad to serve as a legal representative for Jewish organizations and individuals who would like to establish contacts with us in Moscow."

This joyous stir about "the new spring of freedom" was widespread among Soviet Jews, including many Party members. As happens in such cases, exaggerated rumors began making the rounds. So, for instance, it was said that a Jewish delegation from America was already on its way to bring help for the Jewish war refugees in Russia.

Alas, all these rosy hopes were turned to naught. As soon as Stalin felt that he did not need the support of Jews abroad any longer, he began to retighten the screws of his tyranny and resumed his anti-Jewish policy. But that stir called forth in the hearts of the Russian Jews a deep feeling of common Jewish fate and Jewish belonging. The seeds of Jewish awakening were sown then and came eventually to fruition years later with the beginning of emigration to Israel.

If at first Soviet Jews kept at a distance from Jewish refugees from the newly annexed Polish and Baltic regions, they were now no longer afraid to communicate with them freely and asked many questions about Jewish life abroad, and especially in Palestine—a Jewish world from which they had been cut off by force a quarter-century before, living as if on a distant planet.

The Russian-assimilated Jewish writer and journalist Ilya Ehrenburg contributed indirectly to the awakening of national consciousness among Soviet Jews. After the outbreak of the war he went to the front and began publishing a column in the Red Army daily, which was reprinted in other papers all over the country. His articles were extremely popular and avidly read by millions. I once saw in the market an elderly Jewish woman exchanging with an invalid soldier a loaf of bread for a bundle of Ehrenburg's articles.

In his articles Ehrenburg described in a passionate way the German mass killings in the Soviet territories that they conquered. He did not, of course, mention that the massacred were Jews; he just spoke of "Soviet citizens." But the numbers of the murdered in the various cities tallied with the figures of the prewar Jewish population in the respective communities, so that it was clear that the victims were Jews and that Ehrenburg was afraid to be too specific.

In addition to this, one could read between the lines Ehrenburg's veiled intimation that the local populations willingly collaborated with the German murderers in the extermination of the Jews. All this brought home to Soviet Jews the painful realization that all the talk of the brotherhood of Soviet peoples, of socialist reeducation, etc., was a sham; the hatred of the Jews was deep rooted and remained the same as before the Revolution.

But it was not necessary to look for proof of anti-Semitism between the lines of Ehrenburg's articles. You could see its buds with your own eyes in Tamak. Now and then you could overhear in the bread line or in the market remarks like "Hey, Abrasha! Don't send the Gentiles to fight for you at the front while you yourself are hiding here under the apron of your Sarah." Or, "What city have you taken today, Tamak or Tashkent?"

What did the anti-Semites care about the unusually large numbers of Jews, far above their proportion in the general population, who went to the front voluntarily and were killed? Or about the extremely high percentage of Jewish names on the rolls of war heroes who distinguished themselves in battle with the German invaders? The Jew was, as usual, the convenient scapegoat to be blamed for their own suffering and for the military calamity that befell the country.

In addition to the plight of hunger and cold, the Jews were faced with the hostile atmosphere of anti-Jewish feelings in the street. All this caused bitter disillusionment among the Soviet Jews, including many Party members.

* * *

I had a chance to observe the psychological trauma of Jewish Communists right at the VU. A Jewish refugee couple, the Zalkins, from Berdichev, was employed there. Both were zealous Party members and from the very start they deliberately shunned any contact with the Jewish evacuees from Latvia.

Zalkin was the prototype of Boxer in George Orwell's *Animal Farm.* At the meetings of the civilian employees he would be the most vociferous in admonishing us to strengthen "Stalinist vigilance" and to "work harder." He was uncouth, and his intellectual horizons were limited. Like Orwell's Boxer, Zalkin repeated time and again the slogan "Comrade Stalin is always right!" And his speeches were indeed lavishly interspersed with quotations from Stalin, and he uttered the name with the awe of a pious person pronouncing the name of God.

Not long after my arrival in Tamak I had an unpleasant experience with Zalkin, who was in charge of the school's bathhouse. I managed to get a pass to the school's *banya.* On that day I happened to give a test in my classes and therefore asked him to let me take the bath before my turn in order not to be late for school. To my surprise he let loose in a crude manner—"Who do you think you are? The bourgeois president of your congregation going to the *Mikveh* on Friday with extra privileges? You still have to learn a lot about communist discipline!" I did not say a word and left without taking the eagerly awaited bath. It was a silly matter, but it showed the rudeness of his character, and after that day I was even more afraid of him and tried to avoid him.

In March 1942, however, when I came to take a bath, Zalkin stopped me unexpectedly and, to my big surprise, began to chat with me amicably in Yiddish. The epithets he used at the mention of Stalin threw me into consternation. For far lesser offenses against the sovereign "Father of the Peoples" people got lengthy terms in labor camps, and I suspected at first that it was a provocation to get me in trouble. But the passion of his outburst soon made me realize that he was sincere, that he wanted to pour out the accumulated disillusionment in his heart and tell me things that he could not dare confide to any of his even most intimate Soviet friends.

"I don't have to be told by Ehrenburg what my neighbors have done with the Jews in Berdichev," he said. "In 1918 they made a pogrom on us and killed my parents. They don't have to be prompted by the Germans, the 'Pockmarked' has taught them how to do it. Has he not liquidated all the Jewish leaders in the Party?"

He went on, "the Moustached Georgian Killer is not any better than Hitler. He concluded a pact with him, and now he is unable to defend the country. Mark my words, the Germans will yet be here too." I looked at Zalkin with pity. He was a frustrated man. The clay idol that he had built up and worshipped blindly had disappointed him, and he was now without his godless "religion." I did not react to his remarks. Despite his frequent overtures of friendship in the future, I nonetheless distrusted him and remained as cautious of him as before.

SEVEN

My isolation from the free world had begun in July 1940, when Latvia became part of the Soviet Union and a fast process of sovietization and total political coordination of press and radio was ushered in. Nonetheless, one could then still listen to foreign radio stations and find out what was happening abroad.

Since escaping from Riga, however, I was completely cut off from the outside world. Particularly as regards Jewish life, I suddenly found myself to all practical purposes on some strange distant planet. I had no longer any idea whatsoever what was going on in the Jewish world abroad. It was forbidden to listen to foreign broadcasts—a gratuitous and senseless prohibition, because the people in the USSR did not own any radios. They would get their radio news through a contraption in the shape of a cardboard cone attached to wires. These were usually located in public places, street corners and some even in private homes. There was only one version of the news, filtered through censorship. It would come on and go off entirely at the whim of the central station. There was no device on this contraption for turning it on or off.

There were about 20,000 Jewish war refugees in Tamak, but there was no contact or natural cohesion between them as Jews. There were no symptoms of a Jewish community, no signs of Jewish life. There were probably many Soviet Jews with a traditional background who practiced Judaism as far as it was possible under the difficult circumstances, but, afraid to expose themselves to the Stalinist persecution, they did it in secret at home.

As far as I knew, the only exception in Tamak was Reb Mendel, the spiritual beacon in that dark Ural backwater, an unofficial one-man Jewish institution. I could not admire his courage and untiring activities enough.

In the beginning of March 1942, not long after Purim, he began to make preparations for Passover. He told me that he had long ago bought some wheat from a kolkhoznik—it must have cost him a fortune—but the problem was where to grind it. I remembered that I once saw in Akhmadulin's basement an old hand grinder for oats. It looked like a museum piece, and what had drawn my attention in particular was the French inscription of the Belgian manufacturer. I asked Akhmadulin about it. He told me that he had taken it home from the hardware store that he had owned together with Feldman.

I went with Reb Mendel to Akhmadulin. We had a hard time cleaning the antiquated grinder, but with Akhmadulin's help we got it into working order and managed to grind the wheat. The mass which came out had only a remote resemblance to flour. It was rather a coarse brownish sand, a most fitting material with which to bake "the poor bread which our fathers ate in Egypt."

Turning the crank of the antique grinder, I recalled the thrill I used to experience as a boy when accompanying my father and the other Jews of my home town to my uncle's mill to cleanse the millstones for the grinding of the flour for *matzot*.

After long persuasion Sonya Plavnik allowed us to bake the

matzot in her oven. Again I remembered with nostalgia the festive mood of my father and our neighbors and their chanting of the Hallel prayer when baking the *shemura matzot*. We did no chanting, however, in Tamak. Like our fathers on their exodus from Egypt, Menikhes and I baked the *matzot* in a hurry. Out of fear of the Soviet Pharaoh, Sonya—but especially her daughter—asked us to do it as quickly as possible. The walls have ears, and one of the neighbors might notice us perpetrating the horrible political crime of baking *matzot* for Pesach—the greatest menace to the existence of the Soviet regime.

Menikhes gave a *matzah* each, or a piece of it, to his friends. I shared the *matzot* I got with the Orshovskys, Sasha and the other families whom I could trust. Some of them had not seen *matzah* in many years.

The first *Seder* night that year fell on April 1, and Menikhes invited us to his home. We left Raphi with a neighbor and went. The Ural winter had not loosened its grip as yet, it was bitter cold outside and a *purga* was raging.

There were besides us seven other invited guests. Reb Mendel was never out of surprises. He had Passover wine, which he had made from raisins and laced with raspberry juice. Only God knows how he had managed to get those scarce luxuries in Tamak. Since I was the youngest male member at the *Seder*, I asked Reb Mendel the Four Questions. He answered, "We were slaves unto Pharaoh in Egypt." But we understood without words that he meant not "were" but "are"—and also to a Pharaoh no less cruel than the Egyptian one.

The mood at that *Seder* was subdued; it called forth memories of a life that was gone. Each of us recalled the festiveness of past *Seder* nights and thought about the future, wondering where he would celebrate the *Seder* in the coming year and whether he would still be alive the next Pesach.

There was no meat or fish at this *Seder*. The meal consisted of vegetable soup and potato pancakes, which Anna prepared. She also tried very hard to set the table in a tasteful, festive manner. Afterward we sat and chatted for a long time. I had never met any of the other guests before, but we all felt a close kinship and a common fate.

EIGHT

The Ural spring is very late in coming. The winter stretches out like a gigantic prehistoric monster over mountain and valley, covering everything with a heavy blanket of ice and snow. From time to time the sleeping monster would stir and call forth a furious snowstorm such that you could hardly catch your breath and visibility was limited to a few yards.

But at the end of April the northern monster was prodded by the sun to wake up and retreat for several months to the arctic regions. The monster tarried but was finally forced to give in and left with an angry growling and cracking of thick ice on the frozen rivers.

The final transition to spring was sudden; it burst on us almost in the course of one night, and it flowed on wildly. The beauty of nature in the Ural spring was breath taking. In May the scenery all around changed suddenly. The tree-covered hills threw off their dark gray color and replaced it with freshly washed green.

And not only nature, but people too changed their look. They crawled out from their hibernation caves without the heavy rag-like apparel in which they were wrapped during the winter. Gone now were the bulky, formless feminine figures in cotton-padded jackets and trousers, heavy shawls and oversized felt boots. Instead, you saw women in dresses and shoes, with fresh makeup on pale faces.

The hunger and cold of the winter brought for the women unintended results. Without resorting to the self-imposed dieting of their American sisters, they were rid of the traditional Russian female corpulence and looked trimmer and younger. Attractive blue-eyed Leningrad blonds and charming brunettes with fiery black eyes from Odessa mingled with exotic Bashkir women who stood out by their high cheekbones under slanted almond eyes—all of them together forming one unique multicolored blending of desirable womanhood.

I too came out from my winter shell and dressed in a worn European jacket over a field shirt with military pants and high boots. But what did this incongruous apparel matter in view of the beautiful spring? There was in the air the mysterious universal spirit of the rebirth of nature, which transmitted itself to the individual and inspired him with a new will to live.

But the spring brought also a sad realization. Many familiar faces were missing. Asking friends about this or that mutual acquaintance you had not seen in a long time, the answer often was "died." Hunger and cold and disease took a heavy toll during the winter, and Death reaped a rich harvest among the refugees.

5

On the Banks of the Belaya

ONE

THE SETBACKS AT the front finally made me realize that we were in for a long stay in Tamak. My hitherto day-to-day improvisations had to be abandoned; it was now necessary to make long-term plans to survive a long war.

The first step was my becoming a "city farmer." To help alleviate the plight of the refugees, the state put at the disposal of evacuated factories and institutions stretches of land in the vicinity of the town to be parceled out among their employees for vegetable gardening. I joined the group of the Children's Home where Ida worked. Our field was adjacent to those of Dr. Orshovsky and other physicians and medical workers with whom we had become friends. There were no plows available; everybody had to dig his field with a shovel. But even those who could afford to pay someone to do the work for them could not do so because hired help was forbidden as capitalist exploitation.

And so on a Sunday before dawn I set out with the other "farmers" on the six-mile walk to the Belaya River, where our fields were. The land had not been tilled in many years and was overgrown with tall weeds, so even before we could start digging the soil, it was necessary to clean out the weeds and rocks, which was a tedious and back-breaking task. The work could not be finished in one day, so in the next few weeks, whenever I managed to squeeze out several free hours, I would hurry to the field.

The most difficult problem was getting potatoes for seed. In addition to exorbitant prices in the market, Akhmadulin told me

141

that the potatoes the kolkhozniks sold were unfit for planting. He introduced me to a friend of his from a collective farm who agreed to take me along in his wagon to make my purchases. I sold some badly needed pieces of clothing and borrowed money from friends for the trip.

Before I went to the kolkhoz, Mrs. Akhmadulin gave me a lesson in the science of potatoes. She taught me how to recognize a potato which is good for seed, how to distinguish between early and late potatoes, etc. "Pay more if you have to," she said, "but make sure to pick potatoes which have as many 'eyes' as possible." The instruction I got from her proved to be of more practical value for our survival in Tamak than all the teaching I had received at the university.

I left on the arranged day with Akhmadulin's friend for the Budyonny Kolkhoz. During the ride I saw vast fields with last year's grain unharvested. My host, an elderly Bashkir, noticed the astonished look in my eyes. "It is hard to make people bring in a harvest which they are not allowed to use," he remarked laconically. He then told me about life in the kolkhoz.

Once it had been a prosperous village, but collectivization had reduced the farmers to a state of poverty. They labored like slaves for the kolkhoz, which did not even provide them with enough grain for bread for the whole year. In the summer months they had to start buying bread in the black market. The bulk of the harvested grain and other agricultural produce of the kolkhoz was sold to the state at ridiculously low prices.

The main income of a collective farmer had to come from his privately owned small plot adjoining his hut, his cow or a few goats and a number of fowl. However, he was assessed by the kolkhoz administration a certain annual quantity of meat, eggs and dairy products, which he was obliged to sell to the state at very low prices. The rest of his private produce he could use for himself or sell in the kolkhoz market in town at any price he could get.

The collective farmers were subject to many restrictions. They could not move away from the kolkhoz without special permission, and a trip to a city, except for the purpose of selling the produce in the nearest town, required the consent of the kolkhoz chairman. Life in a kolkhoz resembled the state of serfdom in the Czarist era some 100 years before.

From Stalin to Khrushchev to Brezhnev the kolkhoz has been the bane of the Kremlin. The collectivization of agriculture and the resulting lack of incentive for the individual are the main reasons that the Soviet Union, despite its gigantic expanse of fertile land, has been unable to produce enough bread for its population and has to buy grain from abroad.

Plowing with a cow was commonplace in the kolkhoz. But I also beheld a most unusual sight which has remained in my memory—an old man behind a plow and eight women with ropes tied around their bodies pulling it. Most of the able-bodied men were in the army, and the work had to be done by the elderly men and the women.

My hosts sold me some potatoes and then helped me buy the rest from friends. I paid a lot of money, but compared to the high prices in the market it was a good deal. The hostess was hospitable and spread out a big sheepskin on the bench in the living room on which I could sleep, but I hardly closed an eye all night. I was tormented by fleas and bedbugs, and in the morning my body was covered with red spots. When I mentioned it to my hosts, they were surprised. "They never bother us." I had similar experiences on my later visits to other collective farms. Maybe my tiny tormentors just hated foreigners.

My hosts put me on a kolkhoz wagon that drove to the market in Tamak. Upon arriving home, I set about the tedious work of slicing the potatoes meticulously according to Mrs. Akhmadu-lin's specifications. The next Sunday early in the morning I set out with the other "farmers" for our fields, pushing a small wagon that we borrowed from the Children's Home. On the way, however, the wagon broke down. We had to leave it at a hut and carry our sacks of potatoes the rest of the way.

The digging and planting were laborious tasks. My hands were covered with blisters and my back ached, but I experienced a deep feeling of creative accomplishment and an inner satisfaction that, in Tolstoy's words, only the sweat of toiling in the bosom of nature can give to man.

Even after the planting the field commanded my continuous

attention. There always was some work to do. The most arduous labor, however, was the endless weeding, because the weeds just kept coming back as fast as I weeded them out.

*   *   *

In May 1942 the eight-year-old daughter of the Gelbmans died. The cup of tears of the two grief stricken families did not seem to be filled as yet. Once again I witnessed a heart-rendingly sad funeral.

At the burial I ran into Mrs. Rosner from Drohobych, Galicia. In the winter, on being freed from a labor camp, she had come to Tamak together with her son, Arnold, a young man in his twenties. I had become acquainted with the Rosners. They had had a very hard time in the beginning. I had spoken to Menikhes's son-in-law and he got Arnold a job in the oil fields. While there, he met Elvira Martinova, an evacuee from Kharkov who served as Party Secretary at the Ishimbay Oil *Kombinat.* The middle-aged woman had taken a strong liking to the tall, good-looking Arnold, and eventually a love affair developed.

Liaisons with women whose husbands were at the front occurred everywhere and attracted no particular attention. But among the religious Polish refugees this particular liaison caused a sensation and became the topic of widespread gossip. Elvira got an apartment for the Rosners in one of the Oil *Kombinat* tenements. To live in such a house, which had plumbing, gas, electricity and even central heating, was the dream of every refugee in Tamak. But Mrs. Rosner did not enjoy the comfort; she was heartbroken by her son's affair with a married woman.

A few months earlier, I had met Mrs. Rosner on my way to the Menikheses, who also lived in one of the Oil *Kombinat* houses. She had lowered her eyes and sighed. "Believe me, I wish I were still living in the kolkhoz or in the labor camp rather than in this nice apartment which my son got from that woman." I had felt uncomfortable and did not know what to say to her.

I had not seen her since that day. In the emotional atmosphere of the funeral she came over to me and said with tearful eyes, "How much I envy my husband, the devout Antynyr Hasid, that he died in the camp and does not have to see the sort of life our only son leads."

I was taken aback. Maybe it was merely my imagination, but I perceived in her tone a kind of reproach at my being indirectly the matchmaker by having helped her son get the job in the Oil *Kombinat.*

In the end the affair had unpleasant repercussions. Arnold was suddenly dismissed from his job and evicted from the apartment. A few days afterward the Rosners left Tamak, and nobody knew exactly what had happened. Anna told me that Elvira's husband, who was the editor of an army paper and a big Party wheel, had allegedly arranged Arnold's removal from Tamak. Everyone considered him lucky that he had not been arrested by the NKVD and sent to a labor camp.

*   *   *

Toward the end of May Sasha went on an official business trip to Moscow. He was very excited, for both he and his wife had suffered a great deal in Tamak and, having good connections in Moscow, he was looking forward to exploring the possibilities of returning home. Two weeks later, however, he came back very subdued. For the time being, no evacuees were allowed to return to Moscow. Their apartment there was occupied by some military men and most of their belongings and furniture were gone.

The news that Sasha brought back from the capital was very discouraging. People starved and froze during the winter. Most buildings were without heat, and there was no food in the stores. The black market and war profiteering flourished, and the price of food was double that in Tamak. Even more depressing was his description of a war invalid he had seen standing on a busy street corner with a lit cigarette offering passersby a puff for two rubles. "And he had plenty of customers," Sasha remarked.

Sasha's friends told him of the events they had witnessed during the critical days in October and November of 1941, when the Germans had stood at the gates of Moscow. One day there had been a rumor that the Germans were about to enter the capital. Widespread panic had ensued, and people had begun fleeing from the city, rioting in the streets, and looting stores, warehouses and private homes.

And the saddest thing of all was that there had been physical attacks on Jews in the streets. Here and there groups of pro-Nazi citizens with swastikas had marched to welcome the Germans. It was only when Stalin sent his Georgian Guards into the streets and ordered them to shoot on sight any looter or troublemaker that order had been restored. Some estimates claimed that over 4,000 people were shot that day in the streets of Moscow.

The Germans had been thrown back from Moscow, but even now they were only about 70 miles away from the city, and there was persistent talk about an impending new German offensive. When Sasha was there, people still felt quite apprehensive and insecure.

The anticipated German attack on the capital did not take place. Instead, not long after Sasha's return to Tamak the Germans launched a massive offensive in the direction of Stalingrad and the Caucasus, aiming at cutting off the heartland of Russia from the oil and other rich resources in the south and thus rendering the Red Army incapable of further resistance. The Germans made rapid progress toward the Volga, and there was a new stream of refugees from the lost territories.

Some of these refugees reached Tamak. Our mood was gloomy and hearts were filled with new fears. In those days I received a letter from Dr. Bronstein with the surprising news that they were leaving for Central Asia. From his previous letters I knew that he was fairly well established in Yoshkar-Ola. The unexpected push of the Germans toward the Volga, however, made the situation there unsafe, and they resumed their wandering. The letter added sadness to my subdued mood.

* * *

The struggle for survival in Tamak went on. During the summer months I concentrated on the field, but as the potatoes grew, I discovered that I was not the only one interested in them.

One Sunday morning, when a group of us "farmers" came as usual to tend our fields, we were shocked by the devastation wrought all around. Many saplings were pulled out by the roots. It was a cruel and senseless act. The potatoes were hardly the size of small hazelnuts. The thieves had been choosy. They picked only the largest potatoes, leaving the rest to rot and dry away in the sun. About one-third of what I had planted with so much labor and expense was ruined. I had planted some cucumbers also, and they were all plucked off and destroyed.

In order to save what was left, we decided to take turns going in pairs to watch at night. For the daytime we hired a watchman, an elderly World War I invalid. Tolya was no fool; in addition to the pay he also asked for 10 percent of the harvest. We had no choice but to agree.

Tolya built himself a small hut from branches and reeds, and for the nights he left us his antiquated, rusty hunting gun. One probably would not have been able to hit an elephant with it even at a close range, but when fired at night it made a deafening noise that reverberated in the hills around. Afterward I could hear the rustling of leaves and the pitter-patter made by small four-legged friends in their escape from the fields. But they would return before long to nibble on the potato leaves.

I kept watch about one night a week. It was a thrilling experience to listen to the deep silence of the Ural night disturbed only now and then by the leap of an animal in the bushes or the sad call of a lonely bird. A stone's throw away you could hear the murmur of the Belaya, which went on spinning its mysterious dream from time immemorial.

Since our field bordered that of the Orshovskys, I used to go for nightwatches with Volodya. I was glad for the opportunity to get to know him better. When I had first met him he was cool. Now, however, he began to warm up, and gradually we became good friends. We would sit and talk for hours during the night, and he told me a great deal about his activities in the Jewish Self-Defense organization during the civil war and his experiences in various Siberian cities.

There was, though, one topic that he never mentioned—Misha's arrest and his own past Zionist underground work. I was very curious to know what he would have had to say about it. I was often tempted to broach the subject, but at the last moment I would refrain from scratching the wound in his heart. And I felt certain that the scar was deep and had never healed. From things said and unsaid I got an insight into his feeling of guilt and pitied him.

TWO

Thanks to Volodya I also became a "fisherman" that summer. One night in the field while sitting and talking he suddenly said, "Isn't it a shame. We are so close to the Belaya with its riches of fish, and we have not even tried to do some fishing." I agreed with him. We bought an old fishing net in the *tolchok*. It was torn in many places, and we had a hard time mending it. At the crack of dawn after our next night's watch we went down to the river. There were already many people there with fishing rods, and I was surprised to see among them some officers from the VU.

In order not to interfere with the anglers we went a little farther down river. We undressed, tied the strings at the ends of the net to our bodies and waded in. The water was ice cold, and it took a while before we made up our mind to dip into it. We finally swam out toward the middle of the stream. After a while we felt the tugging of the fish, and pulling behind us the semicircle of the long net, we made back for the shore.

Most of the fish escaped from the net, and some of them, even when on the shore, managed to arch in high leaps back into the river. Although each escaping culprit was my "enemy," I nonetheless admired the strong instinct for survival in those mute creatures and how they outsmarted us in slipping back to the source of their life. They were, alas, like human beings; those who are shrewd and strong get away, while the meek and less artful are caught in the net and perish.

We had to repeat our haul many times before we succeeded in catching sufficient fish for both families. The cold water made my teeth chatter, and after getting out of the river I had to rub my stiff body for a long while, but I felt refreshed and invigorated. We dressed and hurried home to be in time for work. The rising sun and the long walk warmed us.

In my youth I was brought up in the Jewish tradition that the purpose in life was to study the Torah and that sport and games were nonsense and a sinful waste of precious time. This hopeless addiction to books and study has remained with me all my life. True, I did not develop a crooked spine or a flat chest, but I have been found wanting in sport. I remember how unhappy I made my physical education instructor at the gymnasium with my clumsiness in basketball and in physical training in general. He was an assimilated Hungarian Jew and had his own theory of Jewishness. "Remember that to be a good Jew means to develop strong muscles," he used to reprimand me. But my shortcomings in sports drove him to desperation, and in the end he gave me up as a hopeless case.

At the time I shrugged off his theory with a sophisticated smile, but coming in contact with real life, I often thought that his concept of Judaism was not so mistaken after all. Unfortunately, the Gentile world cares little for Moses, Isaiah, Amos and Maimonides; the language of Samson, Gideon, Bar Kochba and Dayan is more understandable and appealing to them.

I came to like the fishing and looked forward to it. Each time it was a thrilling experience. But it was not done for the fun of sport; who was in the mood for such things in Tamak? I did it in order to supplement our miserable diet of bread with *kipyatok* and an occasional watery vegetable soup. The fish constituted a most welcome contribution of badly needed protein. It was not much, but the few fish I brought home now and then were of tremendous help.

* * *

Though I enjoyed the fishing, one morning later in the summer I had a frightful experience. We were about to swim out with the net for another try at some fish when out of the blue there appeared on the shore an NKVD soldier on horseback. He shouted at us to get out of the water immediately. I was stunned and frightened to death, anticipating that we were going to be arrested. You were not supposed to ask questions when being picked up by the NKVD. The blue-capped rider ordered us not to get dressed but to take our things and leave right away.

We were so bewildered that we did not even pick up the few fish that we had caught. With our clothes and net in our hands, we ran stark naked to the nearest bushes. I saw then in action the great terror that the dreaded Stalinist secret police drove into the hearts of the people. All along the shore the fishermen were hurrying away on the double. Volodya was even more scared than I; his face was as white as chalk. When I tried to look at the river from behind the bushes, he exclaimed in desperation, "For

God's sake, what are you doing?! Get dressed and let us get away from here as fast as we can!" He was trembling with fear.

I nonetheless took a furtive glance at the Belaya and beheld a gruesome picture. A long line of rafts was gliding by downstream, loaded with dark figures in tatters who were working on the oars or sitting on the floor. At the end of each raft stood soldiers with dogs on leashes. It was a ghost-like view which has remained imprinted in my mind to this very day.

We walked home in a hurry, stealthily turning our heads back once in a while to see whether the NKVD rider was coming behind us. Volodya was very upset and did not speak a word all the way. For some time we were afraid to go fishing, but one morning after our night watch we saw the other fishermen returning to the Belaya, and we too decided to resume our fishing. I learned from Akhmadulin that for many years the Belaya had been off limits to the civilian population. In fact, he said, the lifting of this restriction after the outbreak of the war was considered a relaxation of the regime and was even interpreted as a sign that the labor camps in the northern Ural forests were going to be closed. Gelbman and other Polish refugees told me that while in camp they used to float rafts during the summer months, when the Ural rivers are navigable, as far down as the Kama River. Unfortunately, the hopes that the camps would be closed did not come true. Most of the Polish deportees were eventually freed, but the Soviet inmates remained in the camps, and many more new ones were sent there all through the war.

THREE

The short Ural springs and summers were beautiful, but it is probably the suffering during the long cruel winters that overshadows them in my memory, making me recall life in Tamak as clinging with my fingernails to an icy cliff, struggling desperately not to slip down into the deep frozen abyss below. My recollections of Russia are subconsciously bound up with snowstorms, murderous frosts and ice.

Reading Eugene Zamyatin's moving descriptions of life in Leningrad during the difficult winters of the civil war years after the Revolution, I had the distinct feeling that I too was one of the dwellers in his "Ice Cave." And every time I experienced a raging Ural *purga*, I saw with my spiritual eye Gogol's *Troyka*, his symbolic sleigh harnessed to three horses, galloping through the everlasting snowstorm of Mother Russia.

Nevertheless, I particularly remember the great relief I felt the summer that followed my first winter in Tamak, as if I had crawled out into the sunshine from a never-ending ice tunnel. It seemed nearly unbelievable—no more worries about firewood, walking outside without a topcoat and then later, at the peak of the summer, even without a jacket.

In the summertime the amateur theater gave its performances in the city park. Occasionally, the band of the VU would play there too. The warm weather did wonders for Raphi; he felt much better now and became a lively, active boy. He spent a great deal of time outdoors, and we took him to the park often where he liked to play and run around and enjoyed listening to the music very much.

One Sunday afternoon after the concert he climbed up the stairs to the podium and began to sing "Korovushka Rogovushka," a children's song that he had learned in the *Dyet-dom*. His pronouncing the R's like L's made the childish recitation even cuter, and the people sitting near the podium rewarded him with applause. He enjoyed it so much he kept repeating the song. Every time we came to the park, he would run straight to the podium to give his "performance" and wait eagerly for applause. He was the joy of our life, but his song also brought sad thoughts to my mind. Its lyrics expressed a passionate appeal to the cow, "Oh, you dear little horned cow, please give us children your sweet milk," etc. Even the tots in the Children's Home worry about their food, I thought. Their interest in the cow was not to admire it as part of the animal world but rather as some vehicle to provide them with a little milk for their survival. My heart was filled with concern for our son's future if destiny should decree for us to remain in Russia too long a time.

* * *

We had to harvest the potatoes before their time after all. True, the watching had stopped the wholesale thieving, but we noticed that some pilfering was going on all the time nonetheless. And it was done in a shrewdly planned way—in the fields of those two who just had their watch the preceding night, so that they would not discover the theft until their next night's watch.

It was obvious that Tolya had a hand in it. When he was asked about it, he played the innocent simpleton, swearing by the sacred memory of all his departed relatives that he had no idea who did it. One evening, however, the pair who came for their night watch followed him stealthily from the fields and saw him picking up a bag of potatoes in the bushes. Even though caught red-handed, he brazenly claimed that he had bought them from a kolkhoz friend who drove by to the market, and he invoked all the saints as his witnesses that he never touched anything in our fields. Being helpless against Tolya's tricks, we decided to dig up the potatoes as long as there were some still left. Taught by our shortcomings during the planting, we organized the harvesting in a cooperative manner so that it was more efficient and faster. Nevertheless, it turned out to be back-breaking labor. We gave Tolya only half of the agreed share of potatoes. First he used insulting language and threats, calling us refugee robbers who came here to suck the blood of poor innocent people. Then he began to whine and beg us to show ourselves grateful to him for his "loyal, honest service," promising us all the blessings of heaven where his "saintly mother" would intercede on our behalf. It was interesting to watch the show that the cunning old man put on. He knew full well that actually we should not have given him anything. He had had a good thing going during the summer and made a small fortune by pilfering our fields. The yield of my field was less than half of what it should have been. Tolya and the other thieves had taken away the lion's share. But I was happy with the potatoes I managed to harvest. Who was as rich as I? We were going to have something to eat during the coming months. I had a serious problem of where to keep the potatoes, as there was simply no space for them in our tiny room. Akhmadulin allowed me to store them in his cellar. He lived far from us, and it was inconvenient, but I had no other choice and was very grateful to him.

*   *   *

The summer was not all warm weather and enjoyable sunshine. There were plenty of the worries and hardships that life in Tamak usually brought. The most unpleasant incident, however, came totally unexpectedly. One afternoon when I came home from work, Ida told me that we had "subtenants." An official of the City Housing Department had come to tell her that they were putting some new refugees in our room. He had said that it was only for a couple of weeks, but knowing the housing methods of the town administration, I realized that we were going to be stuck with our subtenants for keeps. The city-owned houses were the regular catchall for newly arrived refugees so we, like most tenants in our city-owned building, were simply ordered to take in new refugees.

In the evening our subtenants came—a woman with her five-year-old boy and mother-in-law. They had arrived the day before with a transport of refugees from the Voronezh region, having fled before the advancing German Army. I did not know how we were going to manage to accommodate six people in such a small room. I was desperate, but there was no choice in the matter, and I consoled myself with the idea that it could have been worse. What would I have done, I said to myself, if the official had simply evicted us, the foreigners, and given the room to this family of a Soviet officer who was at the front? I considered myself lucky that we still remained the titular tenants of the room, and we did our utmost to accommodate the family. Despite the terrible overcrowding we all tried not to be in one another's way and got along pretty well on the whole. But trouble came from an unexpected direction—the very first evening there began an antagonism between Nusia and the old woman.

When Nusia and "Uncle" came home that evening, they had to stride over the mother-in-law, who slept on the floor near the door. There was an immediate exchange of rude words between the two women, but the worst was yet to come. A few minutes later, as usual, the smell of Nusia's roast meat permeated the room. We had long since become immune to it, but the noses of our new arrivals reacted sharply. The old woman made a few loud comments; Nusia opened the door, and there was again a duel of insulting words.

The mother-in-law did act in a somewhat odd way in general. She was very religious and felt unhappy that there was no church in town. Evenings before going to sleep she would take out the icon she had brought along with her, kneel down before it and pray for a long while, but afterward she usually was in a grouchy mood. During the day she was a busybody. Before long she became acquainted with all the women in the neighborhood and learned all the gossip about Nusia and "Uncle." Her animosity toward them grew, and there was hardly an evening when she would not make some comments when they passed through our room.

The tension came to a climax when the daughter-in-law received a telegram that her husband was wounded. The old mother was very grieved and wept all day, and when our neighbors came home that evening she blurted out, "My son has lost a hand at the front, while this young healthy bastard has been living here in abundance and in sin with a limping bitch." Nusia became furious, and in a moment the two women were at each other. The daughter-in-law and "Uncle" had a hard time separating them.

I became very worried. There had been established between us and our neighbors a modus vivendi of mutual tolerance. Now I was caught in the middle and sensed that I was liable to get hurt in the clash between the feuding sides. To my surprise the old woman calmed down afterward and controlled herself whenever our neighbors passed by. She became taciturn in general. Nobody knew that she was working in secret on a scheme.

About two weeks later "Uncle" suddenly disappeared. Evenings Nusia would come home alone and hurry by like a wild tigress, but one could not help noticing that her eyes were red from crying. One evening, however, the storm broke out again, and the two women got into a scuffle. It turned out that the mother-in-law had obtained all the particulars about "Uncle" and reported him to the NKVD. His deferment, which Nusia had obtained for him through her "good connections" for a large sum of money, was revoked, and he was drafted and sent to the front. Nusia walked around in a subdued mood and was no longer as cocky as before. But the tension was there nonetheless, and the situation was fraught with potential danger.

FOUR

Never before, even in the gloomiest days of the German offensive against Moscow, had I seen Sasha in such a pessimistic frame of mind as during the German successes in the Stalingrad and Caucasus regions. "If Hitler succeeds in capturing Stalingrad and the Caucasus," he said, "he may bring Russia to her knees and force her to accept a separate peace on his terms."

The grave situation at the front was reflected in the events at the VU, which had a great impact on my work there and eventually affected deep changes in my entire life in Tamak. One morning as I came to work, I found a large group of cadets lined up in the yard ready to march to the railroad station. During the coming weeks most of the cadets, and with them also nearly all the older officers and instructors I knew, left for the front.

At the same time, however, large contingents of recruits, recuperated soldiers from the hospitals and also new officers kept arriving at the VU. The classes expanded immensely. In addition, short-term courses were improvised in order to prepare replacements rapidly for the badly decimated officer corps at the front. The hectic circumstances made my work even harder. A great many of the civilian employees were drafted into the army too and were replaced by war invalids. Little by little, the familiar friendly atmosphere disappeared. Except for Ryabov and several other people, there were nearly no old friends from Riga left.

Ivanov too left for the front. Ever since he had "discovered" me at the Kazan railroad station, a friendly relationship had existed between us. He was a jovial fellow, and whenever I came to his office for my salary, he would tell anyone who was around the story of how he ran across me, embellishing it each time with some dramatic details for effect. But I was very grateful to him for helping me rejoin the school and did not mind his good-natured teasing and exaggerations. In our chats he used to reminisce about his stay in Riga. Like the other Soviet citizens who had lived there, he too loved the higher standard of living in Latvia and dreamt about the day when he would return there with the VU. Alas, his dream was never to come true; some months later he fell at Stalingrad.

* * *

My relationship with Ivanov's successor, Tsitron, was less pleasant. He came from the front where he had been wounded. He was proud of the medals on his chest and often indulged in telling stories about his distinction in battle. He turned out to be a well-read man. His favorite topic was to demonstrate to me, the foreigner, the "superiority" of Soviet "socialist realism" over the literary forms of "decadent" Western writing. Discussing touchy literary questions with a Communist was a dangerous matter in itself, and I had to be wary. To my dismay, however, Tsitron one day broached the topic of Zionism. I became alarmed and attempted discreetly to change the subject, but he continued trying to persuade me that Zionism was merely a willing tool in the hands of the imperialists in their plot against the USSR, and that the only solution of the Jewish question was the proletarian revolution.

I tried to avoid him, but for some reason he always looked for an opportunity to chat with me. I realized that I was skating on thin ice, yet I was afraid to avoid him entirely, lest I arouse his suspicion. I therefore kept up my "friendship" with him, being very careful not to get involved in political talk. Nevertheless, I felt uneasy; I knew well that if he wanted to, he could easily build up a "case" against me for the NKVD.

FIVE

After the start of the German thrust against the Caucasus, large transports of Caucasian oil specialists and workers began arriving in Tamak. The new stream of evacuees made the overcrowding even worse, and the prices in the kolkhoz market soared even higher. The government set about feverishly to step up the Ishimbay oil output to prepare it as a replacement in case the Caucasus oil fields were captured by the Germans. The oil industry was now given top priority over all other industries in the region, and Ishimbay eventually became one of the country's largest petrochemical industrial centers.

In early July when I went to the kolkhoz market, I noticed nearby a tall, emaciated man of about my age who was trying to sell a pair of ladies' shoes. I had never seen him before, and he attracted my attention. He wore threadbare clothes and shabby boots, but the fine features of his face and his high forehead bespoke intelligence. In my bad habit of staring, I began casting glances at him unobtrusively. His eyes responded with a soft smile, and after a while we became acquainted. Before long Osip Sorokin became one of my closest friends. He was a fascinating and extremely erudite man, with whom one could discuss Plato, Leibniz and Kant; he was one of the most remarkable people I met in Russia.

He and his wife Nadezhda had arrived from the Caucasus about a week before our meeting, and the story of their suffering during the war was quite moving. Osip had taught mathematics and physics at the Higher Institute of Technology in Odessa. When the war broke out, he, like so many others, believed that the enemy would be stopped at the old pre-1940 Soviet-Rumanian border and was in no hurry to get on one of the trains that took evacuees to the east. Before long, however, it was too late; the land blockade of Odessa was complete, and the suffering in the besieged city was terrible. The only narrow avenue of escape left was by boat via the Black Sea.

It was only in October 1941, shortly before the capture of Odessa by the Rumanian and German troops, that the Sorokins succeeded in getting on one of the boats that evacuated people by night. On the journey, however, the boat was sunk by the Germans. A great number of evacuees drowned, but after spending many hours in the cold water the survivors were picked up by another vessel. The Sorokins had lost all of their belongings. The rest of the voyage across the Black Sea was very perilous.

Upon arriving in the Caucasus region they experienced great hardships. Nadezhda, who had caught a bad cold in the icy water, soon developed pneumonia and had to be hospitalized for several weeks. Osip went to work as a plain laborer in an oil field, and the struggle for a living was hard. When the Germans began to advance toward the Caucasus, Osip did not wait too long; he had already learned his lesson in Odessa, and he knew by now about the fate of the Jews in the captured territories. It was not easy, but finally they managed to join a transport of oil workers that left for the Urals.

Upon arriving in Tamak Osip worked very hard in the oil

field, and they lived in a dingy corner with a Bashkir family. Later he did succeed in getting a teaching position at the Vocational Training School of the Oil *Kombinat* and then got a room in one of the *Kombinat's* tenements, which improved his situation somewhat. But the struggle for survival was nonetheless very difficult, the main problem being Nadezhda's bad health.

* * *

August brought with it a sad event. Mr. Kutner suddenly became sick at work and lay in bed with high fever. After a few days he was hospitalized, and it turned out that he had meningitis. His condition grew worse. When I accompanied Gelbman, his brother-in-law, to visit him, he was delirious and did not recognize us at all. He kept talking incoherently about his home town and events in his youth. Kutner was a sturdy man of 40, and he fought hard against the disease. There were ups and downs in his condition, and the doctors said that he had a fair chance to pull through, but about a week later he died.

We were all terribly shaken, and none of us present at the funeral could find a plausible answer to the wailing question the stricken widow was directing to Heaven. Why was the family punished with so much tragedy? The blue heaven above was silent and indifferent to the lamentations below on the hill, and the sun shone as usual. Maybe the refugees sleeping beneath the fresh mounds and the *Kantonists* in the old, overgrown graves were trying to convey to us the answer in the light rustling of the wind in the shrubs, only we, the living, were too preoccupied to perceive it. Each of us thought his own gloomy thoughts about what Fate had in store—to survive and return safely home or to find his eternal resting place here.

* * *

The rapid expansion of classes brought unexpected problems. There were schedule conflicts, and I had to combine classes that were already too large as it was, working very hard to keep abreast of the curriculum. The situation grew difficult for yet another reason. Many of the newly arrived front soldiers, some of them without a high school education, were not even familiar with the Latin alphabet. Their chests were bedecked with medals for bravery, and they deserved to become lieutenants, but they could not follow the regular lessons. It gradually became physically impossible for me to cover my classes all by myself. I discussed the matter with Captain Tychenko, the academic dean, and he told me to hire a part-time teacher to help me out. But it was not easy to find a suitable person. I interviewed a number of candidates, but, to my great disappointment, most of them were unable to say a simple German sentence correctly, not to speak of their thick accents. In the end I selected Valeria Hirschberg, an evacuee from Moscow, where she had taught German and music at a high school. Her late husband was a friend of Sasha. She was a cultured, middle-aged woman. Before World War I she had studied at the Conservatory in Vienna for several years.

She began teaching in August. It was hard for her to adjust to the special army conversational teaching methods, but I helped her cope with the difficulties, and her taking over a few classes somewhat eased my excessive teaching load.

SIX

For many months I had eagerly awaited a parcel from my relatives in America, which I hoped might relieve our suffering in Tamak. Finally one day in August there was a note in my mail from the censor saying that the package had arrived. I was overjoyed.

When I went to Ksenia, she told me that the parcel seemed to have been tampered with. We opened it, and the first thing she did was to take out the newspapers in which the articles were wrapped. "Let us get rid of this stuff quickly before it is noticed by some unwelcome curious eyes," she said, adding with a wink, "You had better write your folks immediately to use only plain wrapping paper."

I was entirely cut off from life abroad and longed very much to read those papers to find out what was happening in the free world. With a sad heart I watched her tear them into small pieces and throw them into the stove, but I was nonetheless grateful to the prudent woman for preventing me from getting in trouble.

We then checked the contents of the parcel against the enclosed list. I was shocked to see that nearly one-third was missing. She gave me a bunch of forms to fill out in order to apply for indemnity. I consulted with Sasha and decided that it did not pay to bother at all. As in all other branches of the Soviet regime, thefts were commonplace in the postal system, and it was useless to complain, for it took years before a claim was acted on. And even if I should get some compensation, the value of the stolen things—which were worth a fortune in the *tolchok*—would be assessed on the basis of the ridiculously low state prices, so the amount received would hardly suffice to buy a few quarts of milk in the kolkhoz market.

Sasha's main argument, however, was that since the parcel came from abroad, it constituted an embarrassing matter to the postal authorities. It was most likely that the NKVD would get involved in the investigation, which could have dangerous consequences for me. I therefore asked Ksenia to forget the whole thing, and took the parcel home as it was.

* * *

The short Ural summer flew by fast. After mid-August the nights grew chilly and the Belaya became too cold for fishing. The air filled with the cold breath of fall. At the monthly meeting of the civilian employees in the VU the question of wood allotments was brought up, but the political commissar made it clear that there would not be any at all. To the daily struggle with hunger was added again the specter of freezing. The cold rains and the chilly dampness were around the corner, and not far beyond the winter waited in ambush like a hungry wolf.

The price of wood in the kolkhoz market was now sky-high. I began looking around for other sources of wood and at this juncture had an excruciating experience with Ilya Tesler, a refugee from Latvia. He had been wounded at the front and sent to a hospital in Tamak. He was discharged as an invalid and contacted his fellow-countrymen in the VU. He was given a job in the supply department, traveling around the countryside to acquire provisions for the school.

A suave bachelor in his twenties, he soon hit it off with the women, and when Miss Lurie introduced him to me, she did not fail to tell me that he lived with Mrs. L., the widow of a Latvian officer who had fallen at the front, and that their relationship was much more than platonic. Tesler was a shrewd fellow and ingratiated himself with his superiors by taking care of their personal supply needs. Before long he was also carrying on a lucrative private trade in provisions, and it was whispered that he shared the profits with some officers in his department.

When I was looking around desperately for wood, an acquaintance tipped me off that Tesler was taking secret private orders for wood. I spoke to him, and after much bargaining he agreed to deliver a truckload of wood for 3,000 rubles. I sold much of the stuff in the parcel to raise my half, and our subtenants consented to pay their half, but the money they were expecting from the husband was late in coming. All they gave me was 250 rubles. Tesler, however, insisted on full payment in advance. I had no choice but to sell practically all the things in the package and give him the money. He promised to make the delivery immediately, yet the days passed, and there was no sign of the wood. Every time I saw him, he gave me a new excuse. Then he suddenly disappeared from Tamak, and nobody knew where he was. It turned out that he had taken many "wood orders" from unfortunate refugees and skipped town with a small fortune. He did not have to worry that his victims might go to the NKVD; if they did so, they might be arrested on the spot for buying stolen state property.

Tesler's cheating me out of all I had was a great calamity and could not have come at a worse time. Some time before Raphi had fallen sick and felt weaker with every passing day. Dr. Orshovsky said that it was the result of malnutrition, and in order to build up his resistance, she began to make regular blood transfusions from me to him. He needed some nutritious food badly, but I now had neither money nor anything worth selling in the *tolchok*.

I knew that it was naive, yet in my desperation I hoped against hope that if I wrote Tesler, his conscience would be moved to return at least part of my money. Therefore I went to Mrs. L. to ask her for his address. As soon as I started to talk she flew into a fit of anger. "Don't mention his name to me! That dirty crook has ruined my life!"

What I heard from her revealed to me another unsavory side

of Tesler's depraved character. With his smooth tongue he had spoken to her about marriage and won her favors. The poor woman, about ten years his senior and with three children in the bargain, lost her head. She had sold the clothes that were left from her late husband and much of her own things to support him in a generous way. He had gone on exploiting her, but whenever she mentioned a date for the wedding, he had found some excuse to postpone it. "He told me that he was going on a business trip to Ufa," she said. "I was the last one to realize that he ran away and have no idea where he is." Nobody ever again heard from Tesler.

*   *   *

I continued giving blood for Raphi, but his condition did not improve. About mid-September he was hospitalized, and Ida had to stay with him in the hospital. There were many cases of typhus in town, and since Raphi had been ill with typhus in Kazan, the doctors suspected that it might be a recurrence of the disease. We breathed a sigh of relief when the alarm proved to be false. Soon, however, he developed pneumonia, and his temperature rose very high. My heart was filled with worry, and the incessant downpour from the leaden sky was like a sad musical accompaniment to my miserable mood. Our subtenants did get the money from the husband in the meantime but were in no hurry to pay me the debt. Whenever I asked for it, I would get a different excuse. With Ida and Raphi away, I spent little time in our cold, damp room. I left for school earlier, and after finishing my work there I hurried to the hospital. On the way back I'd stop at my office in the VU and work there all evening or visit friends. I usually arrived home very late, boiled a few potatoes on the primus, ate and went to bed in my clothes.

One evening in October I found our subtenants packed and ready to leave. I was surprised and asked what had happened. They told me they were leaving on the midnight train for Orsk where the husband was hospitalized. There was embarrassment on their faces; they had apparently hoped to be gone before I came.

"What about the 1,250 rubles you owe me?" I asked.

"The money I got from my husband is barely sufficient for the journey," the young woman sighed. I knew that it was not true, and she caught my quizzical look at the sack with victuals, which they very likely bought that day in the kolkhoz market. She blushed and assured me that they would send me the money from Orsk. Her assurance was seconded by her mother-in-law, who crossed herself and called upon her patron saint to bear witness that they were not "the kind of people to want somebody else's money."

Realizing that it was useless to insist, I made the best of a bad bargain and pretended to believe them. My only consolation was their unexpected departure. I had been resigned to being stuck with them for good and was so excited that I could not sleep all night, fearing that something might go wrong and they would return. The next day before going to the hospital I ran home to make sure that they had not come back so that I could bring the good tidings to Ida.

* * *

Raphi improved, and we took him home, but he was still very weak. With a sick child at home, I had to do something about wood. The only choice I had was to barter away a considerable part of our potatoes for a load of wood, knowing that it meant starving before long. But the menace to Raphi's life from the cold was immediate and had to be averted at any cost.

Several days after we took Raphi home, Galya Yavorsky dropped by to see how he was. She too had stayed with her child, a little girl, in the hospital, and we became acquainted with her there. She was a very attractive woman in her twenties. Later her parents came to the hospital and she introduced us to them.

Looking at Yakov and Sima Tamarkin, I was struck by how Galya incorporated a unique blending of the features of both of them. While the well-proportioned figure, fair skin and delicately shaped features of her face were Sima's, she had, from Yakov, large, beautiful hazel eyes and a bushy thicket of flaming red hair, which lent her a piquant charm. We gradually struck up a very close friendship with the family, and Galya invited us to visit them.

Galya's husband, Yevsey I met only later. But seeing the furnished, comfortable three-room apartment of the family—a very rare thing indeed among the evacuees in Tamak—I realized that what Yakov told me about Yevsey's high status in the industrial hierarchy was no exaggeration. He was the director of a large factory in Dnepropetrovsk, which was evacuated to Tamak after the outbreak of the war. In January, however, he was "borrowed" from his factory and transferred to the Ural Council for War Industry in Sverdlovsk, charged with the task of increasing the production of war matériel. It was a very high position, but he considered it merely as a temporary appointment and decided to leave his family in Tamak. Our friendship with the family enriched me with interesting experiences and knowledge of the inner workings of the Soviet system.

*   *   *

When Nusia passed through our room one morning after the departure of our subtenants, she suddenly said hello to me and began to talk amiably. She had never done so before, but nothing in her behavior astonished me anymore; she was one of the most characterless persons I met in Russia, with the thick skin of a muzhik. She obviously missed "Uncle" terribly and hated our former tenants deeply for depriving her of him. Knowing that they had left without paying me the debt, she reasoned that "the enemy of my enemy is my friend" and tried to talk me into suing them, thus making me a tool for her revenge on them. But I knew better than to get involved with the Soviet courts and turned her down politely.

The recovery of Raphi upon his return from the hospital was very slow. I continued giving him blood, but we were in a financial pinch and unable to buy any substantial food. All we could give him was black bread and potatoes. From our American parcel only two pairs of silk stockings and a few cakes of toilet soap were left. If sold in the *tolchok*, they would have brought several hundred rubles. In view of Nusia's changed behavior, we decided after much consideration to give her a pair of stockings and a cake of soap, in the hope that she would reciprocate by giving Raphi some nourishing food from time to time; she always had plenty. She was thrilled like a child by the unfamiliar fragrance of the soap and marveled at the transparent stockings, the likes of which she had never before seen in her life. But characteristically enough, it never occurred to that callous woman to give our child even as much as a little soup.

* * *

One evening in October when I dropped in on the Orshovskys, I found Esfir lying in bed with a bandaged head. She had been assaulted that morning in the market by a pair of juveniles who got away with her handbag in which she had money and the family's ration coupons. In the struggle with the thugs she sustained numerous bruises and also a few knife cuts. The brutally roughed-up old woman looked very pale and badly shaken, and the family was worried about her health.

Even before coming to Tamak, in Kazan and the other places through which we traveled, as well as on the trains, I had become familiar with the widespread stealing and robbing. Tamak too had, naturally, a number of thieves and muggers who preyed on the inexperienced refugees, especially the women.

Still harder to cope with were the juvenile gangs that consisted largely of orphans or those whose fathers were in the army. They were tough and worked in a well-organized way. It was so reminiscent of the bands of waifs and strays that had been the scourge of the population in the years after the Revolution.

I observed one incident in the market a few months after my arrival in Tamak. A boy snatched a pocketbook from a woman and tossed it to his accomplice, who vanished quickly in the crowd. The woman grabbed the snatcher and cried for help, but the thug remained calm and told her brazenly, "Auntie, I don't know what you are talking about. I did not take your pocketbook, you can search me." A man among the bystanders exhorted the woman to hold on to the boy until a militiaman arrived. "If he is arrested, his friends will find a way to get your pocketbook to the militia in order to free him," he said, explaining that this was a tacit agreement between the gangs and the militia. While the people were waiting for the arrival of a militiaman and telling one another excitedly about their own experiences with mugging, the youth suddenly freed himself from the grip of the woman and darted away. It happened so swiftly that before anyone had a chance to stop him, he was out of sight.

An even more excruciating problem was the discharged invalids whose numbers grew as the war continued. They made the market their haunt, and considering themselves a privileged caste, they were not afraid of the militia. They regarded the proceeds of their pirating as a tribute due them from the civilian population, and so they did it with impudence. They would walk up to a stall in the kolkhoz market, grab something and leave without paying, ignoring the cries of the kolkhoz woman.

The favorite ground for their activities, however, was the *tolchok*. Here they behaved in a "businesslike" manner. Walking around among refugees who offered an article of their clothing or a portion of bread for sale, they acted as would-be buyers and even dickered about the price. Then one of the invalids would grab the object and throw it to a friend, who would disappear with it quickly. Some time later one could see the whole group of invalids standing in a corner of the market passing around the bottle of homemade vodka that they got from some fence for the stolen object.

Alas, there were also instances that bore an overt anti-Semitic character. I once witnessed such a sad case. An invalid took away a shirt from a woman, and she ran after him crying, "Shame on you! It belonged to my husband who fell at the front; I have to sell it to buy some food for the hungry children." He jeered at her "Hey, Sarah, where was your Abrasha killed? In the defense of Tamak probably"—a favorite anti-Jewish gibe alleging that there were no Jews at the front. When the poor woman fetched a militiaman and pointed out the one who had robbed her in a group of invalids, the drunken culprit unwrapped his wooden leg and began fencing off the militiaman with it. The guardian of the law retreated from the scene without doing anything.

Mugging and pirating in the market grew so rampant that it gradually became, especially for women, more and more hazardous to go there. The militia were reluctant to interfere, particularly where invalids were concerned, and people eventually stopped turning to the militia because some of those who did were later "taught a lesson" by the gangs.

Ida too experienced her share of muggings. Several times she was robbed of a portion of bread and once of a blouse that she tried to sell in the *tolchok*. She came home every time upset and heartbroken. She went to the kolkhoz market in August to buy some milk for Raphi, and a juvenile thug snatched her purse. As she was about to scream, he shoved a knife to her ribs and snarled, "Auntie, if you know what is good for you, keep quiet!" She became petrified and watched him silently as he ran away and came home sobbing and scared to death. That was the last straw—never again during our sojourn in Tamak did I let her go to the market.

*   *   *

The natives had predicted a mild winter, yet the harsh frosts and snowstorms set in early. It seemed as though the Ural winter wanted to reassert its sway over the people and demonstrate from the very outset that it did not intend to be more merciful than its predecessor. On top of the daily hardships came the distressing news about the deteriorating military situation, especially at Stalingrad. The scales of the war seemed to be tipping in favor of the Germans. The future looked gloomy, and hearts were filled with fear.

Around mid-October I began not feeling well. I was often tired and feverish, and started having splitting headaches with occasional spells of dizziness. I had never in my adult life been ill and therefore ascribed it to undernourishment, the strain of the daily hardships and overwork, and I hoped that the indisposition would pass before long.

I went on swallowing aspirins but did not get better. After several days I began to feel a tormenting backache. I tried to ignore it but found it more and more difficult to get up in the morning. But I could not afford to be sick and had to carry on my work and the daily struggle for the survival of my family. The pain grew worse. Before long my back became tight and swollen, and bending or sitting down was an agonizing experience; it also became increasingly harder to walk. At night I could not lie on my back; it was now sensitive even to the slightest touch.

One day the pain became unbearable, and I dragged myself

home with difficulty and lay down immediately. I was burning up with fever and could not sleep all night, lying on my stomach and writhing in agony. Ida heard my sighs and groans and asked me what was wrong. "Some pain in the back, nothing serious," I said. Why create panic about myself? There were enough worries over Raphi.

Getting up that next morning, dressing and dragging myself to work was an ordeal; each movement hurt terribly. I could hardly wait to finish classes and went straight to Dr. Orshovsky. She took my temperature—it was over 103. When she began examining my back I saw a sudden alarm on her face. "How have you been able to walk around like this? Your back is one large furunculous swelling; there must be something brewing inside the spine. You have to go to the hospital immediately," she said.

It is difficult for me to figure out in retrospect how I managed the two-mile walk to the hospital that afternoon. On the way to Dr. Orshovsky an icy wind was blowing and a *purga* was in the offing. When I left her, the snowstorm was in full fury, cutting the visibility to a few yards. I dragged on slowly, each step a painful effort. Then I suddenly slipped and fell on my back. A sharp pain ran through my body. I remained lying helplessly, tempted to rest a little and to gather the strength to get up.

The raging of the *purga*, however, kept increasing and sounded now like the howling of a pack of wolves waiting close by to jump on me and tear me to pieces. I was aroused from my lethargy, and after several vain attempts I finally managed to turn over from my pain-wracked back onto my stomach and get on my knees. There was not a living soul in sight to help me. I crawled on for a while on my knees until I reached a fence and, grabbing it, I laboriously scrambled to my feet.

I remember only very dimly entering the hospital building and slumping on the nearest bench, with Dr. Orshovsky's note crumpled in my hand.

6

The Surgery Ward

ONE

WHEN I AWOKE the next morning, my head was heavy and swimming. Through blurred eyes I saw that I was lying in a strange bed and wondered dimly where I was. There were many beds around me with people whom I had never seen before. Their talk sounded like the dull thumping of raindrops on a tin roof.

Some people in white coats approached my bed. I tried to catch what they were saying, but their voices seemed to be coming from a distance. They began examining my back, which felt like a raw, aching clump, and each tap of their fingers came as a sharp stab. I felt great relief when it was over. After a while I was lifted onto something and wheeled away.

After a while I heard a muffled voice, which seemed somehow familiar to me, telling me to count backward from 100. Then the veiled faces over me began to dissipate in the mist, and I was rising slowly and floating weightlessly through space.

As I was put back into my bed, I saw through a cloud strange faces and plaintively I muttered something to them, yet nobody paid any attention to my whimpering. I became ashamed of my tears and closed my eyes to conceal them.

Before long I dreamt that I was on the green meadow behind my parents' house where I used to play as a boy. It was a balmy summer day, and the sun was shining brightly. My brother and sisters and the playmates of my youth gathered around me. They welcomed me merrily and wondered how come I did not recognize them a while ago in the beds. The little girl whom I used to frighten by mentioning the Cossacks asked me why I was crying and what harm the Cossacks had done to me. Soon I joined them in their game, and I was happy as I had not been in many years. Later I was home. My parents welcomed me with smiling faces. I was surprised to see how young they looked. Father, sitting as usual at the table over an open Talmud volume, interrupted his singsong chant and asked me how I was, why I lived so far from home and how come they had not heard from me in such a long time. Mother's face was clouded with deep worry. She was sitting at my bed in which, to my bewilderment, there lay a little boy. I was curious to know who he was and stepped closer to the bed. I saw immediately that he was very ill; he was whining weakly and breathing with a gurgling sound. Gazing intently at his feverish face, it struck me that his features resembled mine. I looked in surprise at Mother. She nodded her head sadly, "Of course it is you, don't you remember?"

Suddenly my body began to evanesce and fuse with that of the boy, and soon it was I lying in bed and burning up with fever. While wiping off the perspiration from my face with a moist cool towel, Mother began in a sad voice: "When you were a little boy you had diphtheria and were dangerously ill. One night your condition became critical. Our doctor said that there was nothing he or anyone else could do to help you any longer. Father was out of town and I was desperate. I wrapped you in a blanket and carried you to the hospital in the nearest town. It was a cold winter night with a deep snow, and I barely made the four-mile walk. When I reached the hospital, I was out of breath. The doctors took a look at you and said that it was foolish of me to bring them a dying boy. But I did not give in. They began working on you and saved your life. About two weeks later we took you home, but you were very weak and lay in bed for many weeks."

I recalled now dimly how, upon recovering, I was taught to walk again. Sitting in opposite corners of the room, my parents would spread out their arms and coax me to toddle from one to the other. My mother regarded my recovery as a miracle and made a vow to God. For a very long time afterward, every Friday upon coming home from Heder, she would give me a basket with hallah, meat and fish to distribute among the needy people in the neighborhood.

Mother went on wiping my sweat and telling me that the pain would go away soon and that I was going to be well again. Then she got up, and all of a sudden both she and Father began to fade away until they vanished completely. The entire scenery of my house and my home town, too, dissolved like blue smoke.

* * *

When I opened my eyes, there was a woman sitting at the bed. I was still in a haze and confused her with my mother, and it took me a while to see that it was Ida and to realize where I was. Gone was the green summer scenery of my home town. Through the window I saw a heavy white blanket of snow, a pale winter afternoon sun reflected in the ice configurations on the window-panes. I was lying flat on my back, which was bandaged tight all around. It hurt terribly, but it was not a piercing pain anymore, it felt rather like a deep throbbing ache. Ida tried to feed me some broth, but I could hardly swallow a few spoonfuls.

A while later Dr. Hornfeld passed through the ward and stopped at my bed. "You gave us a good scare," he said, "but you are going to be alright." (Now I realized who had made me count backward in the operating room.) He said that they had opened a large sore and drained some fluid from my spine but that it was too early to have a clear picture about the disease in general.

I felt giddy and exhausted and, shortly after Ida left, fell again into a deep sleep. Later I was awakened by a sudden stabbing pain. I felt like turning over but recalled Dr. Hornfeld's admonition to lie still on my back lest I upset the drainage tube in the wound. The night outside was as dark as ink. The ward was quiet except for loud snoring and some deep sighs and groans. The dim blue lights over the doors threw eerie shadows. The surging pain did not let me fall asleep again; the rest of the night I spent in a feverish, restless drowsiness.

In the morning I was again taken to the operating room and likewise a few more times during the next days; the tapping from the spine in particular caused me nightmarish pain. When

I was put back into my bed, I would lie there for hours on end in a haze, too preoccupied with myself to care about what was going on around me. Gradually, however, the pain lessened, and I felt somewhat better. I began to get acquainted with my neighbors and to observe my surroundings.

There were over 40 patients in the surgery ward. It was a small world in itself, away from the mainstream outside, and eventually I had an opportunity to get an insight into Soviet life from a new, different angle. A Soviet friend, who had been a political prisoner in a labor camp for several years, once told me: "As soon as the prison doors close behind you, you are overcome with a strange feeling that now you have nothing to lose any longer and you can talk about things in a manner you would have never dared outside."

I observed a similar psychology in the hospital. In view of the frequent cases of death, the ward was considered by the patients as a sort of ladder between life and death, and most of them— regardless of the height of the rung they perceived themselves to be standing on—felt free enough to break the padlock of silence that seems to lock the lips of the Soviet citizen on the outside, and they now indulged in "heretic" political talk.

Years later, reading Solzhenitzyn's fascinating book *The Cancer Ward*, I was reminded so much of the Tamak surgery ward and relived mentally my own experience there. I found striking similarities of behavior between many of the protagonists in the book and some of the people I had met on the ward.

TWO

Several days after the operation I asked Dr. Hornfeld when I could go home. He said, "Be patient, you'll have to stay here for a while." The prospect of a prolonged hospitalization filled my heart with fear for Ida managing alone with Raphi in this cruel wintertime. Yet there was nothing I could do. The hardships and starvation of the past year and a half had apparently weakened my body to the point of being unable to take the blood transfusions I gave for Raphi.

The ward was very crowded; there were even beds in the corridors. Often a new patient was simply put on a mattress on the floor until a bed became available. There was a constant turnover of patients—many came for minor surgery and left after several days. On the other hand there was a seemingly constant group of gravely ill. Most of them were already there when I came. Some of these patients eventually died, others remained even after I left. It was my first hospitalization since childhood, and I was bewildered at first. But soon I fell into the hospital routine and became familiar with the surroundings.

In the bed to my right lay Zhilin, a middle-aged, tall man with a large, bald head. His broad face, with its hollowed cheeks, had a waxen pallor. He was an engineer from Kiev and had had a severe accident at work. One hand was badly mangled in a machine. He kept to himself and read most of the time. It took me a while to get acquainted with him. His wife, a petite blonde, visited him often and brought him good books. When I began to feel better, I used to borrow them.

Zhilin proved to be a well-educated man, with the broad, humanistic knowledge typical of the prerevolutionary intelligentsia. He showed great interest in life abroad and asked many pertinent questions, but he carefully avoided any talk that smacked of politics. Later I saw that there was no love lost between him and the regime. From a casual remark or hint I also sensed that he must have experienced some horrible ordeal during the Stalinist purges in the thirties, but he never said what it was, and I did not venture to ask him. He told me, though, a lot of interesting things about Soviet life in general.

My left-hand neighbor, Umnov, was about 60. His thinning, strawblond hair was woven through with gray, and the extremely fair complexion of his oval face had a slightly feminine blush. Unlike Zhilin, he was outgoing from the very beginning. He introduced himself and said some encouraging words. The features of his intelligent face and the way his dreamy blue eyes gazed above the copper-rimmed glasses, which kept sliding down his nose, resembled features of my old philosophy teacher, so that I somehow assumed that he, too, was a teacher and was therefore very much surprised to learn that he was a farmer from a kolkhoz near Tamak. His left foot had been severely injured by a tractor.

Umnov was friendly and polite to everybody and used a

refined language replete with sagacity. I never heard him utter a curse or a vulgar expression. What is more, whenever he overheard someone say a four-letter word—which usually come so readily and so frequently from Russian lips—he admonished him gently, "Is it really necessary to speak like this?"

Reading Tolstoy's and Turgenev's peasant stories, I had thought that their peasant characters were merely idealized types that did not exist in reality. Now, however, I saw such a peasant in the flesh, as if he had just stepped out of the pages of one of those stories. Later, on my visits to Russian villages, I came across a number of these elderly peasants.

In the morning, when breakfast and the doctors' rounds were over, Umnov would take out a book from under his pillow and read it in deep meditation. His eyes lit up and his lips moved silently, as though he were spelling each word. After finishing reading, he put the book back under the pillow. He would resume his reading after lunch, oblivious again to what was going on around him.

I noticed that he read the same book day in, day out, and I wondered what kind of book it was. But the plain, brown paper wrapper had no inscription on the outside. I was also puzzled at why he kept the book under the pillow and not on the bedside table as did the other patients. Later, when we were already pretty closely acquainted, I dared to ask him about it. He whispered with a smile, "I am sure you are no stranger to this book," and handed it to me. I glanced at it and understood why he concealed it so carefully from unwelcome eyes—it was a Bible!

* * *

I should have actually started with Gavryusha, as he was the first patient to contact me. On the first evening after the operation someone on crutches had hopped over to my bedside and asked whether he could have the broth that was left. I was still in a daze and did not quite understand what he wanted. As I nodded faintly, he grabbed the plate and wiped it clean with a piece of bread. The next morning during breakfast I noticed that he was watching me from his bed. Seeing that I ate very little, he hurried over and, looking imploringly into my eyes, gobbled up the rest of the meal. He did the same at lunch, shortly after I was brought back from the operating room. When he came again during supper time, however, Umnov told him politely to leave me alone, and thereafter he did not bother me anymore.

He was a short, broad-shouldered man in his fifties, with a thick, pepper-and-salt crew cut. His mercurial, greenish eyes seemed to be swimming around all over his wrinkled face. I don't think anyone knew or cared to know his last name or Russian patronymic. All, even the young girl attendants, called him by the diminutive form of his name, Gavryusha, but sometimes they used the more familiar diminutive—Gavryushka. He was a pitiful, tragicomic figure and the butt of many practical jokes.

Umnov told me a little about Gavryusha. He came from the Volga region where he allegedly had once been a well-to-do peasant. During the enforced Stalin collectivization he lost his land and joined the kolkhoz. In the terrible famine that followed the collectivization his wife and only daughter died. He tried to drown his grief in vodka and later left the kolkhoz and became a *brodyaga,* or hobo, wandering through the vast spaces of Mother Russia. He eventually had come to the Tamak region where one winter day he was found lying on the road with frozen feet and was taken to the hospital, where they had amputated his toes. He had to give up his wandering. During the summer he dragged himself on crutches from kolkhoz to kolkhoz, doing easy chores or living from handouts. With the approach of the frosts, however, he went back to the hospital and had become, for the past few years, a steady fixture of the ward all through the winter until the arrival of the spring.

To be sure, Gavryusha was not a malingerer; he needed medical attention all year around. He was alone in the world. Nobody ever came to visit him nor wrote to him. In a "damned capitalistic country" he would have been placed in a home for invalids, but in the eyes of the "Government of the Workers and Peasants" he was a former *kulak* (landed peasant), a declassed element without rights, doomed to be ground to pulp under the wheels of "progressing socialism."

Yet his tenacity and capacity for survival were remarkable. Some gossipy tongues claimed that when the cold season drew near, he would cause his toe stumps to begin to suppurate again in order to be readmitted to the hospital and to find a shelter there for the winter. It was the only means of struggling for existence left open to him. He slept on a mattress on the floor. Only when a patient died or was discharged, did the nurse allow him to occupy a bed temporarily. Yet his happiness never lasted too long. As soon as he noticed a new patient arrive, he would mutter sadly, "Well, another deportation" and hop back to his mattress.

Mealtime was his busy period. He'd closely watch the patients to see who left something on the plate and would hurry over and gobble up what remained. It was interesting to observe his activities during visiting hours. He would hop from bed to bed, indulge in talk and oblige those who would play a practical joke on him with a dry laugh, constantly looking with imploring eyes for a handout. He had a flattering way of his own with women visitors, who would usually give him a bit of the food they brought along. He tried hard to ingratiate himself with everybody by doing chores and offering his services. He had a razor and clippers and was always ready to give a shave or haircut, but he refused to accept money—hinting, though, that a piece of bread or some leftovers would be welcome.

The evening, however, was Gavryusha's finest hour. He'd sit down on a chair in the middle of the ward and sing plaintive Volga songs. All fell silent and listened; some started to hum the melody along. It was astounding to watch the sudden metamorphosis that took place in him—the humbled *brodyaga* and butt of jokes by day, a dignified, self-respecting human being by evening. He used to tell fascinating tales about folk heroes on the Volga who, long ago, rose up to free the peasants from the yoke of a cruel Czar. Many patients would smile sadly; they obviously perceived the allusion to Stalin. His repertoire seemed inexhaustible. I marveled at his picturesque language and power of expression. His voice, too, sounded somehow different at these times; it conveyed a tone of self-confidence. His tales contained a wealth of interesting Russian folklore—pity that nobody wrote them down.

His stories about the horrible suffering of the people during the famine after the collectivization were very sad. In many villages most of the population perished from starvation and the attendant diseases. I recall particularly one most moving story he told about a neighbor of his who, attempting to save the members of his family who had remained alive, harnessed his horses and drove to a distant village, which, supposedly, was not stricken as badly by the famine. When he reached that village he went from hut to hut, begging them to sell him some grain or any other food, but many peasants had been there before him, and the villagers had nothing to sell. In one of the huts they happened to be making *pirogi* that day. He asked them to sell him some. They refused. "We have no use for your rubles. Why haven't you brought along some clothing or shoes as the others do?" the host said. Then he added, in a rather half-joking tone, "You have two horses. Give me one and you can have as many *pirogi* as you'll be able to eat here." The famished neighbor could not resist the smell of this popular Russian delicacy and agreed. The hostess placed on the table all the *pirogi* she had made and also a jug of cold sour cream. Realizing that he was not allowed to take any of the food with him, he ate up everything—to the great amazement of the people who were watching him. When he went out of the hut, however, he suddenly keeled over and died instantly.

Upon finishing a story, Gavryusha would often take out his harmonica and play sad Volga tunes. His eyes were sad as he gazed into the distance, and he went on playing until the nurse put out the lights. He would then hop back to his mattress and lie awake sighing for a long while, apparently thinking of his late wife and daughter, of his village and lost home, of his ruined life.

THREE

My initial hope that I would not have to stay too long in the hospital dissipated gradually as the days passed and there was no decisive change in my condition. True, the violent pain in the center of the swelling was eased, but my back was still sore all over, and new furunculous pockets formed. There was also another trouble attendant on the illness. Before the start of the back ailment I had noticed that my legs were swollen and I had difficulty walking. Now, however, the swelling grew worse. When I stuck my finger into one of my calves, a hole would remain there for a while as if my calves were made of dough. The pulsation of my heart was erratic, and Dr. Hornfeld ordered me to get out of bed often and take a walk. At first it was hard, but I made an effort and with the help of Umnov's cane walked slowly in the corridor.

The hospital meals were scant and of poor nourishing quality. I badly needed some substantial food, yet in view of our extremely difficult financial situation there was no chance of getting it from the outside. Ida was hardly able to make ends meet at home as it was.

Some time after my operation there was a letter from America. My relatives wrote that they had sent us a package. I thought sadly of the great financial relief it would have brought us now, at this crucial time. But I knew that months would pass before it arrived—if at all.

As I was reading the letter, I noticed that Umnov kept glancing at it. He then took the envelope, felt it with his fingers and marveled, "What white, smooth paper!" Envelopes and writing paper were practically unavailable, and Soviet citizens were used to writing letters on pages torn out of a notebook—if they could afford to pay about ten rubles for one in the black market. Otherwise, they used plain wrapping paper (some also wrote on newspaper pages). The sheet of paper was then folded into a triangle shape, with the edges tucked in to hold it together, and the address was written on the outside.

I also received a letter from Berman in Kazan. A few days later we had a detailed letter from the Bronsteins, who now lived in Turkmenia, and they asked us again to move there. The climate was warm and food was cheaper and easier to come by. Reading Mrs. Bronstein's enthusiastic description of the sunny Central Asian weather in this season of the year, I kept glancing sadly at the thick, long icicles hanging down like crooked spears from the roof of the building across and at the dense shower of snow crystals falling steadily from the gray sky.

* * *

The arrival of a new patient usually attracted no particular attention. About mid-November, however, a patient came who aroused the curiosity of the entire ward. He walked in accompanied by the doctor, the head nurse and the director of the hospital himself. The woman who came with him took out of her bundle a pillow, a cotton-padded blanket and bed linen whose snow-white color was in sharp contrast with the washed-out, ashen hospital linen. The nurses busily made his bed and fussed about him. The tall, emaciated man, in his fifties, with a sour, drawn face put on pajamas and a dressing gown (how many ages ago had I worn these luxurious things—I tried to remember) and got into bed with the air of an imperious executive making himself comfortable in his hotel suite, ready for room service.

The news spread fast that the new patient was Zaytsev, the District Party Secretary. The routine of the ward was upset for a while; the talk became cautious and somewhat subdued. Gavryusha, too, made himself less conspicuous and did not give his performance that evening. Before long, however, the people became used to Zaytsev's presence, and things gradually returned to normal.

Zaytsev had chronic stomach ulcers and had come for an operation. His wife, a plump, phlegmatic woman, visited him daily. Except for some perfunctory words now and then, they hardly ever indulged in real conversation. After serving him the food she brought, she would sit down and, with her hands folded over her broad chest, watch him eat. After finishing his meal, he buried his face in the newspaper she gave him and did not seem to pay attention to her presence. She would look embarrassed and begin staring around the ward. After a while she would say goodbye and leave.

The main topic of conversation in those days was the desperate situation of the Red Army at Stalingrad. The people were bitter, and many a tongue became too loose. Zaytsev would listen attentively, and when the conversation got on politically dangerous ground, he would interfere and give a pep talk, quoting lavishly from the passages in the newspapers, which he used to underline with a red pencil.

There were, however, two patients in particular with whom he used to have a running political battle. Agulayev, a burly Bashkir, made no bones about his lack of love for the Russians and would occasionally drop veiled hints that Bashkiria ought to be an independent state. Zaytsev lectured him about what Comrade Stalin had written regarding "the absolute freedom and full independence of all the peoples of the Soviet Union."

Lysko, a Ukrainian with a husky voice, would always rebut Zaytsev's arguments and challenge the veracity of his statements. After such a debate Zaytsev would take a few pills to assuage the pain from his aggravated ulcers. Lysko was a most unpleasant and rude character in general, always ready to insult and pick a quarrel. He called every Jewish patient Abrasha and occasionally made anti-Semitic remarks about the Jewish doctors, too.

He was very talkative and liked to brag particularly about his "feats" in the battles during the civil war. Once, however, he got into trouble. He somehow mixed up his "we's" and "they's," so that it became clear that he had actually fought on the side of the Whites. Zhilin interrupted him and told him that he had better shut up. I could not help feeling malicious joy at Lysko's debacle. After that incident he behaved and left Zaytsev's ulcers alone. He also stopped telling anti-Jewish jokes.

People were sentenced to long labor-camp terms for far lesser heresies than those expressed by Lysko and Agulayev. I therefore simply could not imagine that Zaytsev would not, sooner or later, inform the NKVD about them. Even though I was very careful and never took part in any political talk whatsoever, I nonetheless dreaded the possibility of an NKVD investigation in the ward. I knew that, as usual, innocent bystanders, too, would be implicated in the end. But nothing ever happened. Some days later, before Zaytsev apparently had time to attend to the matter, his ulcers suddenly began to act up violently. He had to undergo emergency surgery and died shortly afterward.

I was puzzled, though, by the fact that Umnov, the Bible reader, had sided with Zaytsev and defended him. The answer to this puzzle I found later when I became familiar with his background. It turned out that he belonged to the sect of the Old Believers who, in the 17th century, seceded from the Russian Orthodox Church. They rejected the priesthood and most of the sacraments and considered all other Christians as followers of the Antichrist. The Czarist authorities in European Russia persecuted the Old Believers, and many of them fled to the Urals and Siberia.

In the middle of the 19th century Umnov's ancestors, with a large group of that sect, came from the Volga region to the Tamak district and founded a number of villages. Umnov told me many interesting details about the old rites and the customs in everyday life that the Old Believers still practice to this day. We talked a great deal about religion, and he would listen with great interest to my explanations of the ethical principles of Judaism. Once I asked how he could side with Zaytsev and his kind who preach that religion is the opiate of the people.

Umnov's answer was typical. "We Old Believers hold that man must not resist temporal force with force. This is why we did not fight against the Czarist persecutors and have also accepted the Soviet rule. Only by spreading the true teachings of the Lord will the Antichrist be conquered."

There were many interesting occurrences in the ward, and I learned much from them about the way of thinking of the common Soviet man and his feeling about the regime. But I will drop for now this thread of the story in order to tell of the calamity that unexpectedly befell us.

FOUR

In the second half of November Raphi suddenly became sick. Dr. Orshovsky found that he had an inflammation in his right ear. The inflammation grew worse, and after a few days there was also a swelling on the skull above the ear. He had to be hospitalized. The doctors suspected mastoiditis and said that a mastoidectomy might become necessary. But the nearest competent specialist who could decide whether or not an operation was unavoidable—and also perform it—was at the University Hospital of Ufa.

Realizing that it would be practically impossible for Ida alone to manage the trip with the sick baby, I asked Dr. Hornfeld to allow me to go with her. He smiled sadly and said, "You are in no condition to leave the hospital even for one day, you would only be a burden." I was beside myself with anger over my helplessness. Ida asked among our acquaintances to find out whether someone was going go Ufa, but nobody was. Meanwhile, however, Raphi's condition grew worse, and the doctors said that the trip could no longer be postponed. We were desperate.

Aid came unexpectedly; the two Silber sisters were going to Ufa and were willing to help. Ida borrowed some money from friends, and the next day, December 2, she came to say goodbye. Only as I watched them all come out of the Children's Ward across the yard, with my son in his mother's arms, and set out on the long walk to the station, did I realize the full depth of our misery—while I was lying helpless in the hospital here, my family was off to another hospital in a strange city, with our son likely to face a dangerous operation.

I had gotten to know the two Silber sisters, refugees from Latvia, not long after my arrival in Tamak. I remember how pitiful they looked in their thin clothes, both shivering from cold. The younger, frail and hardly 16 then, would cling to her older sister like a frozen, frightened bird. Later the older one became engaged to a Latvian refugee who had a job at the VU, but before they could get married he was suddenly sent off to the Latvian Military Unit that had been formed in Russia.

They had had a very hard life in Tamak, and the older sister had decided now to join her fiancé. The younger did not want to remain in Tamak alone and went with her. They were going to the Latvian *Evakpunkt* in Ufa to arrange their departure for the Latvian Military Unit.

* * *

Nine days later I received a letter from Ida. It turned out that the journey had not passed off without difficulties and mishap. They had had to stand in line at the Tamak station for a long time before they could get the tickets. When the train arrived, however, the rush to the cars was so ruthless that they could not get aboard and had to wait for the next train.

When they finally arrived in Ufa, it was already late in the afternoon, and the two sisters had to hurry to the *Evakpunkt* in order to find a place to sleep. They told Ida to wait for them at the station until they came back to help her get to the hospital.

The hours passed, but there was no sign of the sisters, and, to make things worse, a snowstorm started. About nine o'clock Ida gave up waiting and set out alone. She took a tramway and got off about a mile away from the hospital. With Raphi in her arms and a knapsack on her back, she began inching along the suburban street.

The *purga* was still raging, and after a while she felt that her strength was giving out. She wanted so much to sit down and rest for a while on the steps of one of the houses, yet she would not for fear that she might not be able to get up again. Then she suddenly stumbled and fell down with the child. After many futile attempts at getting up she began to cry loudly for help. She saw dimly a figure passing by on the other sidewalk, but the person either did not hear her or did not care to help. After that the street seemed to be deserted. Ida felt that her last bit of strength was going to fail any moment and that they would remain lying there and freeze to death.

Minutes or hours later—she could not tell—she saw a man bending over her. He picked up Raphi and then helped her to her feet, asking where she lived. When she told him that she was coming from Tamak and was on the way to the hospital, he said, "You're still far away from it. Come, let's go to my place; it is right around the corner."

In those cruel times, when the life of an individual was of little value, it was heartening to find people who had not lost their humanity. Mrs. Lavrov, the man's wife, gave Ida and Raphi some warm soup and suggested that they stay with them overnight. But Raphi needed medical attention, and after warming up Ida left the knapsack there and resumed her walk to the hospital. The snowstorm had subsided and walking was somewhat easier, but it was already after midnight when she finally reached the hospital with the sick child.

The next afternoon the Silber sisters came to the hospital. They too had had their share of trouble that previous night. After leaving the *Evakpunkt* they began running about to the hotels and inns to which they had been sent, but could find no place to sleep. About midnight they returned to the station and spent the night there.

Ida wrote that the doctor had begun an intensive treatment

with antibiotics in order to reduce the swelling in Raphi's ear, and only after that would he decide whether or not a mastoidectomy was unavoidable.

In the meantime Ida went through an ordeal of her own. It turned out that at that hospital the mothers—though required to stay with their children in the hospital—had to provide their own food. After the piece of bread and little bit of food that had remained from the trip were gone, she literally starved. She was desperate, and when she could no longer endure the hunger, she asked another mother to take care of Raphi while she went to the Latvian *Evakpunkt* to get some food. When she came back, the Head Nurse wanted to throw her out with Raphi for going away from the hospital without permission. In desperation, Ida went to the Hospital Director to explain the pitiful situation she was in and why she went to the *Evakpunkt.* After much pleading he finally agreed to let her stay and ordered that her daily bread ration be issued to her from the hospital. Thus she lived there on her daily piece of black, tasteless bread and *kipyatok.*

FIVE

I was wholly wrapped up in my worry about our son and was not concerned now about what was going on in the ward. Yet my attention was willy-nilly drawn to the brewing scandal about the disgusting conditions in the hospital. It started when Agulayev was discharged and discovered that some of his personal things were missing. He had a row over it with the nurses, and the hospital director was summoned. Soon there were loud complaints from everywhere. Bed linen and blankets, medicaments, as well as things that belonged to the patients disappeared mysteriously. There were many grievous wrongs all around, and the most violent outburst was about the food. In addition to its very poor nutritional quality, the portions were by far smaller than they ought to have been, and the bread rations were short-weighted.

All these grievances were surely justified; it was an open secret that the hospital employees stole. I was, though, somewhat baffled by the double standard of ethics on the part of the complainants. No average Soviet worker or employee could possibly live on his wages. Everybody would at one time or another pilfer something from his place of work and sell it in the black market. This was not regarded as stealing but rather as merely "taking" from the state that which belonged to one by right. It was the only way to make ends meet and be able to pay the exorbitant prices in the kolkhoz market for the food that the government failed to supply in its stores.

It was therefore odd to watch the sanctimoniousness of the complainants. They were used to "taking" things themselves without any compunctions at their places of work. Now, however, when they were the wronged ones, they argued with indignation and outrage. There was an investigation but nothing changed; things went on as before.

Interestingly enough, there were never any complaints about the physicians. All appreciated their hard work and unselfish efforts. There was an awful shortage of medications (antibiotics were practically nonexistent), yet the doctors, most of them Jewish evacuees, did their best to help the patients.

A quite different story, however, was the service of the nurses. They were rude and callous to the patients. The doctors prescribed medications, but they were seldom given; rumor had it that they would find their way to the black market. If one wanted to get his medicine, he had to threaten that he would "notify the proper persons." At night the nurse on duty would sleep in her cubicle, not caring about even those patients who were recovering from surgery and badly needed her help. No wonder that the patients felt contempt for the nurses and treated them with disrespect. They made disparaging remarks to them and occasionally there would be a nasty row between a patient and the nurse.

The only exception was Yelena Trofimovna, a cultured, elderly nurse. She was courteous with everybody and different in every respect from the other nurses. She enjoyed the appreciation and esteem of all patients, and when she was on duty one could rest assured that he was in good hands and would get his medicine without any fuss. She would drop in frequently during the night and promptly take care of the seriously ill.

I noticed from the beginning that there was some special relationship between Yelena and Umnov. She would often stop at his bedside and chat with him. One night when she was on duty, I saw her come into the ward, walk straight up to him and talk with him in a whisper for a long while. She did so on several later occasions. I thought they must be old friends and paid no particular attention.

*   *   *

When Zhilin was discharged, he gave me a volume of Chekhov's collected stories. "Keep it as a souvenir from me. The stories are delightful. Read them. It will help you keep your mind off the dismal reality," he remarked laconically. Seeing Gavryusha making preparations to occupy Zhilin's bed, I was not exactly happy with the prospects of getting him as a neighbor. But the nurse shouted at him rudely, "The bed is for a new patient!"

A few hours later a man about 30, with a broad, round face and black, curly hair was wheeled in from the operating room and put into the bed. He looked around dizzily, then fell asleep and slept throughout the afternoon and night. When he awoke in the morning, I introduced myself, and to my surprise it turned out that Jacob Burstein was from Dvinsk, Latvia.

He too had a sad story to tell. When the war broke out, he, with his wife and four-year-old girl, managed to escape to Russia. They wandered from place to place and ran into a lot of hardship. In the fall of 1941 they came to the Urals and were sent to a kolkhoz. Although both he and his wife worked very hard, they could not make ends meet and suffered hunger and cold throughout the winter. In the spring they finally succeeded in leaving the kolkhoz and came to Tamak. He got a job in a plant as a truck driver and living became somewhat easier.

Two days before he had driven to the forest to fetch lumber for the plant. On the way back the engine stalled, and he was stuck in the woods. It was night already, and he tried desperately to repair the engine. Unable to afford the sky-high price of felt boots in the black market, he wore only shoes and socks. And so, while working on the motor in the 50-below-zero temperature outside, his feet got frozen. He did not notice it immediately, but after a while he could not stand and could hardly get back into the driver's cabin. When another plant truck finally arrived many hours later, his feet were stiff and swollen, and he was taken to the hospital.

The doctors eventually succeeded in saving Burstein's feet, but most of his toes had to be amputated, and he suffered great pain. We gradually became friends and reminisced together about Latvia. I had visited Dvinsk in the thirties, and he happened to know some of Ida's relatives there. He told me a lot about the cynicism and cruelty with which the small band of Jewish communists treated the Jews of that city, particularly during the mass deportations to Siberia shortly before the outbreak of the war.

* * *

On December 16 I received a telegram from Ida telling me that the mastoidectomy had already been performed. I was beside myself with despair that I could not be near my son at this important time. Three days later Ida wrote that though the operation was very complex, everything seemed to have gone successfully. Raphi was very weak, but the doctor said that, barring some unexpected complication, he was going to be alright. My heart was nevertheless filled with worry.

In those days Umnov too had a worried look on his face. The doctor had told him that there were some gangrenous symptoms in his foot and advised that the infected parts be excised lest the disease spread further. Umnov, however, refused to consent to an operation. His wife and daughter, who came for their regular weekly visit, stayed much longer than usual. They were joined by Yelena, and they all talked excitedly for a long time.

When they left, Umnov told me, "My family says that I'm an old stubborn mule. Yelena too thinks that I ought to agree to the operation." He fell silent and lay pensive for a while. Then he started up and said, "My God! Why did it not occur to me sooner?" He took the Bible from under his pillow and opened it at random. He scanned the opened page, and his eyes lit up. "Read this," he whispered as he handed me the book. I read the passage he pointed out. "For the Lord God will do nothing, but He revealeth His counsel unto His servants the prophets" (Amos 3:7). I did not know what he was driving at and cast a puzzled glance at him. "Don't you see? The Scriptures tell me to seek the counsel of the servant of the Lord," he said. "We Old Believers have no official priesthood. Our spiritual leaders are worthy laymen selected from our midst. We had one in our village, but he died some years ago. Since then we go to the Reverend in Beloretsk. He is a saintly old sage and knows me well. Yelena is going to visit him in the forthcoming Christmas season, and I'll consult him about the operation and abide by his advice."

I was intrigued by Umnov's random consultation of the Bible and asked him where he got it from. "This is an old custom," he answered. "I remember my late father doing it whenever there was an important decision to make." He was very surprised when I told him about the ancient Jewish custom of asking a child to recite at random a verse from the portion of the Scriptures he studied in school that day.

As soon as Yelena finished attending to the patients that evening, she came over to Umnov and they talked in low voices for a long while. When she left, I asked him whether she was a relative or from his village. "Oh no, she is not from this region at all; she comes from Leningrad. But she is a devout Old Believer and has been a close friend of our family since she arrived here some years ago," he said. I was surprised and asked him why she had moved to Tamak. He smiled sadly, and what he told me that night revealed yet another sad tale about the cruelty of the Soviet secret police.

Yelena's husband, Dr. Goltsev, was a noted surgeon at the Leningrad University Hospital. In the turbulent period after the Revolution, however, he came to a tragic end because of a bizarre event that, in a democratic country, would be regarded merely as a practical joke. One day the "Workers' Committee" at the hospital posted on the billboard a "Schedule of Work" for the coming month, listing alphabetically everyone from attendants to doctors, ordering them all to do the daily chores of washing the floors, heating the ovens and suchlike. In order to point out the absurdity of such socialist equality, Dr. Goltsev erased the word "Work" in the Schedule and inserted instead "Operations".

But the patients, most of them wounded soldiers, apparently missed the point of the joke. Assuming naively that they were really going to be operated on by some nurse or clerk, they made a big row. Before long they went to the office of the "Workers'

Committee," broke the furniture and beat up some of the officials. To be sure, later the Soviet government itself canceled such extreme innovations of the "Workers' Committees." At the time, however, Dr. Goltsev was immediately arrested and sentenced as a "counterrevolutionary saboteur" to 25 years in a Siberian labor camp. Several weeks later his wife and three-year-old son were exiled to Siberia. The boy died there some time later. In the remote village where Yelena lived were some exiled Old Believers, and she eventually converted to their faith.

In 1936 Yelena was unexpectedly allowed to leave her exile and was assigned to settle down in Tamak. She was forbidden to return to Leningrad or to travel to any other western part of the country. Since her husband's arrest she had never heard from him again—she did not even know whether he was still alive.

During my sojourn in Russia I was told many a gruesome story about the inhumanity and senselessness of the secret police and the horrible suffering of its victims. Each time I was shaken anew to the depth of my soul. That night, too, I lay awake for a long time thinking about what I had heard from Umnov.

SIX

The days moved slowly in agonizing worry about Raphi and impatient waiting for my discharge. At long last, on December 28, Dr. Hornfeld reluctantly agreed to discharge me. "Don't forget, though, that you are still far from being well and must take it very easy," he cautioned me. "Be sure to come at least once a week to have your back checked and to change the dressing on your wounds."

It was very cold outside as I walked out of the hospital. The sun, a pale frozen disk, looked down indifferently from the clear sky. The crisp air tingled my nostrils and stung my lungs, which for over two months had breathed the thick, lukewarm ward air that was saturated with a peculiar stench of human pus and sweat. I felt weak and shaky in my legs and walked cautiously, as if on stilts, watching every step lest I slip on the icy road. Being accustomed to the hospital environment, I thought the world outside strange. I stopped at the post office to pick up our accumulated mail, and after resting there for a while I continued my walk home.

As I unlocked the door and went into our room, I felt as if I were entering an ice cave. The thick ice layers on the window practically prevented the scant wintry light from penetrating into the room. I lit the stove and went to boil some *kipyatok,* but the water in the pail was frozen solid, like a lump of wrought iron. The only way to get it out was to heat it in the bucket on the stove.

The hot water warmed my insides, and I felt somewhat better. I looked around the empty room, and my thoughts wandered to my family in Ufa. I felt wretched and forlorn and muttered to myself, "My God, when will all this horrible suffering finally be over?" After writing a letter to Ida, I began to work on my preparations for classes, which were to resume the next morning. Soon, however, I was overcome by tiredness and had to stretch out on the cot for a rest. As I lay there exhausted, doubt began gnawing at my heart. Maybe I did overestimate my strength after all. Perhaps I should have listened to Dr. Hornfeld and not hurried to be discharged—I became absorbed in these gloomy thoughts and soon dozed off.

It was nearly evening when I awoke. I felt rested and decided to drop in on the Slutskys to meet Lev. His wife Raisa, with her 12-year-old twin girls and mother-in-law, evacuees from Odessa, lived a few houses from us, and she worked together with Ida in the Children's Home. Lev went to the front immediately after the outbreak of the war. In the beginning there were letters from him. but then they stopped. All inquiries to find out what had happened to Lev were fruitless. His family was desperate.

Raisa bore her anguish with courage and worked hard to keep the family above water. Even more, however, I admired Lev's mother, Rebecca Yosifovna, who had lived with the family since her husband's death some years before. She was the prototype of the wise old Jewish mother of past generations, a species nearly extinct in our days. In the presence of the family she never showed any signs of the despair that tormented her heart. On the contrary, she would always find the proper words to inspire them with courage and the hope that they would hear from Lev soon.

But the months passed and there was no word from Lev. Nobody would speak of it, but it was feared that he had been killed in battle. Not less frightening was the thought that he might have been taken prisoner, for it was known by then that the Germans killed the Jewish prisoners of war.

* * *

I shall never forget a Saturday morning during my first winter in Tamak. I went for something to the Slutskys and knocked on the door, but there was no response. I opened the door and entered. Rebecca was alone and apparently did not hear me come in; she was sitting at the window with her back turned to me, praying. I did not want to disturb her and stood listening to her in silence. She read in a plaintive voice in Hebrew "Our God and God of our fathers. . . . visit us with mercy and salvation. . . . Remember the covenant, the kindness, and the oath which Thou didst swear to our father Abraham on Mount Moriah, and the binding of Isaac his son on the altar. . . ."

I recall the peculiar feeling I had as I listened to the old, heartbroken mother reciting the Biblical story of Isaac. It so eloquently expressed her deep grief about her own only son. I stepped up closer and saw on the yellowed pages of the worn prayer book fresh tears that fell on the faded spots of older tears shed by other mothers of former generations.

When she finished praying, she noticed me and began wiping her moist eyes, somewhat embarrassed, and after a moment she said, "I guess you know why I shed so many tears at this chapter. I give God notice that He had better not try me too much, that I'm only a weak woman, not as strong as father Abraham to be willing to sacrifice my only child, and that He simply must bring my son back to me alive and well."

I marveled at the boldness with which the grieved mother argued with God. It was worthy of the audacity in the dialogues that the famous Hasidic Rabbi Levi Yitzhak of Berdichev used to have with his Creator.

Rebecca's pleading with the Lord, however, was answered only after many months. In June there came a letter from some soldier whose name was totally strange to the Slutskys, telling them in brief that Lev was lying in a military hospital. There were no other details in the letter except for a cryptic remark that Lev was sorry for being unable to write himself. There was also no return address on the letter.

The Slutskys and we helped each other to carry the burden of our worries and to cope with the hardships of daily life. Ida would leave Raphi with them whenever the necessity arose. The twin girls (they were so much identical that for a long time I could not tell them apart, which would amuse them immensely) were very fond of him and liked to play with him. He became attached to Rebecca, and he too called her Grandma and would ask us, "Please let us go to Granny Becky."

The news about Lev made us happy too. I ran over to the Slutskys as soon as I heard it. Though puzzled by the mysterious character of the letter, they nonetheless were utterly joyful to know that Lev was alive. Rebecca had a merry twinkle in her eyes. "You see? We women are not so weak after all. God is a man and cannot withstand our tears for too long. I'm sure that if He had come with His suggestion to Sarah instead of to Abraham, she would have found a way to talk Him out of the whole business." After a moment, however, she added pensively, "But then we would not have this moving story in the Torah. I would miss it terribly; it has inspired me with so much courage and hope in times of despair."

*   *   *

The Slutskys waited anxiously to hear from Lev. But after that letter in June there was no word from him at all. It is therefore hard to describe their happiness when he arrived entirely unexpectedly during my hospitalization.

From the family pictures I had been shown so often I knew Lev as a husky person. That evening, when I went to visit, however, I saw before me an emaciated man with hollow cheeks and gray-black hair. He was only several years older than I, but he looked as if he were in his late fifties. I listened with great interest as he told me about the tribulations and dangers he had gone through since the outbreak of the war, and I realized that he was lucky indeed to have come out of it alive.

He was a sapper and participated in the hard and dangerous rear-guard fighting against the rapidly advancing enemy. Sometime later his battalion was encircled by the Germans. In order to avoid an encounter with the enemy, they hid during the day-time in the forests and at night they tried to make their way toward the Russian lines. They suffered terribly from hunger and cold and sustained heavy losses in the unanticipated skir-mishes with German patrols. After many weeks of untold suffer-ing and dangers they finally managed to get out of the encircle-ment. However, the toll in dead and wounded was very high.

And then something unbelievable happened. As soon as they reached the Soviet lines, they were surrounded by NKVD sol-diers who disarmed them and placed them all under arrest. "We were stunned by this strange welcome and did not understand what was happening," said Lev. "But we were in for a still worse shock. Early next morning we were all lined up and witnessed a horrible scene. Our commander, thanks to whose perseverance and courage we managed to escape, was now accused of 'treason and cowardice in the face of the enemy' and was executed by a firing squad before our eyes."

The other officers were stripped of their ranks and dis-patched immediately to a punitive unit at the front. The rank and file of the battalion was put into a prison camp. (Later, they too were sent to punitive units.)

Lev was "lucky." He had a severe shoulder wound and one of his lungs was pierced by a shell fragment, so he was taken along with the other seriously wounded to a military hospital where he underwent surgery several times. Nevertheless, all through the months in the hospital he lived in constant fear of what would happen to him when he recovered. Knowing the senseless brut-ality of the NKVD, he suspected that in the end he too would share the fate of his comrades from the battalion. This was the reason he was afraid to write to his family, lest he involve them too in the trouble. The letter in June was written by a discharged invalid whom Lev befriended in the hospital. After that, how-ever, Lev did not want to take such a risk again.

One day in October he was discharged. "I did not believe my ears. No interrogation, no reference to my 'crime'; I was simply told that I was invalided and free to go home," said Lev. It was apparent to him, however, that he was not spared out of con-sideration for his invalidism. He rather suspected that due to the chaotic retreat of the Red Army his dossier had been misplaced, and that as soon as it turned up, the NKVD would build up a case against him.

Lev was an engineer and easily could have found a suitable position, but that was out of the question for the time being. His convalescence progressed very slowly. His wounded lung could not stand the bitter cold and the rough Ural weather, so he was forced to stay indoors. Despite his invalidism, however, he lived in Tamak in continuous fear of an unexpected visit by the NKVD. I liked him and eventually we struck up a close friendship. He was well read and in his youth had also received a good Jewish education from his father who, until the Bolshevik Revolution, was a Hebrew teacher. It turned out that he was familiar with Jewish literature and interested in Jewish matters. We discovered that we had many ideas in common and had very enjoyable conversations.

It was already late in the evening when I returned that first night from the Slutskys. As I was about to go to bed, Nusia came home. "Oh, you are here? I thought you would not come back from the hospital anymore," she blurted out in her customary muzhik manner. And without even asking how I was or how Raphi was doing, she limped by to her room. I was stunned and did not say a word.

SEVEN

I had a certain feeling of strangeness as I came to the VU the next morning. It seemed to me that I had not been there in ages. Some more old acquaintances were gone, and there were new faces all around. I dropped in to say hello to Ryabov, and his warm welcome improved my mood. He looked at me intently and asked if I felt like resting for a few days. I knew that it was my emaciated look that made him say it. "I'll start right away; my students miss me terribly," I said. He laughed loudly in his customary congenial manner.

We chatted for a while, and as I was about to leave, he put his hand on my shoulder and said, "Keep your chin up. The wounded German beast is not dreaming any longer of driving us into Siberia but rather of how to crawl back to his lair. The day is not too far off when we'll start packing and be on our way to Riga, and all the suffering will come to an end." I looked at the smiling face of my kindhearted friend. He stood before me broad-shouldered and planted like an oak in his native soil. His optimism rubbed off on me, and I felt reassured. For a while, I too was carried away to Riga.

I was faced with many difficult problems and set to work immediately. During my absence Valeria had had to combine heterogeneous classes, and the instruction was conducted in a rather improvised manner. It was therefore necessary now to sort out the students anew. The classes had to be practically reorganized from scratch in order to catch up with the planned curriculum. After classes I went to get my ration coupons and the money coming to me for the time of my hospitalization. To my surprise, Tsitron greeted me warmly and even invited me for a visit to his home. I was not very enthusiastic about it, but I did not want to antagonize him and promised to do so as soon as I recuperated.

I had a great deal of work and stayed at school until evening. On the way home I stopped at the Slutskys to leave my bread coupons with Rebecca, who had offered to get my bread ration together with theirs. I was very grateful to her because I was hardly up to standing in the bread line for hours in such bitter cold. I felt weak and could hardly wait to go home and lie down. But Lev began telling me more about the dangers and suffering he had experienced while encircled by the Germans. It was a tragic story whose horrors defy description. I listened with great interest, but it got late, and I had to leave. There was an icy wind blowing outside, and the temperature in our room was not much warmer; our firewood supply was so low that I could not afford to light a fire in the stove. I boiled a few potatoes on the primus, washed them down with *kipyatok* and then went to bed in my clothes.

The next day I received a letter from Haifa for the Orshovskys. Work was strenuous, and I felt very exhausted. But Mikhael had not written in a long time, and knowing how anxious his mother was to hear from him, I went at once to bring her the letter. She welcomed me with her unique warmth that always made me feel at home. I was so much indebted to this wonderful family for standing by us in difficult times. They helped Ida take care of our sick child when I was in the hospital, and if not for Riva's untiring medical attention during his frequent illnesses, I really don't know how Raphi would have survived. She also had made practically all the necesary arrangements for his admission to the hospital in Ufa.

* * *

The next morning the heaps of fresh snow that had fallen throughout the night reached the windows, and a pale sun tried to pierce through the overcast sky. It was the eve of 1943, and the mood in general was more optimistic than on the eve of the outgoing year. The German attempts to relieve Stalingrad had failed, and the noose around the more than 300,000 Germans who were surrounded there was tightening. There was a merry bustle at the VU. The officers and cadets prepared a New Year's celebration, and the theater was going to put on a new show, Gorky's "Mother." But I was neither in the mood nor in the physical condition to participate in these festivities. Besides, I had to attend to a more prosaic matter; there were no potatoes at home, and I had to fetch some from our supply in Akhmadulin's cellar.

I set out on the long walk immediately after classes. Akhmadulin was not at home as yet. His wife was surprised to see me, and in her primitive but kindhearted manner she exclaimed, "Gosh, how terrible you look! What happened to you? Where have you been all this time? We thought you had moved away from Tamak."

The bag of potatoes that I carried home weighed hardly 20 pounds, but to me it seemed like an unbearable load, and I had to stop frequently to catch my breath. Recalling the 200-pound sacks of grain I used to carry at Turiba in Riga I sadly realized how poor indeed my state of health was. When I stopped at the Slutskys to pick up my portion of bread, I was in for a pleasant surprise; in honor of the New Year they issued that day on each ration card 200 grams of margarine, half a pound of hard candies and a pickled herring. It is hard to describe how happy the people were with these pittances tossed at them by the state.

I was exhausted by the time I came home and stretched out on the cot to rest a little, but I dozed off and awoke after dark. I had to write to Ida. I lit the *koptilka,* a tiny wick lamp fashioned primitively from a tin can, which I had bought from Akhmadulin shortly after our arrival in Tamak. (Its name, derived from the Russian verb "to smoke" or "to smut," was most fitting: it was very generous with smoke and soot and filled the room with the unpleasant smell of kerosene, but it was extremely stingy with light.)

The cold in the room was beastly, and I was very much tempted to light a fire in the stove, but the sight of the dwindled wood supply made me change my mind. After finishing my New Year's feast of potatoes with a piece of herring (the margarine and candies were stashed away for Raphi) I went to bed and tried to sleep, but sleep did not come. I lay thinking about my family far away and about the pain and hardships we'd gone through during the departing year. Watching the pale crescent moon and the stars swimming out slowly from beyond the Ural hills, I wondered what fate the coming year had in store for us— would it bring the end of our suffering or would we still be starving and freezing in Tamak a year from tonight? But the moon and the stars remained silent and did not answer.

I finally dozed off but was awakened by a sudden noise— Nusia and some visitors were passing through our room. After a while I heard the clinking of glasses and male and female voices wishing each other a Happy New Year. I tried to fall asleep again, but the loud talk and drunken singing in the adjacent room kept me awake for a very long time. Later on, however, I managed to sink into a dreamless sleep and did not even hear when Nusia's guests left.

*   *   *

There were no classes on New Year's Day, and I lay in bed till late in the morning, pondering how wonderful it would be to lie there and rest all day. But I had a lot of paper work and decided to go to the VU and work there in my office. As I was about to leave, Yakov dropped in and asked me to come to see them later. Yevsey had arrived unexpectedly the day before, and the family wanted me to meet him.

Galya and her parents were among our closest friends, and we used to see each other often. But I had never met Yevsey. Nonetheless, I knew a great deal about him. His family was very proud of his brilliant career and talked about him often, and I was naturally curious to meet him in person, but it was not without mixed feelings that I walked to their place in the late afternoon. I had had my share of unpleasant experiences with fanatic Jewish communists and was not therefore sure how to behave toward Yevsey, who occupied such a high position in both the Party and the administrative hierarchy.

Yevsey was not at home when I arrived; he had gone to his factory and was expected back at any moment. We exchanged small talk. The mood in the house was cheerful; the family was happy with Yevsey's visit.

When Yevsey walked in, I looked at his expensive fur-lined leather coat, his tall sable hat and fancy leather-trimmed felt boots. It was all in such conspicuous contrast to the shabby winter apparel one was used to seeing all around. He was a tall, handsome man in his thirties, with light-brown, curly hair over his high forehead. His eyes were lively, and the energetic features of his face expressed intelligence. Sima brought in a bottle of Georgian wine and a box of chocolate candies. I had not seen such luxuries since leaving Riga and understood that Yevsey brought them along from Sverdlovsk, for in the land of socialism such things were out of reach of simple mortals; they are reserved only for the upper echelons of the Party and the Establishment—the new aristocracy of Soviet society. Yevsey poured the sparkling red liquid into the glasses and proposed a toast to the final victory over Hitler in the coming year. I wholeheartedly joined in. I felt at first somewhat jittery in his presence and hardly participated in the conversation. His friendly demeanor and the warmth of his personality, however, gradually melted away my reserve, and before the evening was over, we talked freely as if we had known each other for a very long time. He was a fascinating conversationalist and rather well-informed about life in the West in general. I enjoyed the talk with him very much, and the evening passed quickly. I knew, however, that he had to take a plane to Kuybyshev very early in the morning and excused myself early.

The temperature outside was way below zero, but Yevsey's optimism warmed my heart. He intimated that great events were in the offing that would surpass by far the battle of Stalingrad. I felt invigorated and even tried to walk briskly, listening to the echo of my steps in the empty street, and went to bed with rosy hopes in my heart that the new year was to bring changes for the better in our difficult life.

*   *   *

On January 3 I got a letter from Ida. She wrote that the process of healing was coming along satisfactorily and that barring some unexpected reversal, Raphi could be discharged before too long. There was also other good news that day—the Germans had begun to withdraw from the Caucasus region. I realized that this was what Yevsey meant with his cryptic remark about forthcoming great events.

Knowing that the Sorokins would be happy to hear the news, I dropped over on my way home. On his visits to the hospital Osip had told me that he was very worried about Nadezhda's deteriorating health, and when I entered their room, I was taken aback to see how much worse she looked than two months before. But I attempted to appear cheerful. "I have wonderful news for you! The Fritzes have started to run from the Caucasus!"

Osip was enthusiastic and said to Nadezhda, "Soon the Caucasian oil workers will begin to return home, and we too are going to move with them. In the warm Black Sea climate you'll get well again before you know it." Nadezhda showed happiness and even smiled. Nevertheless, I could not help noticing the tears that began to well up in her beautiful, large eyes. My good friends indulged in reminiscences of their life in the Caucasus region and talked with nostalgia about their home in Odessa. I too became involved in their blissful dreaming and promised to visit them after the war. Then Nadezhda began to doze off, and I left quietly. Osip shook my hand with a deep sigh. No words of explanation were necessary; I understood his tormenting concern over Nadezhda's grave illness.

Walking home I became immersed in gloomy thoughts about the plight of those two close friends as well as about our own suffering. We were all so helpless to escape from the terrible reality of Tamak. It was snowing, and the flakes caught in my eyelashes froze into pearly crystals.

7

The Longest Winter

ONE

THE TIME AFTER my discharge from the hospital was one of the most difficult periods in my sojourn in Tamak. The hunger and the cold became unbearable, and I realized that subsisting on black bread with *kipyatok* and a few boiled potatoes now and then would hardly help me regain my health, yet I was helpless to do anything about it. I had nothing left that was worth bartering in the market for food, and the few—hundred rubles I got from the school could not be touched—I needed them for the expected trip to Ufa to pick up my family.

The time for me to see the doctor was overdue, but I felt too weak to make the long, arduous walk to the hospital and postponed it from day to day. On January 6, however, I began to feel a stabbing pain in my back, and when I came home in the evening, I saw that one of the closed wounds was suppurating again.

The following day I went to the hospital. Dr. Hornfeld examined me and shook his head. "Didn't I warn you not to hurry with your discharge? How can you expect to recover on your starvation diet outside? I'm afraid you may yet have to be hospitalized again." His ominous words filled me with apprehension, but I did not have the faintest idea of how to get any substantial food.

I went to the ward to see how my old friends were. It was a strange feeling to look in as an outsider at a place where I had spent more than two months. My bed was now occupied by an old Bashkir whose sickly, pale face was furrowed with age. Bur-

201

stein had left a few days before, and other acquaintances too were gone. Umnov greeted me cordially. "I have been waiting for you to drop by; I want to show you something." He got his Bible and took out of it a sheet of paper. "Read it; it is the answer from our Reverend, which Yelena brought me," he whispered with a merry twinkle in his eye. I glanced at the letter. One could see immediately that it was written by a trembling old hand. The writer still used the obsolete, prerevolutionary Russian spelling and composed the letter in a flowery classical language spiced with Church Slavonic and Biblical expressions.

Umnov's holy man, who signed himself "Arkhip, the humble servant of the Lord," was against surgery and concluded his letter with a verse from Jeremiah (17:14): "Heal me, O Lord, and I shall be healed; save me, and I shall be saved: for Thou art my praise." When I told Umnov that this verse was recited by pious Jews thrice daily in their prayers, he was thrilled. "How remarkable! I'm sure Reverend Arkhip knows about it, he is a very learned man."

Umnov was in good spirits. "Do you see now that I have been right all along in refusing to consent to the operation? I want to go home soon; my leg will be healed without any surgery." Then he asked how I was coming along and what the doctor had told me. "Everything would be all right if I only had some nourishing food. But you know my situation; I simply can't afford to buy it, and without it Dr. Hornfeld thinks that I'll wind up in the hospital again," I answered.

Umnov thought for a moment and then said, "I have an idea. My wife will visit me tomorrow. Before coming here, she usually goes to the kolkhoz market to sell some produce. Be there early in the morning and she will take care of you." He wrote a note and told me to give it to her. I was moved and could not find the right words to thank him. He waved his finger at me. "Don't you get emotional about it! I'm sure you'd do the same for me if I were in a tough spot."

I set out on my walk home, thinking about Arkhip's letter and about Umnov's deep faith and kindheartedness. That simple Ural peasant was one of the few shining exceptions in a society that worshipped crude atheism and was callous about the fate of the individual. It was probably by association that Menikhes came inadvertently to my mind. He visited me only shortly after my hospitalization. Sometime later Anna came and told me that her father was sick in bed with asthma. I was worried about him and had intended to visit him after my discharge, but they lived very far away, and it was hard for me to walk there. Since it was not too much out of my way home, I decided to drop in.

Reb Mendel was happily surprised to see me. He embraced me, and I could not help noticing that his eyes became moist. He felt better now and was out of bed, but the doctor had ordered him to stay indoors for some time. I related my experiences in the hospital, and he told me about the happenings among our mutual acquaintances and what was going on in town in general.

Talking about Umnov, I asked him if there was any connection between Umnov's consulting his holy man and the absolute faith of the Hasidim in their rabbi. "You may be right there," he said. "Like us Jews, the Old Believers suffered greatly from persecution under the Czars and are familiar with our traditions." Then he spoke about the *Subbotniks* and other Judaizing sects among the Russians and their untold suffering at the hands of the Czarist regime and the clergy of the Russian Orthodox Church.

It was still dark outside the next morning when I hurried to the kolkhoz market to find Mrs. Umnov. She greeted me warmly and asked how it felt to be out of the hospital. "My husband seems to miss your company very much," she said. "I saw him yesterday," I said and gave her his note. When she finished reading it she took my bag and went into the stall.

As I watched her putting into my bag two bottles of sour milk, a jar of melted butter, cheese, eggs and various kinds of vegetables. I calculated hurriedly that all my money plus the 150 rubles that I had borrowed from Menikhes the day before would not suffice to pay for it. When she handed me the bulging bag, I asked her, somewhat embarrassed, how much I owed her. She smiled. "I'm very busy now; we'll figure it out some other time. Eat it in good health and get well soon!" I felt a lump in my throat as I groped for the right words to thank her and to reassure her that I was going to pay her as soon as I could. The food literally helped me survive those crucial days.

TWO

Finally the impatiently awaited day came; on January 21 I got a telegram from Ida to come for them. Making the 80-mile trip by train, however, was a frightening prospect. It was difficult to get a ticket in the first place and then loomed the struggle to board a train amidst a stampeding crowd. Sasha advised me to take the so-called milk-run train which was supposed to be less crowded. It left about midnight, but in order to have a better chance to buy a ticket, I set out on the three-mile walk to the station early in the evening. The temperature was way below freezing. The milky moon watched me dragging on slowly along the slippery, icy path.

After standing in line for a very long time I finally succeeded in buying a ticket. As soon as the noise of the arriving train was heard in the distance, people rushed outside. Some ran toward the train and jumped on it even before it stopped. The shoving was exhausting, and after much effort, one of the conductresses let me in. To get a seat was out of the question. I remained standing in the corridor, engulfed by a solid mass of passengers. Later I managed to squeeze through to the wall and leaned against it with my back so that it was not elbowed so much.

The train was slow and halted at every small stop, where kolkhoz people with sacks and baskets got aboard and the pushing and shoving would start anew. Despite all my caution my back hurt from the bumps and jolts it sustained. I became worn out and dizzy and was tempted to slip down to the floor and sit there, but it was quite impossible to do so. It is hard to describe the relief I felt when we finally arrived in Ufa at 4 A.M. It was too early to go to the hospital, so I went into the station and sat down. I was exhausted and sleepy, but recalling my unpleasant experiences at the Kazan station I was afraid to fall asleep and merely drowsed, ready to slip out in case of an unexpected checking of papers.

While sitting there I overheard a conversation in Polish on the bench behind me. I turned around and saw two young men who noticed my attention and fell silent. "I didn't mean to eavesdrop," I apologized. "I'm from Czechoslovakia, a neighbor of yours."

They moved over to my bench, and we began to chat. They were Jewish refugees from Poland, and after their release from a Ural labor camp they had moved to Ufa. They volunteered for the Polish Army and were now leaving for a military training center. During our talk one of them asked me if I knew that Klement Gottwald was in Ufa. I was skeptical and shrugged it off jokingly. "What would the leader of the Czechoslovak Communist Party want in Ufa? To organize the Czech masses here? I'm sure that Stalin would like to have him somewhere closer to him."

But the young man reassured me that it was true. The other day he had run into a former classmate of his who worked in the Polish section of the Comintern. She had told him that together with the Polish section, the Czech and some other sections had recently moved to Ufa. I continued to chat with the young men until their train arrived and they left.

* * *

Little by little it became light outside, and I left the station and took a tramway. After getting off there was still a considerable distance to walk to the hospital; I could hardly wait to see my family. It was breakfast time when I arrived, and Ida was in the ward feeding Raphi. When she came out, I felt a twinge in my heart upon seeing how thin and worn out she was. I could not go into the ward and could see Raphi only through the door. He looked emaciated, only skin and bones. The white bandage around his head accentuated even more the paleness of his face. While waiting for the doctor Ida told me about the terrible anxiety she had gone through after the child's operation, when his condition was at times critical, and also about her own many hardships. In addition to the suffering from hunger, some articles of her clothing and other things had disappeared mysteriously. She had a strong suspicion about who took them but was afraid to report it; it would have been useless to do so anyway. The biggest loss was Ida's cotton-padded jacket, a garment indispensible for survival in the Ural winter, and I simply did not have the money to buy another one at the extremely high prices in the black market.

When the doctor came, he gave us disappointing news—he

wanted to examine the child thoroughly and take some X-rays later in the day, so that he could not be discharged until the next day. I had anticipated going back home the same day. Now, however, I was suddenly faced with a new problem—where to stay overnight. I was appalled at the prospect of having to spend the night at the station.

Ida suggested that I try the Lavrovs, who had rescued her from the snowstorm on her walk to the hospital. They were very nice people, and Mrs. Lavrov had come to the hospital a few times to see how Raphi was doing. I went there immediately and was in luck. Mrs. Lavrov was at home and gladly agreed to accommodate me for the night. I had not slept a wink the night before and was dying to take a nap, but she had to go out for the day, and I did not want to stretch her hospitality so far as to ask her to let me remain alone in the apartment. I went back to the hospital, but Ida was in the ward, and the nurse told me that she would be busy with Raphi the rest of the day, taking him to the various checkups, and that I could not stay.

I decided to go to Gottwald. Looking back I can't quite explain even to myself why I did so. I was aware that going to a Comintern office might be a venture tantamount to entering a lions' den. One factor in my decision was probably the fact that I had no place to stay during the day and loathed both alternatives left to me—either to sit in the railroad station or to ride around in the cold streetcars. I suppose, however, that the main reason was my being cut off from Czech life since leaving Czechoslovakia, so that I was eager to get some information and know what was happening.

I took a tramway and went to the address I had from the Polish refugee, arriving at a shabby, wooden three-story building in a downtown side street. There was no sign outside to indicate what offices were located there. After some hesitation I entered. I was stopped by a civilian whose stern look and authoritative bearing told me immediately that he must be an NKVD man. "Who are you and what do you want here?" he asked me in a strict voice.

"I'm from Czechoslovakia and would like to see Comrade Gottwald," I replied. He slowly examined my ID card from the VU and asked a series of questions. "Do you know Comrade

Gottwald? Are you a communist? How did you get out of Czechoslovakia? When did you arrive in the USSR? Have you traveled around much here? Who are your friends?" I felt sweat pouring out and regretted my coming there, but it was too late to back out. He jotted down my answers and told me to wait in the lobby.

I glanced around. From the many doors alongside the corridors I judged that the building must have been previously a hotel or a dormitory. The walls and the ceiling were peeling and dirty. They had not seen the painter's brush in years, and it was hard to tell their original color. The NKVD man was on the phone for a long while; then he came over and told me to go to the second floor. I walked up the squeaky wooden staircase and knocked on the indicated door. There was no answer. After waiting awhile I opened the door and entered. No one was in the room. I sat down and waited. From the adjacent room came the noise of a typewriter.

A few minutes later the door to the other room was flung open, and in came a stocky middle-sized man. Despite the beard that he now had, I recognized at once the notorious firebrand of Czechoslovakia's Communist Party. He greeted me coolly, and his restless, deep-set eyes pierced my face. I knew that the NKVD man had given him all my answers over the phone, yet he began asking me various questions about my background, to what Czech political parties and organizations I had belonged, etc. Then he got up and started pacing the room, puffing incessantly on his pipe. Suddenly he shot at me the question that I had expected all along (I only wondered why the NKVD man did not put it to me in the first place). "How did you find out that I'm in Ufa? Who gave you the address?" To avoid getting my Polish acquaintance and his girlfriend into trouble, I said that I had heard it from a Czech refugee whom I had met on the train, giving my fictitious informant some common Czech name. He looked at me askance. His haughty smirk told me that he did not believe it. I felt uneasy and did not think any longer of what I wanted to talk to him about but rather of how to leave unscathed as soon as possible. He kept pacing the room and finally asked me the purpose of my coming to see him. I composed myself and said that I wanted to know whether the Beneš Government in exile in London had set up in the USSR an organization to help Czech refugees, similar to that maintained by the Polish Government.

"No. There is not any. We don't believe in charity," he retorted rudely. "The only thing I can advise you is to join the Czechoslovak Military Unit that has been formed. But then"—he eyed me from top to toe—"in your physical condition, what kind of soldier would you make? No, it won't do. And what with your wife and sick child coming out of the hospital you would all be only a burden to us."

Seeing that any further talk would be useless and that he was impatient to end the meeting, I thanked him for his time and said goodbye. As I reached the door, I said hesitantly, "Could you give me the address of the Czechoslovak Embassy? The German Consulate in Riga took away our Czech passport and I'd like to get a new one." He glanced at me sternly and answered, "I can't tell you the address; you have to get it through the routine Soviet channels."

Thus ended my frustrating meeting with Gottwald. I felt trepidation as I left his office and was walking down the staircase; it occurred to me that the NKVD man might be curious and ask me more questions. But he did not stop me, and I heaved a sigh of relief when I was out of the building.

Interestingly, I was not too surprised at the results of my talk with Gottwald. I did remember his fiery speeches from the rostrum of the Prague Parliament, in which he promised to hang, after the proletarian revolution, "all enemies of the workers' class" on the lampposts in the streets. But before going to him I had thought that the calamity of our country and our common fate as refugees ought to have mellowed his rough temperament and that he would be more responsive to the plight of a fellow-countryman. I was shocked only by his rudeness and indifference to the fate of the individual. After all, I did not ask him for a personal favor, just for some harmless information. I have often thought about that encounter with the future ruler of Czechoslovakia who subsequently carried out the sovietization of that country and, after his communist putsch in 1948, destroyed the last vestiges of her democracy, later staging the cynical monster trials and murdering his Jewish comrades in the leadership of the Party.

What puzzled me most at the time, however, was the very fact that the Comintern had moved to that remote Ural city. Gottwald's eagerness to find out how I knew it and his strict admonition not to mention it to anybody only increased my bewilderment. The answer to that puzzle came in May, when a surprising political event shed some light on the mystery.

* * *

I walked away from the Comintern building as fast as I could and returned to the hospital. Ida was still busy with the child, and I could not see her. I was faced again with the same problem—where to spend the afternoon. The nurse told me that the University Library was not too far away. I left a message with her for Ida and went out. It was a wonderful feeling after such a long time to be in a place of higher learning again. The library was large and had a rich collection of interesting books in various languages. I browsed around until evening fell and then went to the Lavrovs.

Matvey and Klavdia made me feel at home. They lived alone and had their share of worries. Their only son was in the army, but his wife and children got stuck in German-occupied territory, and they had not heard from them since the outbreak of the war.

Matvey, who worked in the City Administration, was an intelligent man, and I learned much from him about the recent turbulent history of Ufa. After the Revolution it was the site of the anti-Bolshevik Constituent Assembly presided over by Yekaterina Breshko-Breshkovskaya, called "the Grandma of the Russian Revolution." (After the Bolshevik seizure of power, she had fled Russia and lived in Prague, where I had a chance to see that legendary old revolutionary.) The civil war years brought much suffering to the city. It changed hands several times between the White, the Red and the Bashkir Armies. The vengeance and mutual retaliation among the factions were cruel. A particularly sad chapter was the Stalin purges of the 1930's, which devoured thousands of innocent people. Many relatives and friends of the Lavrovs disappeared without a trace. We talked until late in the evening, and I had an interesting stay with those kind, hospitable people.

THREE

In the morning I went to the hospital, and after finishing all the formalities we set out on our walk to the tramway stop. The cold was beastly, and Ida shivered terribly in her light clothing. I saw that she would not be able to endure the trip home without a cotton-padded jacket or some coat; she barely made it to the tram stop. In our desperation we decided to seek help at the Latvian *Evakpunkt*.

It was not much warmer in the streetcar than outside, but at least we were protected from the icy wind. We finally arrived at the *Evakpunkt*. The secretary looked at us and sighed. I realized what a pitiful picture we must have presented—Ida frozen and shivering from cold, and I myself emaciated and weak, holding a sick child with a bandaged head in my arms; and all three of us in tatters. We told her in what a terrible predicament we were, particularly in view of the thefts in the hospital. She went in to her boss and after some time she came back with an order to the warehouse of the *Evakpunkt* to issue us winter clothing and warm underwear, felt boots, fur caps and gloves. The state prices I paid were astoundingly low. We also bought three blankets and other articles of clothing, which we needed very badly.

We put on the warm clothing and walked to the tramway. Ida felt better now, and her mood improved. The streetcar was very crowded; after much difficulty we got in and finally arrived at the railroad station. We could not board the 3 P.M. train and went back into the station. The next train was not due till 9 P.M. Ida therefore went with Raphi to the so-called Children's Corner, a special room set aside in the larger stations for mothers with infants, but she was told that there was no vacant place there. The same thing had happened to us on several other occasions. On the door to that room a large poster portrayed a smiling Stalin holding a happy baby on his lap and praised the leader's great love and care for children. In reality, however, the few cribs there were reserved for VIP families only.

We had no choice but to wait in the station. Finally getting on the train was an arduous task, and after great effort we succeeded in squeezing through into a corner and sat down on the floor.

It was nearly midnight when the train arrived in Tamak. We set out on the long walk home. It snowed hard, and the visibility was poor so that I had to walk slowly with the sleeping child in my arms. The cold in the room was beastly, but we were too exhausted to light the oven and went to bed in our clothes. I lay awake for a long while thinking about my experiences during the past two days and about the difficulties ahead of us. Nevertheless, I gradually fell asleep with the blissful feeling of being together at home at last.

* * *

In the morning it was not easy to make up my mind to crawl out of the bed, it was so cold. But the dim yellowish morning light that was attempting to filter through the thick ice layers on the window kept reminding me that it was time to get up and go to work. I got up, lit the oven, then went for water. There was as usual a line at the pump. Getting water in the wintertime required great skill to avoid slipping on the icy surface formed by the spillage around the pump, and what with the condition of my back it was a frightful venture. Only a few days before a refugee woman from our building had fallen at the pump and broken a leg.

It would be difficult to describe to the American reader the heavenly pleasure of sipping boiling *kipyatok* on a freezing winter morning. I put some dried black-bread crumbs into it and gulped it down avidly. The hot water warmed my entrails, and I felt better. Ida and Raphi slept peacefully atop the good old Russian brick oven, which was beginning to get warm. I put some more wood into the oven and left quietly for work.

There were many things to attend to at home, and I returned immediately after classes. On the way I stopped at the post office. There was a letter from Dr. Harkavy; that wonderful woman was anxious to know how Raphi was doing after the dangerous surgery. We also had a letter from the Bronsteins; they exhorted us as usual to make up our minds and move to them in Central Asia. Walking home in the deep snow and sub-zero temperature, I thought about their descriptions of the warm weather there, how they walked outside without topcoats. It seemed to me so unreal, as if they lived on some other planet.

I was pleasantly surprised to see Rebecca as I came home. It was an idyllic picture to behold Raphi cuddled up in the lap of his favorite *babushka*. The room was fairly warm now. The rays of the pale sun refracted in the thawing ice on the window panes and played shyly in the shadows on the oven. Despite its blackened walls and sooty ceiling the little dingy kitchen seemed almost cozy now. After a while the twin girls came, too. Raphi had always liked to play with them, but now he remained limp and passive and only smiled at them sadly. It broke my heart to realize how weak he still was.

FOUR

When the Slutskys left, we began deliberating about what to do. The best thing, of course, would be if Ida could resume work in the Children's Home the next day. First of all, she and Raphi would be warm during the day. And, of course, the hot lunch they would get there was of the utmost importance in those difficult days. The question, however, was whether Raphi was fit yet to attend the *Dyetdom*. We decided therefore to consult Dr. Orshovsky. She came over to take a look at Raphi and said that he should stay at home for some time until he recovered. We were placed thus in a very difficult situation. With the sick child at home, the room had to be kept reasonably warm. Yet our wood supply was ominously low and would be gone before too long. I had hardly enough money to buy even a small bundle of wood in the black market. We began to look over the things we had bought at the *Evakpunkt*. It was a difficult choice; each piece was equally essential for our survival in the winter. After much soul-searching we decided to sell Ida's blanket and mine and also some articles of our underwear.

I took the sacrificial items to Akhmadulin. He assessed them and said, "They will bring you about 500 rubles. With the kolkhozniks charging now, in the middle of the winter, an arm and a leg for every log, all you can get for that is just enough wood to last a few weeks. You must find a more reasonable source." He went with me to his friend with whom I had previously bartered our Penza children's snowsuits for wood. Unfortunately he had no spare wood.

I racked my brains what to do. It occurred to me to turn to Jacob Burstein, maybe he could help me. I set out immediately to his place. I had his address but did not know in what part of town it was. I stopped several passersby, but none of them had ever heard of that street. An elderly Bashkir woman finally directed me to some distant suburb. It was already evening when I reached that out-of-the-way alley. I could not make out in the dark the numbers on the small huts and had to go from door to door until I found the place at last.

Jacob was not at home yet. I knew his wife from her visits to the hospital. The Bursteins lived in a rear alcove; to reach it one had to walk through the rooms of a Bashkir family with whom they stayed. There was no stove in the dingy room. They paid their rent by supplying the firewood for the entire hut. "We give them all our wood allotments from the plant, but they go on constantly asking for more. To get a little bit of warmth from their oven in the kitchen we have to keep our door open around the clock, but it doesn't help much, and we freeze plenty nevertheless," she sighed.

When Jacob came in, I glanced at his feet and remarked, "I'm glad to see that you have felt boots." He replied with a sad smile, "Oh yes, my boss finally issued them to me. Not that he had a change of heart. I had to have my feet frozen first to make him realize that I can't drive a truck to the forest without felt boots."

"How are your feet?" I asked.

"They still hurt, especially when it is cold. One toe in particular gives me trouble and doesn't let me sleep at night," he said. He paused and then continued. "Who knows? Maybe it's all for the best. I used to go through an agonizing experience each time my deferment came up for renewal—what would happen to my family if I should be drafted? Last week, however, when I appeared once again before the Draft Commission, the doctor took a look at my toes and said, 'Incapacitated permanently for military service!' So I don't have to worry about a deferment."

Jacob's words reminded me of a tragicomic story I had once

read, and I quickly suppressed the chuckle that it called forth in me, lest it be noticed by the Bursteins. The story is about the *prizyv* (draft) in Czarist Russia and goes, in brief, as follows:

The Jews, who were subjected by the Czarist regime to cruel persecution and discrimination, were not too enthusiastic about serving, and for very long terms at that, in an army where they would experience open humiliation and sadistic treatment. Small wonder, then, that the *prizyv* would be a terrifying prospect both for the draft-age young men and their parents.

And on the Sabbath before the *prizyv* in particular each mother would shed copious tears in the synagogue and pray fervently to God to save her son by some miracle from the dreaded military service. One of the various suggestions to the Almighty as to how to perform that miracle was that He grant her son some physical defect—only a temporary one, naturally, merciful Father in Heaven!—so as to be rejected by the *prizyv* commission. One mother, however, remained unperturbed all through the services. "What is the matter with you? Your son is going to the *prizyv*. Why, then, aren't you imploring God to save him? Or is your heart of stone and you don't care," her neighbors indignantly reproached her. The woman replied calmly, "I'm lucky; I don't have to worry a thing about my son—thank God he is a genuine cripple."

I told Jacob about my purpose in coming to him. "I'd like to help you, but it is very risky," he replied.

"I'm aware of this," I said, "but you are a friend and must help us in our predicament with our ill child."

He shook his head, "Sorry, I'm afraid to do it."

I decided to offer him a whole sack of potatoes. He exchanged meaningful glances with his wife. I realized that the offer of such a large quantity of the scarce commodity, for which they would have to pay a fortune in the kolkhoz market, was too tempting to be turned down. "All right," Jacob said after a moment. "One evening soon I'll bring you a truck load of wood."

*   *   *

It looked like the beginning of a *purga* as I started the long walk home through the dark alleys and streets of the suburb. I felt great relief at the prospect of having solved the problem of wood. However, recalling how much labor and sweat, time and money it had cost me until I harvested the potatoes, my heart was filled with sadness. I realized what acrobatic skill it took to walk on the tightrope of survival. Here I barter away our supply of potatoes for wood only later to have to exchange a portion of bread for a few potatoes and then in turn to sell some article of clothing to buy a piece of bread. "My God, what a vicious circle!" I thought with horror.

The next day I went to Akhmadulin's cellar. As I finished filling the sack, I felt a twinge in my heart when I saw how ominously few potatoes were left for us. I borrowed a hand sled from Akhmadulin and set out on my way home. From a hill over the creek came the gleeful yelling of children sledding down on their improvised toboggans. But to me the high heaps of snow, blown by the *purga* onto the road during the night, were only an exasperation, making the pulling of the loaded sled a gruelling task.

I waited up for Jacob till very late that evening, and likewise for the following five nights. On the sixth night he came at last. We unloaded the wood in a hurry, and as we were heaving the sack of potatoes onto the truck, he whispered to me, "It was not an easy task to accomplish; believe me, I'm scared stiff." I did believe him; for I too was trembling with fear, thinking that something might go wrong and that the NKVD would come any minute to arrest me.

I did not have to worry now about firewood for the near future, Jacob had not been stingy with the wood, and its quality was good. Yet I could not enjoy it and lived in continual trepidation that some untoward incident would precipitate this transaction into trouble for me. Then one evening I spoke to Sasha about it. He listened to me and then said in his usual, good-humored manner, "When will you finally stop being a naive Western schlemiel? Thieving and pilfering have become a way of daily life with us and are commonplace. First of all, you personally did not steal state property but paid for it with your honestly hard-earned potatoes. And as to Burstein? Most likely nobody will ever find it out. And even if some superior of his should accidentally get wind of it, he'll be smart enough to keep his mouth shut, because he himself, no doubt, has by far larger thefts and embezzlements on his conscience. Sasha's reasoning assuaged my fear somewhat. Nevertheless, I went on being concerned over the matter for quite some time.

FIVE

Dr. Hornfeld examined my back and shook his head; the process of healing was slow and unsatisfactory. He warned me again that I must absolutely have some nutritious food. I knew it all too well myself. But my main concern had to be Raphi, to get food for him and nurse him back to health. I dropped by the ward to see how Umnov was and found him in good spirits; he was to be discharged and was waiting for the kolkhoz wagon to pick him up the next day. "I feel bad about being unable to pay my debt now and want to assure you that I'll do so as soon as I can," I said.

"Don't you begin to fuss about it again," he replied. "On the contrary. With a sick child on your hands, I want you to feel free to turn to us whenever you are in need." He became pensive. "I have learned much from you and shall miss you. You must promise me to come to Tishina to visit us." I gladly promised him to do so, for I too had gotten to like and respect that gentle and upright Russian peasant.

*   *   *

It is hard to describe the great jubilation that was called forth by the German surrender at Stalingrad on February 2, 1943. To be sure, according to some war historians the battle of Kursk that came later was, by virtue of its strategic importance and the enormous amassing of troops and weapons, more decisive for the beginning of the rout of the Germans from Russia. Those who witnessed the events inside Russia, however, will agree that Stalingrad marked the turning point in the war on the Russian front, for none of the following victories contributed so much to the boosting of the morale of the army and the people as the Stalingrad victory. After a continuous chain of humiliating defeats since the outbreak of the war, it showed that the Germans were not invincible and restored self-confidence.

In Tamak too, despite the hunger and cold and the struggle to survive, the victory at Stalingrad generated a festive mood. True, the end of the war was not in sight as yet, and much bloodshed, tears and suffering still lay ahead. But the light at the end of the dark tunnel was dimly visible and inspired hearts with courage and belief in the ultimate defeat of Hitler.

On the Sunday after the Stalingrad victory there was an assembly at the VU. "All cadets, officers, faculty and employees must attend," read the announcement. I looked around at the audience; only a few of my old acquaintances were left by now. The school looked more like a hotel for transients. The new *politkomissar,* the successor of Popov, who had left for the front some time before, delivered a long, bombastic speech. He extolled the great wisdom of Stalin in leading the glorious Communist Party to the victory over fascism. Then he suddenly began to upbraid the officers and cadets for lacking revolutionary zeal and exhorted them to shape up and to double their efforts.

His words baffled us. "We have not heard this tune in a long time" Straus whispered to me. Immediately after the outbreak of the war, the Soviet leadership had changed its tactics. Knowing the great "love" of the people for the regime, it prudently enough did not call on them to fight for "the socialist achievements of the Revolution" but rather appealed to their Russian nationalism to rise to the defense of the beset Motherland. Hitler's invasion was compared to that of Napoleon, and the war was proclaimed as the Great Patriotic War. The role of the Party was pushed quietly into the background, and instead, time and again, the patriotism and heroism of the Great Russian People in past generations were stressed.

This change of tactics had brought a certain loosening of the screws of Party control in general, and as a corollary to this liberalization censorship too was relaxed. It is interesting to note that many works of prose and poetry that would never have been allowed to be printed earlier did indeed appear in the period between the outbreak of the war and Stalingrad.

Somehow the people wanted to believe that that relaxation had signaled a sincere change in Stalin's policy, that the dawn of a new freedom was on the horizon. The *politkomissar's* speech, therefore, came to us as a shock. It augured ill about things to come, and the changes for the worse were not too long in coming. Shortly after Stalingrad the tone of the propaganda in the press and radio began to sound more and more like the prewar days. The icy Stalinist wind was blowing again, and the screws of Party control in all facets of life were slowly tightening.

The consequences of that turn for the worse were felt in the VU immediately and affected me personally. They were eventually to bring about a drastic change in my position there and in my life in Tamak in general. I'll tell about this later. For now let me continue for a moment the account of daily life. We had an extremely difficult time then. We tried desperately to nurse Raphi back to health, but we had run out of money completely. The blankets and the other things that had been rejected by Burstein as barter for wood were sold one by one in order to buy a bottle of milk or a bit of substantial food for our child.

On February 25 Dr. Orshovsky came again to examine Raphi. She said that the scars from the surgery were healed and removed the bandages. He was still weak and haggard, but she said that he could start attending the *Dyetdom* the next day. We were very happy; it greatly relieved the pressure of our difficult situation.

* * *

Shortly after Stalingrad the routine at the VU was upset once again. Large groups of cadets with their officers were sent to the front and new replacements began to arrive. There were rumors about an impending reshuffling in the school, and about mid-February the avalanche of change came closer to me; my immediate superior, Captain Tychenko, the academic dean, left suddenly.

It was a terrible blow. Even though I had not struck up as close a friendship with him as I had with his predecessor, Logunov, or with Ryabov, there was nevertheless a friendly relationship between us. A high school principal in civilian life, he was efficient in educational matters and appreciated my work. I enjoyed his confidence and esteem, and he gave me his fullest cooperation. Without standing on ceremony I would drop in on him often to discuss problems frankly.

That Tychenko, a frail man in his fifties and only a reserve officer at that, was sent to the front surprised everyone. It was indicative of the horrible decimation of the officer corps at the front.

Among the new officers was a Lieutenant Colonel Dolgikh, whose arrival drew attention. It was the first time that an officer of such high rank had come as a replacement. Besides that, he was well into his sixties already. To my misfortune he was to become Tychenko's successor.

We are prone to speak of "love at first sight." I believe, however, that the same can be said of its opposite—antipathy and mutual dislike. At least this was true of Dolgikh. Soon the reputation of his rudeness spread. The employees in his office immediately felt that he was different in every way from the other officers. He deliberately drew a circle of arrogance around himself. The secretary, Varya, a gentle refugee teacher from Kharkov, could not stand his whims, and in the very beginning she transferred to a lower-paid position in another office. I was therefore hesitant to go to Dolgikh on my own to introduce myself. I wanted to wait for things to develop, but unexpectedly he sent for me to come to see him at once.

I entered his office with an uneasy feeling. I saw immediately that the description Varya had given me was accurate. He greeted me coolly and remained aloof. His small, grayish eyes—set in a disharmony with his broad, owlish face and huge, bald skull—kept staring at me intently. I felt uncomfortable. Substituting in my imagination his rimless pince-nez with a monocle, I saw for a moment a Prussian officer and felt a slight shudder down my spine. After a while he suddenly asked me to give him a report about the German department and the work in the classes. I briefed him in detail. He listened and then remarked off-hand, "A lot of changes will have to be made around here."

"There is always room for improvement," I remarked, "and I'll be glad to make some suggestions." He interrupted me rudely. "I'm not in the habit of asking my subordinates for advice but of giving them orders, which they have to carry out without questioning."

I was dumbfounded. Never before had I been spoken to in such a tone by anybody in the VU. My reputation there as an educator was established, and I enjoyed the respect of both the students and the administration. I realized that Dolgikh was indeed different from all the Soviet officers I had known. His entire behavior boded ill.

Still worse was the experience Valeria had with him the next day when he summoned her to his office—something which Tychenko had never done. She was in tears when she returned. He was rude to her and even used insulting language when she attempted to argue with him. "It is incredible!"—she shook her head. "That man is an anti-Semite of the old 'Black-Hundred' brand. You don't know them. But believe me I can smell one a mile away." She was very upset and wanted to go immediately to talk to the *politkomissar.* But I asked her not to be hasty. In the evening we spoke to Sasha. He advised us against undertaking any steps for the time being. "It is a very serious matter, let us wait and watch his next moves," he said.

At first I found some consolation in the fact that Dolgikh started to interfere in the work of the other departments as well. The heads of those departments, however, seasoned officers, resented his meddling and complained to Ryabov. But I, a foreigner and a Jewish refugee at that, who lived in the shadow of constant fear of the NKVD—what could I do? I was glad that nobody had bothered me so far and was afraid to get involved in a controversy with a superior. I had no choice but to put up with it and hope that, after having displayed his authority, he would simmer down and leave us in peace.

* * *

Dolgikh was sort of a puzzle. He kept to himself, making no friends in the school. His bearing and even the way he dressed were peculiar. While the other officers were usually simple in behavior and paid no special attention to outward appearance and pomp, he was very fussy about ironing his uniform and shining his boots and insignia. I remember an important fact that struck me as strange: he had no medals on his chest—an unusual thing for an officer of his rank. It was apparent that he had not come from the front. The official version was that he had already been pensioned and was called back to active duty only recently. In the beginning I ascribed his rude behavior to his unhappiness about having been recalled to service. Gradually, however, I came to realize that his bitterness had deeper roots and that his arrogance, too, was merely a front to conceal something in his past and to hide his lack of self-confidence.

I recall one instance that strengthened this suspicion. At one of our meetings he began to demonstrate to me how classes ought to be conducted and also what kind of exercises and exams should be given. Realizing that he had never before been connected with the field of education and that he had no idea about teaching, I decided that it would be useless to reason with him from a pedagogical standpoint and that the best thing was to listen calmly to his amateurish suggestions.

Then he started to recite bits of German phrases, which he apparently remembered from his high school days. "You see? This is how one has to study German!" he exclaimed enthusiastically. His pronunciation was atrocious, and the German words were terribly distorted. I had a hard time suppressing a smile. But seeing how eager he was to show off, I remarked, "Your knowledge of German is impressive." The fleeting glee that appeared in his nervous, watery eyes told me how much his vanity was flattered. After a while, however, his wrinkled face resumed its stern expression, and he continued talking to me in his usual arrogant manner.

Working with Dolgikh was unpleasant; it grew harder to endure his meddling and whims. The worst thing, however, was the anti-Semitic undertone I felt in his dealings with me. On one occasion I was about to mention it to Ryabov, but I felt that he had enough headaches as it was with the changes that were in the offing and did not want to burden him with my problems. Thus, to my daily struggle to make ends meet was now added this worry about Dolgikh.

* * *

The package from America finally arrived at the end of February. Luckily, this time it had not been tampered with, and nothing was missing. I can't describe how elated we were with the parcel, musing sadly how much it could have helped us in the desperate straits we were in during the past months.

I know how trivial and unbelievable it must sound to some readers to fuss so much about a shirt, an article of underwear, a pair of stockings or a piece of soap—things that are taken for granted in our country of plenty. I understand; for I too would probably never have believed it if I had not myself experienced the privations of these articles in the land of socialist achievements. To this very day in the Soviet Union getting a package from abroad is like hitting the jackpot, and the lucky recipient is the envy of all his neighbors.

We badly needed each and every piece in that parcel, but we could not afford such luxury for ourselves. We could look at each item only in terms of how much food it could bring. I used to be very careful when writing abroad. But my relatives, it seems, were able to read between the lines, for the assortment in this package was more practical than in the first one.

Inostranny (foreign) things especially brought good prices because of their superior quality and fashion. The women were crazy about them. Each piece had its particular value. In this respect I needed Akhmadulin's expertise and waited for him to come over and give me his estimate.

Selling or bartering, even your own belongings, was actually illegal. Nevertheless, everybody did it. It became a necessary way of life, since the government stores (and there were no private stores) sold you nothing but the daily bread ration. Realizing that trying to stop the forbidden trading in the *tolchok* would be like attempting to plug a dike with a finger, the authorities looked the other way. Occasionally, however, the militia would raid the *tolchok* and confiscate the things the refugees offered for sale. True, they were seldom arrested, but they were put on the list of black marketeers, the last thing which I, as a foreigner, wished to have happen. Therefore, when I wanted to sell some item of our belongings, I would ask Akhmadulin to do it for me. I paid him a commission, of course, and he was reliable in every way.

* * *

The package contained some soap, an extremely scarce commodity in Russia. Toilet soap in particular was worth its weight in gold. Figuring that it should not be too difficult to quickly hide a piece of soap in the pocket in case a militiaman showed up unexpectedly, I decided to take the risk of selling one piece myself to buy some food.

I hurried to the *tolchok*. Sure enough, as soon as I displayed the cake of toilet soap, its colorful wrapper drew the attention of the daughters of Eve. *"Amerikanskoye! Amerikanskoye!"* they whispered, and their eyes popped out. Before long there was a circle of women around me, and I felt ill at ease lest I be noticed by a militiaman. I actually had no idea how much to ask, but I said, "100 rubles." A few women began to haggle with me about the price.

After a moment a young woman in native dress came up close to me. She touched the soap and smelled it, inhaling the exotic aroma with the ardor of a pious Jew sniffing the spice box during the *Havdalah* ceremony. Quietly she handed me a crumpled 100-ruble note and hurried off, followed by the envious looks of the other women. I could easily have sold many more pieces, but I had been afraid to take along more than one cake. It occurred to me then that I was a poor trader and should perhaps have asked more than 100 rubles. (As a matter of fact, Akhmadulin later told me that my suspicion was right.) I was extremely happy with the 100 rubles, and hurried to the kolkhoz market and bought a bottle of milk for Raphi (for 40 rubles!). There was not much I could buy with the rest of the money. After shopping around I purchased a few onions and a bit of pot cheese and returned home. We made mashed potatoes and washed them down, as usual, with *kipyatok*—a royal banquet!

I went to sleep happily. Later in my sleep I was in our field at the Belaya. To my great surprise I dug out not potatoes but pieces of fragrant soap. The Orshovskys and the Slutskys looked on in amazement and said, "How come we get out only potatoes?!"

"Dig deeper," I replied. They did so, but to no avail. I felt embarrassed and carried a pile of soap cakes over to them.

I woke up in the morning to the gray reality of the cruel winter. After work I went to the hospital. Dr. Hornfeld was not there, and the nurse merely changed the dressing and told me to come next week. I took along some pieces of clothing to Umnov, but was told that he had been discharged several days before.

Two days later I went to the kolkhoz market early in the morning before leaving for work. Mrs. Umnov and her daughter were very glad to see me but refused to take my gifts. "You badly need each piece in the parcel now to help you nurse yourself and your child back to health. You'll pay us on another occasion," they argued. I was deeply moved by their humane understanding but insisted that they must accept the things. They finally took them, reluctantly. Then Mrs. Umnov said with her usual broad smile, "But this is too much anyway for what I gave you." And once again she filled my bag with eggs, cheese, melted butter and various vegetables.

SIX

The paradoxes of life were unbelievable. We lived in a very fertile region where before the Revolution food had been plentiful and cheap, but now even the kolkhozniks did not have enough bread. Endless forests stretched far and wide all around, yet firewood was scarce and expensive. The Urals, rich in minerals and all kinds of natural resources, had large salt-processing installations, but one had to pay about 25 rubles for a cupful of salt in the black market.

The collectivization of agriculture and the nationalization of all the land, industry and commerce put a bureaucratic stranglehold on everything and stifled the initiative of the individual, causing chronic stagnation and foundering of production, supply and distribution. As a result there was a constant shortage of everything, and the people were hungry and cold.

Nearby were the rich Ishimbay oil fields. Nevertheless, kerosene was not available in the stores, cost a fortune on the black market and was hard to come by besides. Being indispensible for our cooking on the primus and lighting of the *koptilka*, it consumed a considerable part of our meager budget. As long as Prusis was still at the VU, he used to sell me a little kerosene at state prices now and then. After his arrest I had gone to his successor, an officer whom I did not know. He looked at me askance and retorted curtly, "No kerosene for civilian employees!" I never went to him again.

Sometime after my discharge from the hospital, Straus introduced me to a lieutenant, a man in his late forties, who happened to be in his office at the time. We chatted a while, and when Muleyev left, Straus told me that he was the new supply officer, replacing Prusis's successor, who had left for the front.

In addition to the worries about food and firewood, we also were practically out of kerosene. But I had no money and did not know what to do. Muleyev seemed to be a congenial man, and I decided to try my luck with him. He was very friendly and, without any fuss, sold me a can of kerosene. It is hard to describe how happy I was.

Muleyev turned out to be an intelligent and interesting person, and we talked often. He had been the manager of the Tamak railroad station and had been mobilized only recently. He came from a prominent Bashkir family that had lived in town for generations and played an important role in Bashkir cultural life. (His brother, to whom he introduced me on one occasion, was the director of the Bashkir Teachers' Institute.)

In the first weeks after my arrival in Russia I was intrigued by the organizational structure of the Soviet Union. Besides the "independent and equal" 15 republics, there were also many autonomous republics and autonomous regions. In theory it all sounded wonderful. Recalling the woes of Czechoslovakia and other European countries with their minorities, I thought that the Soviets had found the ideal solution to the vexing minority problem. Had not the communist propaganda kept on trumpeting about the "absolute equality and freedom" of all nationalities in the USSR?

However, during my sojourn in the Tatar Autonomous Republic and my visits to the Chuvash and Mari Autonomous Republics I noticed that something was fishy. To use a cliché, they were neither republics nor autonomous. I observed the same thing when traveling through other autonomous regions. Everywhere people were afraid to answer my naive questions; neither did I get any answers to these same taboo questions in Tamak. It was not until I became closely acquainted with Muleyev that he enlightened me about the inner workings of the Bashkir Autonomous Republic. When I got a deeper insight into the so-called autonomy of the minorities, however, I realized that it was a sham, a Soviet ruse to continue the old Czarist policy of Russianization.

To be sure, after the Revolution there was a short revival among the non-Slavic nationalities. Even the smallest tribes in Siberia and Central Asia, which numbered only several thousand souls each, and had never before had alphabets of their own, were given alphabets in the Latin script. In 1935, however, Stalin ordered that all Latin alphabets be abolished and replaced by Cyrillic script. This edict, designed to accelerate the Russianization process of the minorities, was enforced also on the Moldavians, a Romance people who had used the Latin script for many generations. But the transition to Cyrillic was not peaceful. There was general dissatisfaction among the non-Slavic peoples, and the intelligentsia in particular put up resistance to the enforced change. Many of them paid with their lives, and thousands were sent to labor camps—a sad chapter in Soviet history that is hardly known in the free world.

* * *

Paper in general was a scarce commodity. Newspapers were used as cigarette paper and would bring a good price in the *tolchok*. I often saw people, even total strangers, approach one another with the formula—"Want to smoke? You the paper, I the *makhorka*," or vice versa.

Books too served as cigarette paper. Interestingly enough though, only books of the Soviet era, which were usually printed on the same poor-quality paper as newspapers, were in demand. A book of prerevolutionary vintage was of no use to smokers because its thick, solid paper was unsuitable to roll the *makhorka* in. A dull Soviet novel describing the love affair between a kolkhoz girl and her tractor would, therefore, bring a far better price in the *tolchok* than a Dostoyevsky novel published before the Revolution.

To buy a Russian newspaper in a store was nearly impossible. It would be somewhat easier, however, to get the Bashkir daily, provided you went early in the morning to wait for the delivery of the papers. (I did not smoke, but it was the only way to have some toilet paper.)

I knew no Bashkirian except for some single words that I picked up in the street or the market, but I would glance through the paper for those words that were familiar to me. I noticed immediately that Bashkirian had some characters that did not exist in Russian, but I did not know their function. I also discovered that there was a similarity between Bashkir and Hungarian words. After I became acquainted with Muleyev, my linguistic curiosity prompted me to ask him about these matters. He explained the grammatical basics and the historical development of the Bashkir language. It was an interesting experience in comparative philology.

In the beginning Muleyev, who was a Party member, would be very cautious in his talk. Once as he was elaborating on the principles of vowel modifications, with which the Bashkir language is replete, I asked him in an off-hand manner, "Why has the Latin script been abolished? In my opinion, it seems to be best suited to precisely render these nuances." His face suddenly turned pale and his Mongolian high cheekbones quivered slightly, and after a moment he replied, "We Bashkirs are very proud to be privileged to use the same Cyrillic alphabet as the great Stalin does." He changed the subject at once.

Later, when our relationship became closer and he was no longer afraid to trust me, he told me a great deal about the stubborn Bashkir resistance to the Cyrillic script and the cruel Stalinist persecution of the Bashkir intelligentsia. He also confided that many of his relatives and friends were the victims of the purges in those horrible years.

* * *

At the beginning of March I went to Dr. Hornfeld again. He examined my back and said, "Well, it looks better now; I think you are on your way to recovery at last." I was very happy to hear the good news. He dressed my back again and told me to come to see him in two weeks or so.

While there I looked in on Nadezhda, who had been hospitalized the previous week. The tuberculosis of her lungs had taken a turn for the worse. I looked at the emaciated young woman, and her beautiful large eyes, seeming even larger now because of her thinness, shone with a strange light. I could see that her condition was worse than it had been, but I tried to be cheerful. "How much I envy your going to the warm shores of the Black Sea where you'll soon forget the *purgas*," I said, nodding toward the window, outside of which a snowstorm was visible. She became animated and chattered away, telling me how much she was longing to bathe in the hot sun again. Then she paused, and her moist eyes gazed dreamily into the distance. The sad smile on her dry lips told me that she was not sure about it, and I too grew sad.

On the way home I stopped to visit Menikhes. Several days before Anna had dropped by to tell me that he wanted to talk to me. He looked better now but was still bothered by his asthma and left the house only seldom. I told him about my difficulties with Dolgikh. He was pensive for a moment and then said, "I'm afraid this is only the beginning. I know his kind of Jew-hater. He is going to give you serious trouble. Can't something be done about it before it is too late?"

1943 was one of the cyclical years in the Jewish calendar with an added, second month of Adar, and thus Passover was still about six weeks away. But Reb Mendel was already worried about *matzot*. He told me that Sonya Plavnik had suffered a slight stroke a few weeks ago and asked me to see how she was and find out whether it would be possible to bake the *matzot* at her place.

* * *

The next evening Sasha dropped in. He was very upset as he took out a bundle of *Einikeit* issues. "Read carefully between the lines and you'll learn what Hitler is doing to the Jews in the occupied territories!" He was beside himself. "We here are forced to be silent. But the Jews in the free countries, why don't they cry out and try to awaken the conscience of the world, which seems to be indifferent to the slaughter of the helpless Jews?" After a while we came to speak of Dolgikh. "Maybe Valeria is right, and we ought to talk to the *politkomissar* or to Ryabov," I remarked.

"Not yet," he replied, "I'm sure Dolgikh is bound to make a serious political blunder. So let us wait and give him enough rope."

Sasha was planning to make another trip to Moscow in the near future. He hoped that now, after Stalingrad, it would be possible to get a permit to move back to Moscow. He was very optimistic about the military situation and thought that very soon there was going to be a large-scale Soviet offensive that would roll back the front far away from Moscow. He paused and then said pensively, "If only *you* in the West would open the Second Front, Hitler could be finished off before too long." I smiled at his stress on the word "you." The Second Front was on everybody's mind, and it was a very frequent topic of conversation. The protracted war brought suffering, and the people were vexed and angry at the Western Allies for their delay in starting the front. How often would I hear from my Soviet friends the agitated question, "When will the Second Front be finally opened?!" The intonation of the words had the ring of a personal reproach—as if I had a direct telephone line to London and Washington but was too lazy to use it.

As Sasha was at the door he suddenly turned around and said, "Oh, I almost forgot! A friend of mine told me that in January Ilya Ehrenburg's daughter had been in Tamak." He regretted very much that he had missed meeting her. Sasha's parents, like Ilya's, came from Kiev, and they knew each other. He also attended the gymnasium together with Ilya. He told me a lot of interesting things about Ehrenburg and his controversial reputation. "His character certainly leaves very much to be desired," Sasha said. "He would sell his soul to the devil for the sake of his career. He has the facility of a cat and always lands on his feet. Believe me, he is a very shrewd man. Otherwise he would have been liquidated by the Georgian long ago. This is the only way to survive here," Sasha sighed. Speaking of Ehrenburg's daughter, he told me that her husband, a promising writer, had gone to the front as a war correspondent immediately after the outbreak of the war and was killed there in 1941.

Getting the *Einikeit* used to be an event. Sasha would lend the newspaper to many evacuees, and it became worn and stained and got to be nearly illegible. He therefore asked me to read through the copies immediately and then give them to Valeria the next morning. I sat up reading until late in the night by the dismal light of the smoking *koptilka*.

The awkward Soviet spelling of the Hebrew words alone went against my grain and irritated me. But worse was the stereotyped Party line of the paper. Its timid and obsequious tone towards Stalin generated a revulsion in me. Reading the *Einikeit*

I used to have a strange feeling that I was not reading a *Jewish* newspaper at all but rather an awkward Yiddish translation of *Pravda*. Nevertheless, despite the strong feeling of aversion the paper evoked, I would read it avidly from beginning to end—it constituted the only tenuous link with the Jewish world. Sasha was right; one had to read between the lines to detect the veiled allusions to the horrible fate of the Jews in German-occupied lands. I had, of course, no idea then about the dimension of the vast extermination of the Jewish population that took place. But what I read, as well as other ominous hints that trickled through, sickened me and gave me terrible nightmares.

*   *   *

But life in Tamak went on. The days of March crawled on in hard and frustrating work at the VU and in strenuous efforts to cope with the hunger and cold. Yet a situation is never so bad but it might not become worse. One day a general arrived at the VU. There was agitated talk and guessing all around. Straus, who was usually well-informed about what was going on in the school, said that General Glinka was the new commander of the school. I was stunned by the news. As long as Ryabov was head of the VU, I felt more or less protected from Dolgikh. His becoming Glinka's deputy and thus only second-in-command made me apprehensive.

Glinka, about 60, had been wounded at the front and was incapacitated for field service. His left arm dangled helplessly, and he always wore a black leather glove over his crippled hand. Both in appearance and character he was entirely different from Ryabov. The son of a poor peasant, Ryabov had started as a private and, by virtue of his innate talent and intelligence, had made his way upward through the ranks. Still, he remained the same genuinely folksy man, modest and friendly to everybody. He never pulled rank, was much respected by faculty and staff and was very popular with the students. I often saw him sitting at a table in the mess hall and chatting amiably with a group of cadets.

Glinka, on the other hand, had begun his career as a lieutenant in the Czarist Army and was a flashy officer. Unlike Ryabov, who lived with his family in a modest apartment, he immediately set up an extravagant household, with orderlies attending to his services. He was correct and courteous but kept his distance from the officer corps and the cadets. He came to Tamak alone, and before long he had a lot of female companionship. Rumor had it that the food for the lavish parties that he threw at home was delivered from the school kitchen.

One of the results of Stalingrad was the introduction of epaulettes. The innovation came as a psychological shock to the average Soviet officer who was proud of the fact that the Red Army was a people's army. Heretofore addressed simply as *kommandir*, he was to become again an *ofitser* as in the Czarist era. It went against the grain. But nobody dared to openly question Stalin's sudden "cult of the uniform," and after Glinka's arrival the fuss about epaulettes and other trappings got into full swing. (It is interesting to note that only after the war did it become known that the gold braid for the epaulettes had to be ordered at the time from Britain.)

When I met Ryabov in his new, tightly fitting uniform, he smiled and, pointing at his shiny epaulettes, jestingly said, "How do you like it? I look like the Czarist commander of our division in World War I. I only hope you won't have to call me 'Your Excellency' before too long, as I had to address him."

* * *

The talk about an imminent reorganization was persistent, and I dreaded especially some unexpected move from Dolgikh. But strangely enough, he bothered neither Valeria nor me, and we even dared hope that he would leave us in peace.

But the blow suddenly struck. And it came in an entirely different way than I had expected. One day in April Ryabov called me to his office. He chatted with me amiably, as usual, but I noticed some embarrassment on his face. He caught my inquisitive glance and said, "You know that I have a soft spot in my heart for you, and it hurts me to tell you that German will be phased out at the end of the spring term. Dolgikh proposed it during my trip to Moscow directly to Glinka who accepted it immediately, and there's nothing I can do now to change the situation."

I saw that Ryabov was genuinely sorry. He put his hand on my shoulder and said, "Don't fall into despair. German has not been abolished for good, only suspended temporarily. When we return to Riga, you will resume teaching again. In the meantime you will remain in the employ of the VU; I shall find some suitable work for you."

I brought the news to Valeria and advised her to start looking around for another job. Several days later, however, Dolgikh suddenly ordered her to hand over her classes to me. "You should have seen the satisfied gleam in his eyes and the smirk on his face as he told me that I was dismissed immediately," she related with tearful eyes. I was outraged. Although Valeria taught on a part-time basis only, her contract ran until the end of the term. It would have been useless to argue with Dolgikh, so I went straight to Ryabov and explained to him that Dolgikh's action was illegal. The order was rescinded.

About a week later Dolgikh called me to his office. He threw an imperious glance at me as I entered, but then his eyelids swiftly dropped over his eyes to conceal the smug satisfaction in them. Trying to sound as official as possible, he said, in an ice-cold tone, "By order of the commander of the Military College, German is to be discontinued at the end of the term." A fleeting smile on his bloodless lips revealed the great pleasure he derived from that announcement. He looked at me slyly, waiting for my reaction. But I did not want to give him the satisfaction of entering into an argument and said, nonchalantly, "I'll fold up the German department in time and hand over all its records in order."

I was very distressed with the new situation and worried about my future. My patience with Dolgikh had not paid off. Maybe I should have spoken to Ryabov, and also to the *politkomissar,* long ago. It might have averted Dolgikh's action, I reflected. But what was the use? The damage was done.

On the other hand, however, Dolgikh had also played out all his trumps and could not harm me any more than he had done already. But was not anti-Semitism illegal and punishable according to the Soviet Constitution? I was very anxious to unmask Dolgikh and also—why pretend to be a forgiving saint?—to take revenge for his meanness.

"Valeria, Dolgikh has made his political blunders, now we can talk to the political commissar," I said. We decided to take Varya along. I had been closely acquainted with the former *politkomissar,* Popov, since Riga. I did not know his successor, but I knew that he was a fanatic communist and would be interested in what we were going to tell him. He listened attentively and asked us many questions, jotting down Dolgikh's slurring expressions. "This seems to be a serious political matter. Anti-Semitism is considered a counterrevolutionary act and can't remain unpunished. Give me time to look into his background," he said as we left.

I had mixed feelings about our meeting with the *politkomissar.* It was gratifying to see his determination to do something about Dolgikh, but on the other hand I was worried that the NKVD might get involved in the investigation.

Sasha was very annoyed by Dolgikh's accomplishment. He felt like a lawyer who had just lost a case. "He seems to be shrewd and had Glinka do the dirty job in a legal way," he said. "I believe, however, that it will yet turn out to be a Pyrrhic victory for him. The *politkomissar* has started the ball rolling. Unfortunately I'm going to Moscow in a few days. After my return I'll look around for someone who could possibly help to find the hidden skeleton in Dolgikh's closet."

*   *   *

Life is strange and full of surprises. Help against Dolgikh came unexpectedly from a person from whom I would never have expected it. Several days later, when I came as usual for my pay to Tsitron, he said, "I must speak to you. We can't talk here; please come to my home in the evening." I was puzzled about why he wanted to talk with me. Being afraid of him, I had turned down his previous invitations and also avoided meeting him at school as much as possible, but this time there was some urgency in his tone, and he spoke almost in a whisper. I went to see him anticipating another lecture on Soviet literature or the world revolution. He was very cordial but looked upset. After exchanging a few bits of small talk, he came to the point. "I met Varya. She told me what Dolgikh has done to you and that you saw the *politkomissar.* I carry some weight in the Party and intend to do something about Dolgikh. Please tell me all the details."

"You know that as a foreigner I could be badly hurt. I'm scared that the NKVD may enter into the picture," I said.

"You don't have to be afraid of that," he retorted. "I assure you that no harm will come to you. The point is that all three of you are Jewish, and it is certainly no mere coincidence that he has been picking only on you from the very outset."

I described to him my own and also Valeria's and Varya's encounters with Dolgikh, his abusive language and particularly his clumsily concealed anti-Jewish remarks. He wrote down everything. "It must not be tolerated that such a 'Black-Hundred' rotten character get away with it scot-free. There is one drawback though—his native town is still occupied by the Germans, and it will take some time before we can find out all the details of his past. But don't worry; we'll get him eventually."

Tsitron was silent for a moment and then, to my surprise, spoke in Yiddish. "I know that you mistrust me, and I don't blame you for it. In my talks with you I gave you ample reason for suspicion. But I want you to believe me that I'm your friend." He fumbled about a while for the right words and continued. "In my youth I was a Zionist. My dream was to go to Palestine as a Halutz. Then came the Revolution and I became a Bolshevik; I even joined the Red Guards."

He paused, and his eyes gazed into the distance, trying apparently to recall some faded memories from his youth. "Many of my Zionist friends were put in labor camps, others succeeded in escaping to Palestine. I, however, believed that only the proletarian revolution could solve the Jewish question and turned into an ardent communist." He looked at me and sighed. "But the tragic fate of the Jews during the present war, and especially the eagerness of the Soviet population in the occupied regions to assist the Germans in the mass killings of the Jews, has irreparably shattered my Communist faith."

He went on pensively. "The war will end, and you'll leave this country. If you happen to be in Palestine please tell my friends that they were right and that I chose the wrong path." (Tsitron recalled that one of them lived in Rosh Pinah and gave me his name. On my later visit to Israel I met him and gave him Tsitron's message. There is another interesting footnote to the story—Tsitron died in Russia in the 1960's, but his son with his family eventually arrived in Israel, thus completing the circle of the return to Zion that his father had dreamt of in his youth.)

We chatted until late in the evening. Tsitron told me many interesting things about his life. "You know, I'd like to change, but I'm caught in the web of circumstances. Besides, I'm too old, and maybe I don't have the courage either," he said with a sigh. I now felt closer to him and pitied him for his tormented soul. He was not the only Jewish communist I met in the Soviet Union who wrestled with himself to find peace of mind.

SEVEN

Spring came to the Ural land. The icicles fell from the roofs, shattering on the ground with a glassy tinkle. The ice on the river began breaking up and floated off with a groaning and grinding. An apricot sun caressed the earth, melting the snow and exposing the heaps of garbage accumulated during the long winter. Before you knew it the ice and snow were gone, remaining only in the gullies.

Our group was again allotted its potato fields; luckily they were now much closer to town than last year. On May 1, early in the morning, I went to our field. There was a lot of weeding and cleaning to be done before the earth would be ready for digging, and I worked hard all day. But of what use was the field to me without potatoes for seed? Unfortunately, Akhmadulin's kolkhoz friend from whom I had bought potatoes the previous spring had died some months before. The only one who could help me now was Umnov. Thursday morning before work I went to the market and spoke to his wife, Glasha.

"Sure. We'll fix you up. Come with me in the kolkhoz wagon to Tishina today," she said.

Ordinarily this proposition would have been most convenient for me. But I was about to stop teaching any day now and was very busy in school, so that I could not take off from work on a weekday. I told her that I would come by train the next Sunday. First I sold some clothing and borrowed some money from friends. Then I managed to get a train ticket at the station. I took the train at dawn. The car was very crowded as usual, but luckily I had to travel only three stops. I got off the train and set out on the four-mile walk along a muddy field road.

The early-May morning was beautiful. It was so peaceful all around. The freshly washed sun was rising in the azure sky; its rays reflected in the wet, reddish soil and enticed the worms to creep out to the surface to warm up. I entered some woods. The startled birds interrupted their morning concert, then suddenly took off. The swinging branches sprayed me with large drops of water from the rain that had fallen in the night.

I came out of the forest and walked on down a sloping meadow. A little farther I met two women who were driving the kolkhoz herd to pasture. They stared at me curiously. The younger one halted and, her mouth wide open, stood there gazing after me for a long while. Then she suddenly started running to catch up with the herd.

Before long Tishina, spread out in the valley below like a giant spider, came in sight. Here and there pillars of bluish-white smoke came out of the chimneys. They curled above the hut roofs like huge snakes and then slowly dissipated in the air. I reached the edge of the village. At one of the huts a man was working in the garden, and I asked him where the Umnovs lived. He came over to the wattle fence and told me how to get there. The people in the yards turned around to look at me. As I crossed the village square, an old woman with two pails of water in her hands stopped and remained standing, as if glued to the spot. Apparently wondering who the stranger might be and what he wanted there, she gazed after me until I turned into the next street.

I found Umnov in the yard attending to the fowl. He still walked with a cane. He welcomed me warmly, embracing me in the Russian manner. A shaggy dog, warming himself in the sun near the barn, came over growling and sniffed at me. After a moment, however, he returned quietly to his place.

"How is your leg, Vasily Ivanych?" I asked.

"It is coming along fine," he replied, adding animatedly, "You know? On Easter we drove to Reverend Arkhip to attend his services. He reassured me again that I'll be able to walk without a cane soon."

When he finished his chores, we went inside. Glasha and Dunia, their daughter, were busy cooking. I sat down and took out the presents I had brought. Umnov marveled at the gloves. "Just look how fancy these foreign things are made. I'll have to wear my Russian mittens over them, else I'll soil them." Dunia sniffed the cake of American soap, and her eyes lit up with delight. Glasha examined the silken scarf, felt it with her fingers and then joked. "What does a plain peasant woman like me need such an elegant scarf for?" I could not help smiling, however, as I saw her walk over after a while to the mirror and wrap the scarf around her head. She turned her head into different positions and looked at herself with beaming eyes. Vasily noticed it and jestingly called at her, "Hey, old woman, don't you doll yourself up too much! Or maybe you want to find someone younger than me?" She laughed loudly and, blushing like a young girl, took the scarf off.

After breakfast Vasily and Glasha went to services. They asked me to join them. I would have liked to watch the ancient rites of the Old Believers about which Umnov used to tell me in the hospital, but I was afraid to attend religious services in an unknown place; one never knew where danger lurked. I said that I was exhausted from the long walk and wanted to rest a little.

Dunia stayed at home. We chatted, and she told me a lot about herself and her family. Her husband had left for the front shortly after the outbreak of the war. When her only son, 19, was drafted, she moved in with her parents. Her brother too was in the army, and they had not heard from him in a very long time.

Dunia went to a neighbor for some chore, and I sat thinking about what she had told me. The war brought so much suffering to everybody. I wondered, though, why Umnov had never mentioned all this to me. But then he never complained and was always content with his lot. I looked around the house. The spaciousness of the hut and the decent furnishings indicated that he had been a well-to-do farmer before the collectivization.

When Dunia came back she continued, "You know, my husband has been wounded three times already. My son too was badly wounded and lay in a hospital for a long time, but they don't want to send him home."

I felt sincere sympathy for her. "The realization that your dear ones are in constant danger must be a terrible torment for you and your parents. I do hope that they all come home alive and well."

"*Nichevo* (it doesn't matter). If the good Lord has apportioned them a long life, they'll survive the war. If not—there's nothing we can do about it and have to accept it," she replied in a calm tone. I was not really taken aback too much by her words. I had had similar experiences in Russia before and came to realize that these people, and particularly the peasants, bore their suffering with resignation. I remember how shocked I was at first when, shortly after my arrival in Tamak, I overheard a woman in our building telling a neighbor, "I just received a telegram that my Grisha was killed at the front" and then added with a stoical calmness, "Well, he probably had no more years to live."

True, the three centuries of Mongol enslavement left a deep imprint of Asiatic fatalism on the Russian soul. But I guessed too that it was more the long suffering as well as the absence of freedom, first under the Czars and then under the communist regime, that made the people bear their misfortunes with equanimity, value life less than in the West and view death with a certain indifference.

The Umnovs returned from services. "How large is your field?" he asked me. I told him. He went with Glasha to the barn. When they came back, he said in an embarrassed tone, "We have been out of flour for quite some time and have to use more potatoes. We just checked our supply; I'm afraid we can't sell you all the potatoes you need. Dunia will go with you to our friends to buy the balance."

We got a handcart and started out immediately, stopping at various huts. The people were friendly, but most of them complained that they had barely enough potatoes for their own use. In some places Dunia would take a look at the potatoes and say that they were not good for planting. After much walking around we finally bought some. Dunia did all the talking and haggling and managed indeed to purchase at a very reasonable price. She smiled. "How do you like me? Couldn't I make a shrewd *kupchikha* (merchant woman)? But don't you have any compunctions; they have more money than you, and it won't hurt them to sell below the current kolkhoz market price once in a blue moon." She thought a moment. "I believe that together with the potatoes from us you should have enough for planting. But I imagine you could use some for your household also. We might as well do it now before returning home." We turned off into a side street along a beautiful pond, and once again she showed her business ability and succeeded in buying some more potatoes.

It was already after three o'clock when we came home. Dunia gave her parents a detailed report on how we had fared in each hut and also related the news she had heard around the village. Glasha served the Sunday dinner. The food was simple but tasty, though not too plentiful. She sighed, "Once we had plenty to eat and everything was cheap. But collectivization has ruined us; they squeeze out the last drop of sweat from us and give us precious little in return . . ." Vasily interrupted her. "It's a sin to complain. We must thank God for what we have."

Dunia gazed into the distance and said pensively, "I'd like to travel and to see how other people live. I know only Tamak and a few other small towns around here. I wonder if I'll ever see a real big city."

"After the war you can visit us in Czechoslovakia. We'll show you big cities with many interesting things," I remarked.

She became animated. "Really? You'll remember us simple peasant folks?"

I rebuked her gently, "How could I ever forget such wonderful people as you and your parents."

Then her eyes became clouded again and she sighed, "But I don't know if they'll ever allow us to leave the kolkhoz."

The Umnovs told me many interesting stories about Tishina and the life of the people. It was a pretty large village, with over 600 huts, and had been prosperous once. Collectivization, however, upset everything and brought impoverishment to all. Many farmers, and especially Old Believers—though far from being *kulaks*—were exiled to Siberia, and their huts were given to Communists who moved into the village. At first, those Old Believers who were left in Tishina were persecuted and excluded from kolkhoz matters. Later, however, the communist management realized that it badly needed their farming know-how and gave them a voice in the administration. The religious suppression, too, was somewhat relaxed eventually.

*   *   *

Later in the afternoon relatives and neighbors began to drop in, mostly women and elderly men. (I saw very few younger men in Tishina; most of them were in the army.) I chatted with them and learned a lot about their life and work. They too were curious and asked me many questions about myself and about life in Czechoslovakia. One young woman wanted to know the size of the private plot a kolkhoznik was allotted there, how much cattle and fowl he was allowed to own, how many *trudodni* (workday equivalents) he was awarded by the kolkhoz, etc. The question was too "hot," and I was in a dilemma as to how to handle it. After some hesitation I told her, "You see, each country has its own way of life; we have no kolkhozes at all." She was surprised. "What? No kolkhozes? Then every peasant can own as much land as he wants and have as many cows and chickens as he desires?"—she could hardly believe it.

When night fell, the visitors began to leave; early in the morning they had to go out into the kolkhoz fields to their assigned work. I too had to go to bed early in order to be able to get up at the crack of dawn and return with the kolkhoz wagon to Tamak.

The bed in which I slept was thoughtfully equipped by Glasha with two large pillows and an eiderdown quilt similar to the one I used to have in my parents' home. Although I had slept little the previous night, I nevertheless could not fall asleep for a long time. I was excited by the events of the day, but I believe that it was more because of the softness of the bed, for I had not slept on such a soft bed since leaving Riga and was unused to it.

Anyway, whatever the reason, I lay wide awake, gazing at the indifferent moon that was swimming out of a shroud of clouds, thinking about the strange fate that brought me to Tishina. The singing at the other end of the village petered out, and the dim lights in the huts went out one after the other. The quiet of the night was now disturbed only by the monotonous croaking of the frogs in the pond. Then the Umnov dog suddenly began to bark, probably informing his colleagues that some foreigner was sleeping in his master's house. Before long there came responses from all over the village, and the angry growling and barking went on for a long time.

I dozed off at last and sank gradually into restless dreaming. My mother was tucking me in bed and whispering, "You look so tired and frozen from your endless traveling around, cover yourself well with the eiderdown quilt and have a good rest." Later I felt that someone was shaking my shoulder. I muttered sleepily, "Please Ma, let me sleep a little longer; it is too early to go to *Heder*." But the shaking did not stop, and I reluctantly opened my eyes—Umnov was bending over me. "Get up; the kolkhoz wagon will be here soon."

I jumped out of the warm bed and dressed in a hurry. Glasha was already busy in the kitchen. After a while, Dunia too got up and went with a milk pail to the cowshed. Both women had to leave soon for work in the kolkhoz fields. I ate a plateful of buckwheat gruel with fresh milk—it tasted delicious. Then I heard the wagon rolling into the yard, and I said my goodbyes. As we were about to pull out of the yard Glasha ran over and handed me a bag with vegetables, several bottles of milk and other dairy produce. "It is a little present for your child," she whispered. My heart was filled with emotions, and words would fail to describe the gratitude I felt to that kindhearted family. The wagon rolled noisily over the gravel along the empty street. Before long we turned onto the road. It was growing brighter. Little by little the sun began to rise, and its first rays burned small holes through the white mist.

I did not know the old driver of the wagon nor the woman accompanying him, but we soon became acquainted and indulged in friendly talk. The lean kolkhoz mare was in no particular hurry and proceeded at a slow trot. The driver put the reins around his neck, and winking at the horse, said with a smile, "The old girl knows the way to the market better than I." Then he took out his *makhorka* pouch and started rummaging in his pockets. "Old scatterbrain that I am! I forgot my paper at home. Well, no smoke till Tamak," he cursed under his breath.

I tore a page out of the Bashkir newspaper I had with me and gave it to him. His eyes shone with happiness. He offered me some *makhorka*, but I told him that I did not smoke. Glancing at the newspaper the woman joked, "You see? We stupid peasant heads were born here, yet we don't know Bashkirian. But look at him—he can even read a paper."

"Not exactly; I buy the newspaper for a quite different purpose. . ." They stared at me a moment and then burst out into loud laughter. The driver ripped off a triangle from the paper, licked its edges with his tongue and made a long, thin cone, which he stuffed with *makhorka*.

Matches too were scarce and very expensive on the black market, and people used them thriftily. Each match would be split in two in order to double the number of the matches. One would go to a neighbor to borrow a brand or a few live coals in order to kindle one's own stove or *koptilka*. I watched the driver lighting his cone; he did it in an ingenious way indeed. He took out a quartz pebble and dexterously struck at it with a broken horseshoe until a spark finally caught in the piece of cotton under the pebble. Then he puffed hard at the cone and inhaled with great delight, letting out large rings of bluish-black smoke, which rolled over our heads and dissipated slowly behind the vehicle.

We drove on and chatted about life in the kolkhoz. Eventually the conversation turned to the topic of how to achieve the best results growing potatoes. The bits of good advice I got from my companions turned out to be very useful to me.

We fell silent. I thought with satisfaction about the load of potatoes I was carrying home, which made the difference between survival and starvation in the coming year. Not less precious to me, however, was the wealth of impressions I took along with me. It enriched me with an insight into the life of a Russian village, a facet of Soviet life heretofore only vaguely known to me. The sad faces of the simple, friendly people in Tishina are still fresh in my memory.

EIGHT

We finally arrived in Tamak. I barely had time to carry my load from the wagon into our room, when I had to run to work. And work was hectic. A few days later my teaching at the Military College came to an end. "You'll get an extra month's salary as remuneration for your vacations, which you have not taken since Riga," Ryabov told me. Actually, my vacation time and the countless hours of overtime teaching amounted to much more. But I had done it voluntarily as a contribution to the war effort and would never have asked to be paid for it. I understood that Ryabov wanted to help me, and I was grateful to him; I needed the money very badly. But even more important was the extra month's worth of bread coupons that came with the money. I appreciated it the more since with my new job both my salary and ration coupons were to be much lower than before.

I commenced my new work immediately. I was put in charge of the distribution and supervision of the textbooks and army manuals. At first I felt depressed by the change, but fortunately I shared an office with Straus, who helped me overcome my blues. "And I thought you were a sensible man!" he would rebuke me. "What darn difference does it make what kind of work you do? The main thing is to survive the terrible war. You don't know how lucky you are to have your wife and child with you. I'd be willing to dig ditches if only I could have my family here."

I had become friendly with Straus while still in Riga, and our friendship grew even closer in Tamak. We confided our worries to one another and talked frankly about political matters. Due to the hurried evacuation of the VU he had not managed to take his family along, and he was worried about their fate in Riga. Interestingly enough, being Lettish he was more afraid of what the Lettish fascists might do to his wife and children than of the Germans. For in the eyes of the Latvian Nazi collaborationists he was a traitor for joining the Red Army in the first place and then escaping to Russia.

Straus was an intelligent man with liberal ideas, which he had never made a secret even while serving as an officer in the Latvian Army. After the semi-fascist Ulmanis putsch in 1934 he was, therefore, put into a detention camp. He told me a lot about his suffering there. Once he had attempted to escape and was shot in the leg by a guard. He had lain in the camp hospital for a long time, and since then he walked with a slight limp.

I was not exactly thrilled by the nature of my new work, but I soon adjusted to it. There was one advantage—it brought me relief from the heavy strain and responsibilities of my former position and above all from the aggravations with Dolgikh. Nonetheless, my new job entailed responsible duties and constant chores. I had to make regular rounds in the barracks and the various billets of the cadets all over town to check that the textbooks were in order. Due to the acute shortage of paper, pages would be torn out and used as cigarette paper. Still worse was the sale of books in the black market that were reported as "lost" or "stolen." A cadet would not mind at all having to pay a ruble or so, the official price of the book. However, since it concerned not only army property but also classified military material, each case had to be investigated, an official report written and handed in to the administration.

The most unpleasant chore used to be when a group of cadets were dispatched to the front unexpectedly. All their books had to be collected and thoroughly checked, which meant leafing through each book from cover to cover to make sure that no pages were missing. I would have to work throughout the night in order to finish before the group's departure early the next morning.

About mid-May I met Ryabov in the school yard. The surprise made my eyes pop out—he wore a general's uniform. I was very happy for him and congratulated him heartily.

"This calls for a toast," I said.

"I'd like to, but I'm leaving for the front in a couple of days," he replied. The news filled me with worry; I sensed intuitively that the departure of my loyal friend who was my mainstay in time of need did not bode well for me. As if reading my gloomy thoughts Ryabov looked into my eyes and said, "Be patient and stick it out in your present position. After the war I'll be again the head of the VU and things will return to their prewar routine."

"Come back alive and well," I told him.

"I'll see you in Riga," he said to me as we parted.

I gazed after him until he disappeared in the entrance of the building and suddenly I felt my eyes getting moist. Call it premonition, if you want. But I was overcome by the strange feeling that this was the last time I was ever to see Ryabov.

* * *

I know that to some readers it may sound strange when I fuss so much about potatoes. I understand; in retrospect, I too have looked at it from their viewpoint. But I always recall the story Yakov once told me about his experiences in a Siberian labor camp.

Before the Revolution he had a small textile store. When the Bolsheviks seized power, he became impoverished, but he tried hard to eke out a meager livelihood. In 1928, when the NEP was liquidated, his shop was shut down. Sometime later he was suddenly arrested. "I couldn't find out why. I never had any employees, nor did I ever indulge in black market dealings. They simply shipped me off as 'a bourgeois exploiter' to a slave labor camp without any trial," he related.

He spoke at length about the food in camp. The daily diet consisted of a slice of black, gluey bread with tea and one watery soup with a few frozen cabbage leaves in it. And on that miserable diet the prisoners had to fell trees in the forest from sunrise to dark. "I don't know how I survived; the inmates died like flies," he sighed. I listened to his sad tale with great interest; his experiences and personal observations were indeed moving. "At first," he continued, "the topic of conversation used to be mostly women, and one's fantasies and dreams would be of an erotic nature. Gradually, however, one stopped talking and even dreaming about a woman and dreamed about a big loaf of the tasteless bread and a full pot of the smelly soup so as to be able to fill his stomach at least once."

The sadism of the NKVD guards and their methods of humiliating and tormenting the prisoners were unbelievable. "They would have us bathe in the *banya* together with the women inmates. But strangely enough," Yakov remarked with a sad smile, "the sight of female nakedness didn't excite us. The nude men and women stared at one another with indifference. Our sexual desires were extinguished by the long starvation and hard labor." He also told me that most women stopped having their menstruation a short time after their incarceration.

After languishing in camp for over four years Yakov was released as unexpectedly as he had been arrested. One winter morning, when the prisoners were already lined up to leave for work, a guard called out his name and ordered him to return to his barracks. "I was trembling with fear that I was going to be thrown into the 'lockup'—the most dreaded punishment, because sometimes a prisoner would freeze to death in that outside bunker. I racked my brains to remember what camp regulation I had violated, but try as I would I came up with nothing."

Then an NKVD sergeant came and ordered him to pack. "To pack; what mockery!" Yakov said. "All I had was a small bundle of ragged underwear. When I came to the office, I saw three other prisoners with bundles in their hands. After a while all four of us were put into a sled and driven out of the camp. I was puzzled as to where we were going; to another camp, I thought resignedly." The ride through the deep snows of the Siberian forests seemed endless. After driving on for over nine hours they came to a small railroad station. To their great surprise the prisoners were told by the guard—who had warned them at the outset not to talk to each other and then had not spoken a single word to them throughout the ride—that they were free. He gave them their documents and some money as "pay" for their labor in camp and then left.

"I didn't believe my ears and thought I was dreaming," said Yakov. "After a tortuous 12-day train journey I finally arrived home entirely unexpected. Sima nearly fainted as I entered; she hardly recognized me. I stared at myself in the mirror and saw an elderly, emaciated man with a pale, wrinkled face and gray hair—I looked 20 years older than before my arrest."

He paused and then continued. "I was very weak. You know that Sima is not a bad cook. She did her best to get me back on my feet. For a long time, however, whatever I ate—whether it was fresh buns with coffee or soup and meat—it would taste to me like the food in camp, and my thoughts would wander off to that vile place. And to this day, in my dreams, I often long for a huge chunk of that tasteless bread and a large pot of that smelly soup."

At the time I wondered why Yakov talked so much about the food in camp. Later, however, I came to realize the great significance it had for him. It had been vital for his survival in the most critical period of his life. The same goes for my potatoes. Thanks to them we managed to survive the terrible hunger and plight in Tamak. Small wonder, then, that my potato field keeps on appearing in my dreams to this very day.

* * *

Nadezhda had come back from the hospital some weeks before as there was not much they could do for her there. Her condition did not improve, but she seemed to be holding her own. In the first days of May she even went outside to sit in the sun. Osip felt encouraged and tried desperately to raise the money for their return to the Caucasus.

Then her condition worsened unexpectedly, and she was bedridden again. The doctor said that her illness was exacerbated now by heart trouble. On May 16, when Osip came home from work, he found her dead in her bed. He was inconsolable in his deep grief. After the funeral he locked himself in his room and refused to see his friends. I came every evening, but he told me through the door that he would rather be alone. The fourth day he finally let me in. I looked at him and was shaken—before me stood a heartbroken man, aged by years.

I felt deep sympathy for Osip and tried to console him. Our friendship grew even closer, and we would meet now more frequently than before. He did not speak any longer about returning to the Caucasus. I understood—he wanted to stay near Nadezhda as long as possible. Strangely enough, he rarely mentioned her name.

One evening sometime later, in the middle of a chess game, he suddenly started. "I never told you how I met her. It was over six years ago, the beginning of a new school term. She was in one of my classes, a slender girl with sparkling, coal-black eyes and a beret covering her shoulder-length raven hair. I could not help noticing her, but I paid no particular attention to her until once, when I finished my lecture, she walked over and asked me bashfully to explain some mathematical problem. Then we walked out together and took a streetcar, still talking about mathematics. When she got off, I gazed after her as she was crossing the square, with the springy gait of a young gazelle. I did not admit to myself that I kept thinking about her and could hardly wait to see her in the next class."

He then told me about his courtship, how they got married several weeks later and about their blissful life together. "She longed very much for a child. But she was barely 18, and the doctor said that she was still too frail to give birth. We decided to wait. Then the war came. And now she has gone childless to her grave in this inhospitable frozen Ural earth," he sighed.

We finished the chess game in silence. I had an eerie feeling, as if Nadezhda's shadow were hovering in the room. Osip walked me to the corner of the street next to the river. He was staring in the direction of the distant hill across the river, where Nadezhda lay buried. I stood a while watching him walk back slowly, apparently in no hurry to return to his empty room.

*   *   *

Sasha returned from Moscow on May 18. I went to him in the evening. Their apartment was still occupied, but Sasha had assurances that it would be vacated in the near future. The Levins talked excitedly about their forthcoming return home. After a while Valeria dropped in. She was satisfied with her new job, but she told me that she intended to go back to Moscow together with the Levins.

Sasha brought a lot of interesting news, and I was all ears. He said that despite the impressive recent victories the situation was not as rosy as it appeared on the surface. The German recapture of Kharkov had shown that they were still capable of undertaking massive counterattacks, which brought confusion into the strategic plans of the Soviet command. It was rumored in the capital that very serious blunders had been made at Kharkov that caused immense losses in men and matériel. Stalin, in his customary way of making others pay for his own mistakes, had had a number of generals shot, and many more heads were to be chopped off.

Due to the Katyn affair and the subsequent severing of diplomatic relations with the Polish Government in exile by Moscow, something went sour in Stalin's relationship with Churchill and Roosevelt. As a result, said Sasha, the very opening of the Second Front was now in doubt. There was a mood of frustration; people felt that Russia alone could not defeat Germany. There was persistent talk in Moscow that Stalin was about to make some dramatic gesture in order to straighten out relations with the Western Allies. But nobody knew the nature of the expected gesture.

Sasha went on relating a lot of other interesting news. Thanks to his connections with Party people who were in the know he was well-informed about things that were never even mentioned in the papers or on the radio. Sometimes I thought that it was mere speculation on his part. Before long, however, it would usually turn out that Sasha was indeed right.

The "bombshell" came on May 22. I did not believe my eyes as I read in *Pravda* an official announcement about the dissolution of the Comintern. People were astounded and puzzled, but they were afraid to talk about it. Nevertheless, the fact was welcomed with concealed satisfaction and seen as a sign of forthcoming relaxations in internal matters too.

I was anxious to hear what Sasha had to say, and I stopped at his place. He shook his head. "I'd have never guessed that this was to be Stalin's gesture; I rather thought it would be some concessions on the Polish problem. But I must say that the Pockmarked is a master tactician of deceit. He well knows that nothing will dupe the naive capitalists more than the dissolution of the Communist International, the instrument for spreading the revolution all over the globe."

He then told me that it had been known for quite some time that the pragmatic Stalin did not particularly like the Comintern people, whom he considered a bunch of unworldly theoreticians sitting in an ivory tower. He had a special grudge against them for supposedly giving him inaccurate evaluations of the situation in Germany and in the Western countries. "I think that the dissolution of the Comintern is one of the Georgian's shrewdly calculated tricks in order to kill two birds with one stone—to get even with the Comintern members he dislikes and also to fool Roosevelt and Churchill. Because this is by no means the Comintern's demise, only its temporary suspension until such time as he deems it suitable to reorganize it according to his own liking," said Sasha. "This is also why he has tucked away out of sight in the Urals your Gottwald and some other Comintern favorites of his—to groom them secretly for their future roles as rulers of their respective countries to be sent on the heels of the advancing Red Army to carry out the process of communization."

Interestingly, when I was in Ufa some time later, I happened to pass by the building where I had met Gottwald. To my surprise I saw over the entrance a sign with the name of some Mining Trust. Out of curiosity I asked Lavrov to find out what had happened to the former occupants of the house. After cautious asking around he managed to discover that one night several weeks before they had unexpectedly moved out and left for Moscow. Sasha's prediction of May 22 seemed to be correct.

8

The Circular Road

ONE

O N MAY 30, when I went to Tsitron for my salary, he said, "I'm afraid I have very bad news for you" and handed me a circular. I read it; it was an order from General Glinka to the effect that all civilian employees at the VU were dismissed as of the end of the month. I was speechless and numbed, hardly listening to Tsitron who was trying to console me that I was not the only one hit by the unexpected blow.

The next day I went to Glinka and asked him to rescind my dismissal. I explained to him that as a foreigner I would be placed in a dangerous situation and that it also would be practically impossible for me to get another position in this backwater town. He was very polite to me. "I do realize your special predicament. I know also that you have rendered dedicated and valuable service to the Military College. General Ryabov spoke very highly of you. Unfortunately however, there is nothing I can do about it. The order came from higher up and concerns all military institutions; we must replace all civilians immediately with demobilized war invalids."

I then asked him for a letter of recommendation. He dictated to his secretary a very nice letter. I was especially pleased to hear him mention that the VU was going to rehire me later. The letter, and that stipulation in particular, proved later to be of tremendous help to me in many a precarious situation. As I left his office, he said, "Don't consider yourself a stranger and feel free to turn to me whenever the need arises."

Thus ended my 3½-year career at the institution that had

enriched me with many interesting experiences, most of them pleasant ones. I acquired there loyal friends who helped my family and me to survive in an extremely difficult period. Alas, most of them are dead now, but they live on in my memory. When I finished my employment at the Military College, my heart was filled with apprehension—a new painful chapter in my life in Tamak was about to commence.

I knew that I was faced with a difficult course now. As long as I was with the VU I felt more or less sheltered. Few people knew that I was a foreigner; I simply passed off as a Latvian evacuee. Seeking a new job, however, entailed filling out questionnaires. Somebody might become curious and ask questions, and it would come out that I was a foreigner; an untoward accident could bring it to the attention of the NKVD.

I therefore was not too eager to get a new job right away. The monthly salary of a few hundred inflationary rubles did not mean much anyway; you could live on it only for several days. On the other hand, it would not be "healthy" to go around without work for too long. I asked my friends to keep their eyes open for some suitable job.

Tsitron was the first person to find one. He spoke to a friend of his, the head of a section at the District Industrial Planning Office, who was willing to employ me there. But there was a serious drawback—that institution stood under the direct supervision of the Party. I wanted rather to find some place where I could be inconspicuous and draw as little attention as possible. Therefore I decided to wait and see how things would work themselves out.

* * *

That evening I dropped in to the Slutskys. Lev's health had improved somewhat with the arrival of spring, but the doctor said that his injured lung could ill stand the harshness of another Ural winter. The family was therefore planning to move to Raisa's brother in Central Asia. We talked, and then Lev asked me, "What is actually keeping you in Tamak now? Why don't you come with us? Life will be easier there. First of all, you won't have to worry about firewood, which devours a good half of the living expenditure here."

He was right, yet it was easier said than done. The warm climate of Central Asia used to be the dream of the refugees in Tamak who suffered so much from hunger, cold and disease. The harvest of death was particularly rich during the winter. Small wonder that the approach of springtime would cause a stir, and people would talk about moving to Central Asia. The dream, however, came true for only a few of them. The local authorities, though eager to get rid of the evacuees, did not lift a finger to help them leave. Only the war invalids and their families could get train tickets and some other assistance. The others had the choice either of paying a lot of money for a ticket under the table or of leaving without a ticket and then bribing the conductors all along the journey.

Despite the high expenses and the many hardships involved, some would venture out on the long, arduous trip. But not all succeeded in reaching their destination. An illustration of these ordeals is the sad story of Foma.

There lived near us a refugee with her 16-year-old boy. Her husband fell at the front in 1941. The previous winter she had become ill and had died some weeks later. Being all alone in Tamak, the boy wanted to go to his married sister in Tashkent. Neighbors helped him sell the few belongings that were left, but the money did not suffice to buy a ticket on the black market, so he decided to travel as a stowaway.

For about half a day he managed somehow to hide and duck the conductress. But then she accidentally discovered him and threatened to throw him out at the next stop and deliver him to the militia unless he gave her 150 rubles. When he gave her the money, she locked him up in her cabin and told him to stay there. Some hours later, however, a new conductor came, and he had to be bribed too. And so it went down the line of conductors who relieved one another during the following days.

On the fifth day Foma ran out of money. When a new conductor came, Foma offered him his watch. But he refused to accept it. "Only hard cash!" he snapped, and then put him off the train at some Kazakhstan station and handed him over as a vagrant to an NKVD guard. The orphaned boy tried to explain the circumstances that had forced him to go to Tashkent, but to no avail; he was arrested and put in jail.

After ten days he was unexpectedly released and—who can fathom NKVD logic?—although being then actually much closer to Tashkent than to Tamak, he was ordered to return home. He sold his overcoat, watch and other things and bought a ticket. To keep alive he begged bits of bread and food on the train and at the stations. After an excruciating journey he finally arrived in Tamak about mid-April. He was in a pitiful condition indeed.

After listening to Foma's moving tale I spoke to Reb Mendel. He raised some money among his friends, and I asked Muleyev to help Foma book a ticket at the station, and several days afterward he was on his way to Tashkent at last.

When I came home from the Slutskys I lay awake, trying to think out my dilemma. Perhaps we should go with the Slutskys. We were worn out by the hunger, cold, frequent illnesses and hospitalizations. On the other hand, I asked myself, "Is it prudent to venture the move? Who knows what awaits us there? Here I have made some loyal friends and also sunk my roots—albeit feeble ones. Perhaps that remote Eden is only a mirage built up in the minds of suffering refugees."

I lay musing until very late but could arrive at no conclusion. The angel of sleep finally came and carried me off on his wings to a balmy land with tall palm trees and endless green orchards. I just had to stretch out my hand to the low branches to pluck off all sorts of fragrant fruit and eat to my heart's content.

TWO

I woke early in the morning and was brought back to the dismal reality of Tamak—I remembered that there was not a single potato in the house and that Raphi had not had a drop of milk in many days. I wrote a letter to the Bronsteins, asking them to explore all possibilities of our settling there. In case we decided to move to Central Asia, it would be good to have this option open as well.

The shock of my dismissal was wearing off, being gradually replaced by a feeling of stoic resignation to whatever fate might have in store for me. I took a piece of soap and went to sell it in the *tolchok* and then went to buy some food. It has often been my experience in life that an unexpected coincidence helps you extricate yourself from your dilemma by prompting you to make a sudden decision, and so it happened now.

In the market I ran into Gelbman. We had not seen each other in a long time and stopped to chat. I told him about my dismissal from school and that we were considering leaving for Central Asia with friends. I was surprised to hear that he was planning to go to Orenburg in the coming days. He said that there was a *Delegatura* (representation of the Polish Government) there that helped the Polish refugees. A townsman of his who lived in Orenburg had written him that there was a chance of leaving for Iran. Then he remarked, "Maybe you ought to come along with me. There have been negotiations about a federation between Poland and Czechoslovakia after the war. Why don't you explore the possibilities? Perhaps they'll help you leave the country." The glimmer of hope, of being able to get out of Russia, fired my imagination, and I agreed at once to go with him.

However, going to Orenburg was not a simple matter at all. To get there by train one had to first go north to Ufa, then west to Kuybyshev and from there southeast to Orenburg, altogether a roundabout route of over 1,000 miles. While one still could get a ticket to Ufa with difficulty, the rest of the journey would have to be made on the main Trans-Siberian lines where tickets were available only to passengers on a *komandirovka*. Apart from that, it would be dangerous for a refugee foreigner to travel on those trains.

Orenburg lay about 250 miles southwest of Tamak, and Gelbman intended to hitchhike there. He had found a kolkhoznik, Grisha, who was willing to give him a ride in that direction. We discussed the problems and decided that we might as well start out that afternoon. On the way I dropped in on Yakov to borrow some money. He gave me the money and said, "I think it is frivolous to go on a wild-goose chase."

"You are probably right, but I would never forgive myself for having failed to explore such a rare chance to leave the country," I replied. I then stopped at the *Dyetdom* to bring the news to Ida. She was very apprehensive over my venture. Nevertheless, she prepared some *sukhari* (dried slices of black bread) in a hurry. I put the food and a clean shirt and underwear into a knapsack and left for the market to meet Gelbman.

We paid Grisha, and he said, "Wait for me at the wagon. I'll come as soon as I finish selling my produce and buy something in the *tolchok.*" We waited for a long time, but there was no trace of him; his stall was closed already, and he was not in the *tolchok* either. We looked all over the market and finally found him sitting beyond the stalls drinking with two women. We reminded him that it was time to leave, but he continued to pass around the bottle of vodka unhurriedly—most likely bought with our money—and to retort "*seychas*" (right away). We finally persuaded him to leave.

When we reached the highway, Grisha and the two women started anew to take turns at the bottle. They offered us a swig too, but we said that we did not drink. They became tipsy and began to sing. The younger woman, Shura, especially was in high spirits and cracked jokes. For some reason she put me in the doghouse from the very outset. "You're too skinny and dried out like a poker." But she apparently took a liking to Gelbman and his full beard and suggested that he come and live with her in the kolkhoz. Grisha sneered at her, "Hey, we know that your husband has been away in the army for a very long time, yet I'd not advise you to sleep with one of the refugees. You'd be disappointed. They aren't real men. Why, they don't even know how to drink vodka!" All three of them burst into roaring laughter. The haggard kolkhoz horse turned its head around to see what was going on in the wagon.

We drove on slowly. Grisha was in no hurry. The early-June afternoon was beautiful; not a single cloud in the azure sky. The wooded hills around us were covered with a fresh green. As we approached the crossroads where the wagon was to turn to the kolkhoz, the older woman said, "We aren't really as bad as you may think; we only try to drown our sorrows in vodka." They really seemed to be kind people. They sold us some cheese, onions and pickled cucumbers that they had left. "Go straight ahead; the station is ten *versts* (about ten kilometers) away," they said.

We walked for about an hour and then asked some women who were returning from the fields how far it was to the station. "Ten *versts*," they replied. We were puzzled and thought we had lost our way. But the women said we had not, and they were right. It turned out to be an experience I had had before and would have later—the Russians, and the peasants in particular, care little about the precision of distance and time.

And why should they? *Nichevo!* There is no hurry. So, for instance, it took me some time to realize that if someone says "it is the sixth hour" it does not necessarily mean "six o'clock" but could be somewhere between 5:01 and 6:00. As it turned out, we actually walked nearly 16 *versts*, but the kolkhozniks preferred a simple round figure.

* * *

We arrived at the station only after nightfall. The doors were locked, and it was dark inside. There were no lights in the adjacent buildings either. We walked around a while, but there was no living soul in sight. We sat down on the platform near the electric bulb over the station entrance, had a bite and then stretched out to rest.

As we were about to doze off, we heard footsteps approaching, and soon a figure appeared in the semidarkness around the corner. The man seemed to be as startled as we were.

"Who is there?" he called out in a trembling voice.

"Passengers waiting for a train," we replied and told him our destination. He came over warily and said, "Your train left three hours ago; the next one is due only at five in the morning."

The old night watchman sat down near us. He told us that this was the last stop of a 30-mile narrow-tracked spur from Yermolayevo and also that there was no railroad connection between Yermolayevo and Orenburg. He then told us about his son who had fallen recently at the front and about his own experiences as a soldier in Poland and in Austrian captivity in World War I.

It was getting late, and he stood up. "It's going to be pretty chilly in a while. If you can spare 20 rubles, I could give you a place to sleep." When we gave him the money, he took us to one of the passenger cars that stood on a sidetrack. "Don't worry; I'll wake you up before your train comes," he reassured us as he left.

"I have never before seen such tiny cars; they seem to be made for children," I said to Gelbman as we were lying down on the bare wooden bench. "I have," he replied. "As a matter of fact, these cars remind me of bygone happier days when we used to travel to our Hasidic Rabbi by a mini-train like this one here. I still remember the joyful spirits and singing of the Hasidim there. Who knows what happened to them and to the Rabbi under Hitler."

Gelbman then dozed off. I too tried to get some sleep, but the air was too stuffy. I went to the other end of the car and opened a window. It was pitch-dark by now and I sat gazing at a lonely light in the distance. Who would still be up that late? Joyous people celebrating some happy occasion or a worried mother awake with a sick child? It was so quiet all around that I could hear the clattering of a vehicle on the road over a mile away.

The air got rather chilly, and I shut the window and returned to my place. Gelbman was snoring loudly, his beard heaving rhythmically on his broad chest. I wondered what he was dreaming about—his Rabbi or Shura? I lay wide awake for a long while reflecting on whether the trip was a futile attempt, a Don Quixotic tilt with a windmill. Would we ever succeed in escaping our entrapment in Russia?

I finally dozed off. Early in the morning I was suddenly awakened by a thunderous clatter, like an avalanche of falling rocks. I looked outside—the train that we had to take was rolling into the station. There was no sign of our watchman. Being afraid somebody might notice us, we hurriedly got off on the side away from the station, mingled with the arriving passengers and went to the waiting room.

There was a long line, but to our pleasant surprise we had no trouble buying tickets and getting aboard. The miniature train was crowded and went at a snail's pace. After an hour and a half we arrived safely in Yermolayevo.

The train took us southeast, somewhat off our route, but it still moved us a bit forward. We had not had anything warm since the previous morning and looked around for the *kipyatok* tap, but there was none at that station. A militiaman was eyeing us suspiciously, and we started to walk away from the station. It was too late. He caught up with us and asked for our papers. He looked at them again and again, but each time he seemed to get more confused, and after a while he ordered us to go with him to the militia station.

Then Gelbman got an idea. He showed him a letter from the *Delegatura* and said that we were on our way to join the Polish Army and fight the "Fritzes." The letterhead "Polish Government" made an impression on the provincial militiaman. He gave us back our documents and told us to walk a few miles along the road to a *stolovaya* at the crossroads where we could get a lift on a truck.

It was a close brush with danger, and we drew a sigh of relief as we walked away toward the road. When we arrived at the *stolovaya,* we asked around for a ride but had no success. We wanted to go inside, but the waitress said that it was for truckmen only. After some begging, however, she let us in and sold us a watery soup, with several *lapsha* (broad, dark noodles) swimming around in the plate. It felt wonderful having something warm in our stomachs.

We then went outside to try our luck anew. After half an hour we at last found a driver who agreed to take us for about 20 miles. We paid him and climbed atop a load of metal bars. The highway was bumpy and full of holes, and we were bounced up and down on the bars. Before long we could not stand it any longer and stood up, holding on fast to the truck walls lest we be blown off by the strong wind.

At the next crossroads the truck turned east, and we got off. We tried for some time to solicit another lift in our direction but then gave up and set out on foot. We walked on for two hours, sweating and swallowing the dust whirled at us by passing vehicles. At long last, a truck gave us a ride to a town eight miles away.

* * *

When we arrived there, we went to the one institution one is bound to find in every Soviet town—the kolkhoz market. There were refugees in that backwoods town also, and we stopped to talk with some of them. They advised us not to return to the highway but rather to take another road, which ran due south. We asked around for a ride, but it was too early for the kolkhozniks to return home. We decided not to waste time and started out walking again.

There were no trucks on the road, only a horse-drawn vehicle now and then, but we had no luck getting a ride. It was hot, and we dragged on slowly, taking a short rest from time to time. Later we managed to get a lift in a kolkhoz wagon. The driver, an elderly Bashkir, asked where we were going. We told him. "Oh, that is very far away. You'll have to walk many days to get there," he said. When the vehicle had to turn off to the kolkhoz, the driver said, "The sun is going to set soon and you'll need a place to sleep. Stay in our kolkhoz overnight. In the morning a wagon goes to town to fetch supplies for the kolkhoz store; I'm sure they'll take you along." We accepted his suggestion.

It was already dusk when we arrived in the kolkhoz, and our driver let us off at the hut of the peasant who was to drive to town. He wanted an exorbitant sum for the ride. We tried to reason with him, but he remained adamant. Then came the problem of lodging, and he again asked a price that even a Hilton Hotel manager would hesitate to ask. The sly Bashkir knew that we had no choice and took full advantage of us.

When bedtime approached he scratched his head. "There's no place here for both of you; one of you has to sleep at my brother-in-law's who will accompany me on the trip." We were apprehensive over getting separated—who could tell what the old fox had up his sleeve. Yet, again, we were helpless. I heartily detested him by now and volunteered to sleep across the street.

My new host was the exact opposite of his brother-in-law—a taciturn simpleton who hardly uttered a word all evening. No less striking was the contrast between the two sisters. While the first one, a phlegmatic woman, did not participate in the "negotiations" and merely stared at us, the other was talkative and inquisitive. I was dead tired and could hardly wait to go to bed, but she pestered me with intrusive personal questions. Observing those two couples I wondered if some humorous angel in the Heavenly Matchmaking Bureau had not played a practical joke and mixed up their dossiers.

When the light was put out, I felt a pricking all over my body. From previous experience with sleeping in kolkhoz huts (with the laudable exception of the Umnovs) I knew at once what it was—the army of fleas and bedbugs launched its attack to make my night miserable.

I cleared away the ragged bedding and lay on the bare bench, but it did not help much. I then stripped to the waist, but the little tormentors continued to beset me, so that I hardly got a wink of sleep all night. In the morning my body was covered with red dots, as if I had been suddenly stricken with spotted typhus. I did not bother to mention it to the inhospitable hosts, for I knew what the answer would be—"they never bite us."

I went to the other hut. Gelbman's experience in the night was similar to mine. "My wife will take you outside the village while I go for the wagon," the host said. We guessed that he did not want to be seen moonlighting with a kolkhoz vehicle. She took us through the back door and led us along byways across meadows to a cluster of bushes at the bend of the dirt road. We waited in the bushes for a long time, but there was no trace of our hosts. We began pondering whether to return and try to retrieve our 150 rubles or to forget the whole matter and set out on foot, but after some time we saw the wagon coming and got in.

As soon as we started out, the smooth-tongued Bashkir began. "You know, we're actually taking a great risk giving you a ride. Some neighbors saw you and might report us to the kolkhoz manager."

Smelling further extortion, we cut him short. "We don't want you to get into trouble. Just give us back our money and we'll get off."

"No, no; stay here," he exclaimed and never broached the topic again. He then tried to show himself as amiable and chatted on, telling us about their miserable life in the kolkhoz—a story I had heard so often before. After a while he asked, "You're from Poland? It is near Turkey, isn't it?"

"Somewhere near there," we retorted.

"And how is life in the kolkhoz there?"

"Exactly the same as here," we said, and changed the hot subject. My host remained silent throughout, only nodding his head to whatever his brother-in-law said.

Toward noon we pulled over to the roadside. "Just to give the horses a breather," said our talkative driver. Now I was to behold a picture I had never seen before. The two Bashkirs performed the process of urination while kneeling on one knee. I watched them in astonishment. When they finished I asked why they did it that way. Our chattering friend cast a surprised look at me and said, "And how else can you empty your bladder completely?!"

They untied the horses and let them out to graze. Then they sat down to eat. We were anxious to continue the drive and asked them to hurry.

"Uspeyesh!" (what's the hurry?!), they retorted. After finishing their lunch they stretched out for a leisurely nap in the shade under the vehicle. We were desperate but had no choice and decided that we might as well wash up a little in the creek nearby. It felt marvelous to soak our swollen feet in the cool water and to wash the accumulated sweat and dust off our bodies.

* * *

When our friends woke up, we continued the drive, and several hours later they let us off at a crossroads. We set out on our walk. The sun was baking, and we got tired, but none of the passing vehicles wanted to give us a ride. We dragged on slowly all afternoon, taking frequent rests until we reached a very long and steep hill. We were exhausted by now and the climb was an ordeal.

When we finally reached the top, we beheld a change of scenery—gone was the typical rolling Ural country. Before us lay an endless flatland, with vast grain fields stretching in all directions.

The walk downhill was somewhat easier. The sun in the west was declining, and we began to worry about where to spend the night. There was no village or even a hut in sight. We considered sleeping in a haystack in some field but were afraid that we might be discovered and arrested as vagrants—the last thing we could afford to have happen to us.

As we walked on discussing what we were to do, we saw a cluster of houses and large buildings in the distance ahead. At first we thought it was a town or some big plant, but then we noticed a water tower and silos whose silver-gray color reflected the rays of the setting sun, and we became unsure as to what the place might be. We decided to stop there anyway and try to find lodging for the night.

When we came closer to the place we saw a huge sign "Sovkhoz Red Ural" over the gates. We went inside. There was a bustle everywhere, people working in the storehouses or busy loading or unloading trucks and horse-drawn vehicles. We asked around for a place to sleep, but nobody could help us. One of the workers advised us to try the houses of the *rabochiy posiolok*, a workers' settlement similar to those I had seen near the big factories in Soviet cities, which spread out beyond the fence.

As we walked in that direction we met an elderly man with a clipboard chart in his hand. He eyed us suspiciously and asked what we wanted there and who we were. When he heard "Polish refugees" he pricked up his ears. "From Poland, you said?" and he began to speak to us in Polish.

It turned out that Podwalski, one of the sovkhoz overseers, was a Pole from Grodno. In 1905 he had participated in the abortive revolution against the Czar and was arrested and sent to hard labor in the Urals. Upon serving his term he was not allowed to return home. He settled down in the region and got married, and he appeared to be entirely Russianized by now. Nevertheless, he was delighted with the opportunity to converse in Polish and spoke nostalgically about the town of his birth. He was eager to hear about life in his old homeland, and Gelbman was generous with his descriptions. He then took us to the sovkhoz *stolovaya* where we had soup and buckwheat porridge. We chatted on late into the evening. It was my first visit to a sovkhoz, and I learned from Podwalski a lot about its organizational setup and inner structure.

While the kolkhoz (collective farm) was formed by the forced collectivization of the fields previously owned individually by the peasants of the village, the sovkhoz (Soviet farm), an entirely state-owned enterprise, was founded on government land or on estates expropriated from the former landed gentry. (This sovkhoz belonged to the latter type, and Podwalski showed us the large mansion of the former owner, in which the sovkhoz administrative offices were housed.)

There are also other basic differences between a sovkhoz and kolkhoz. For instance, the kolkhozniks get a share—though a very meager one—of the collective crops. Furthermore, they are allotted small private plots whose produce belongs to them. They also may own a restricted number of fowl and cattle. The sovkhozniks, however, don't have these privileges. All are state employees and are paid regular wages, as in a factory. A sovkhoz is run on the same principles as any other industrial enterprise, and its entire produce belongs to the state. There are dormitories for the single people, and the families live in the *rabochi posiolok*.

We were put up for the night in a vast barn loft. I was dead tired from the long walking, and my back ached in the bargain. I dug myself into the soft, warm hay. Its sweet aroma worked like a gentle anesthetic and soon lulled me into a sound sleep.

Early in the morning Podwalski put us on one of the trucks that took grain to the railroad station in Orenburg. As we drove on, I saw the same sad picture I had seen so often before—vast stretches of untilled land and unharvested crops. Before long we left the territory of the so-called Bashkir Autonomous Republic and entered the Province of Orenburg, which belonged to the Great-Russian Republic.

The flatland scenery gradually changed to a level, steppe-like landscape. After some time Orenburg came into sight. The River Ural, an endless greenish-gray serpent, was winding its way forward. After a four-day arduous and eventful journey, during which I gained many interesting experiences and impressions, we were finally arriving at our destination.

THREE

The truck let us off at the freight yards, and we began making our way to the station across the vast maze of tracks. Orenburg was an important center of transportation. Ever since its founding in 1735 as a military fortress, it had served as a base for Russian penetration into Central Asia. We walked around a while at the station, which was crowded with people, many of them in colorful Asian costumes. I was surprised though to see many evacuees as well—it seemed that the stream of refugees had not as yet stopped.

We then went to Gelbman's townsman, Sperling, but he was

not at home. The house where he lived served as a lodging center for Polish refugees. It was very crowded, and many had to sleep on the floor. Gelbman was now in his element and walked from group to group to look for familiar faces. I, however, felt out of place and followed him mechanically. Before long he discovered some former fellow labor-camp inmates, and they indulged in a lively exchange of news about mutual friends.

When Sperling returned, he took us to the *Delegatura* office to register. We were assigned places on the floor in one of the rooms and issued some "dry rations." The five-pound loaf of white bread I received made my eyes pop out—I had not seen white bread since leaving Latvia.

Sperling told us that some snag had recently developed in the departure of Polish refugees for Iran, but that things would soon start moving again. I sensed that he was in the know and confided my delicate problem to him. He thought a moment and said, "A friend of mine is an official of the *Delegatura*. I believe he can help you." He went to see him but was told that he was out of town and would return in a day or two.

Next morning he went to the *Delegatura* again, but his friend was not back as yet. I had no choice but to wait in suspense. Gelbman and Sperling went to look around for a place to live and also to explore the chances of finding work. For me, however, it was premature to worry about such matters, and I stayed at home.

I listened to my neighbors who were telling one another about their travails in the camps and afterward in the kolkhozes. Then I overheard one of them saying that he was going to the market to sell his loaf of white bread. My funds were very low, and I decided to join him. As we approached the kolkhoz market, he advised me, "Don't be in a hurry to sell. Look around a while. If you're lucky and run into the right kolkhoznik, he'll pay as much as 300 rubles."

After selling our loaves we walked around in the market. To my great surprise, there were grapes as well as other kinds of fruit on sale, things that I had not seen since my departure from Riga. The Kazakhs who brought those luxuries from Asia asked astronomical prices, but they had enough buyers nonetheless.

I had a feeling of guilt for selling the white bread, which I had intended to bring to my son. To make up for it somehow, I bought him an orange (for 30 rubles!). My companion too bought some fruit and then went home, but I was not particularly anxious to spend the day in that dingy, crowded place and decided to get acquainted with the city.

* * *

As I was walking away from the fruit stand, I saw that an elderly man kept looking at me. He followed me, and when he caught up with me said, "Forgive me if I seem inquisitive. But I overheard you talk with your friend and noticed that your Yiddish accent is not Polish. I see that you are not a Soviet Jew either—what landsman are you?"

I had had ample unpleasant experiences of casual acquaintanceship with curious Soviet Jews who then turned out to be fanatic communists and therefore sized him up warily. His grayish-blond beard and the gentle smile in his eyes, however, dispelled my suspicion. "You seem to have the keen perception of a Jewish scholar," I said—quoting the fitting Hebrew phrase. His eyes lit up with a warm glow, and we began to chat. He then asked me to accompany him home. I gladly accepted his invitation.

I walked on with Nahum Sandler, and we sat down in a park. Before long we talked like old friends, and I listened to his moving stories with great interest. He was an evacuee from Kherson, in the Ukraine. Before the Revolution he had had a store in his home town in the Kherson Province. He described the suffering of the town's Jews from the pogroms in the civil war. Many were massacred, among them his parents—a sad tale that is part of the martyrology of Ukrainian Jewry in that tragic period.

The Bolshevik seizure of power brought him impoverishment. His store was shut down, and as a declassed bourgeois he was denied a chance to earn a livelihood. "The worst suffering came from the local *Yevseks* with their sadistic methods of persecution and humiliation," he sighed. "When I sensed imminent arrest and deportation to Siberia, I left all our belongings behind and hurriedly escaped with my family to Kherson where I eventually found work in a tailor cooperative."

When we arrived at his place, his wife, who was mending a shirt and struggling to rethread her needle, looked at me curiously over her spectacles, which were riding on the tip of her nose. He told her who I was. "Well, if we have such a rare guest let me make some tea," she exclaimed. While she was busy with the primus, he told me that they lived there with their daughter and son-in-law who had been evacuated with their factory to Orenburg.

Sandler came from a family of devout Braslaver Hasidim and was steeped in the lore of that typical branch of Hasidism. His Hasidic stories were fascinating, and time flew by fast. When his wife began to prepare supper, I wanted to leave, but they insisted that I stay for supper. We went on talking. Later we heard a key turn in the door, and Sandler stopped in the middle of a Hasidic tale. As soon as the daughter and her husband entered, they exclaimed—"Ma, look what we got today!" and hurried to her.

When they came back from behind the curtain that divided the room in two they noticed me and eyed me in surprise. Sandler introduced me to them. They were polite but aloof. The meal passed in an uneasy mood. Sandler was taciturn now and seemed to be immersed in thought.

I left immediately after supper. Sandler walked me to the bus stop. We walked a while in silence, then he said, "There is so much I want to tell you; come let us sit in the park for a while." When we sat down, he began, "I noticed the expression on your face as my children were fussing about the 'treasure' they brought from their place of work. The most tragic part of our life is that the younger people don't grasp the depth of their misery. They never knew a better life and believe that Stalin has given them paradise on earth. Let me illustrate the point I want to bring out with a story I heard many years ago from an old Hasid in Uman, where I used to go for Rosh Hashana to pray at the grave of our great Rabbi Nachman."

It would be futile for me to try to render the story with all the eloquence and idiomatic Hasidic flavor Sandler gave it. The reader will have to be satisfied with a brief, pale substitute.

It seems that this disciple of the Baal Shem Tov, the founder of Hasidism, decided to follow the example of his great master and

tour the countryside to bring the teachings of Hasidism to the
poor ignorant Jews in the hamlets. He hired a teamster with a
wagon and set out on his travel.

One afternoon, in the middle of nowhere, the rabbi discovered with horror that one of the four *tzitzith* (fringes) on his
religious undergarment had a blemish. "Stop the carriage at
once and let me off. You drive on and get me somewhere a
fringe that is fit according to Jewish Law," he told the driver.

"Rabbi, it is very dangerous for you to remain here alone.
Night will soon fall, and the robbers who roam the woods might
attack you. Let us drive to the nearest inn," he said.

"Don't you know what a grave sin it is to go more than four
paces without proper fringes?!" the rabbi rebuked him. The
teamster tried to argue with him, but nothing doing—the rabbi
got off and sat down under a tree.

The teamster drove around until he found a roadside inn. He
related the rabbi's plight to the innkeeper who gave him a new
fringe and said, "100 rubles."

"100 rubles?! Why, a fringe costs only a few kopecks. You must
be joking," the driver exclaimed.

"100 rubles. Take it or leave it," the innkeeper retorted curtly.

The driver gave him the money, cursing under his breath.
"Shame on you, you ruthless brigand, for extorting 100 rubles
from a poor rabbi who would rather risk his life than violate a
precept of the Torah." When he returned to the rabbi and told
him in outrage about the innkeeper, the rabbi gently hushed
him. "He must be very poor and probably needs the money to
marry off an overaged daughter or to send his children to a
yeshiva. Besides, the higher the cost to fulfill a commandment of
God, the greater is the merit in His eyes."

After replacing the fringe they resumed the drive. As they
drove by the inn, the innkeeper stopped the wagon and asked
the rabbi to do him the honor of staying there overnight. The
teamster shouted furiously, "Up to some more extortion, you
accursed highway robber?!" and wanted to drive on. But the
rabbi calmed him down and went inside.

The innkeeper served a sumptuous supper and then lodged
the rabbi in his finest room. In the morning, when the rabbi was
about to leave, the innkeeper went to his room and asked him to

bestow his blessing on him and his family. After the rabbi blessed him, the innkeeper gave him 100 rubles.

"I don't get it," said the rabbi in bewilderment. "You took 100 rubles for the fringe, and now you are giving me such an exorbitant sum for the blessing. No, keep the money and use it for a meritorious purpose. You seem to be a poor man."

"You are right, rabbi. I'm very poor, barely eking out a meager livelihood for my large family," he replied. "I'm only an ignorant Jew and don't understand these matters. But I figured that it would not have made a big impression in heaven if you had paid for the fringe a mere few kopecks and I, on the other hand, would have given you only a ruble or two for the divine blessing.

"Now, however, can you imagine the sensation you'll cause when you appear—after 120 years—before the Heavenly Judge? Why, He'll assemble the souls of all great rabbis and announce to them—'Just look at My dedicated servant! Not only did he endanger his life for the sake of the fringe, but he also paid 100 rubles for it.' And, without any trial, you'll be led with fanfares to your well-deserved place of honor in paradise."

The innkeeper continued with a heavy sigh, "My appearance up there will cause little fuss. And why should it? My balance sheet looks bad indeed. The column of good deeds is very short. That of my sins, however, is endless—many violations of the Sabbath and holidays, omissions of prayers and so on. The accusing angel has a sly smirk on his face as he goes on noisily tossing one demerit after the other onto the black scale, which keeps weighing down ominously.

"My defender, however, is silent and sad. He fishes out some small merit now and then and puts it shyly on the white scale, which, however, hardly moves. But then he throws a heap of gold rubles—they don't accept paper money up there, you know—onto the white scale, which begins to descend swiftly. His eyes light up, and he declares triumphantly—'You see? Such a poor man and he gave 100 rubles to the rabbi!' My accuser hangs his head in shame, and I'm shown to my humble corner in paradise."

"Now you see, rabbi? the innkeeper concluded, "how the same 100 rubles have performed an invaluable service to both of us."

A blissful smile appeared on the rabbi's face. He lifted his eyes to heaven and prayed. "O Lord, see how eager this unlearned Jew is to fulfill Your commandments, but his poverty prevents him from doing so. Bless him therefore with Your threefold blessing so that he can perform many good deeds in comfort."

And, as the old Uman Hasid assured his listeners, the innkeeper soon became very rich. He married his daughters to Torah scholars and indulged in the pursuit of good deeds and charity all through his long life.

When Sandler finished his story he said pensively, "In a free country you can go with your hard-earned money to a store and buy food and anything else to your heart's content. But what big deal is that? Material goods, like freedom, are valued only after you lose them. My children earn good monthly wages, which, however, are not enough to live on even for one week.

"But Stalin in his 'great wisdom' has established an ingenious system. From time to time our children get a slice of margarine, a herring, a shoddy article of clothing and suchlike at the factory. They bring it home and thank Stalin for his 'generosity' (you saw their elation today when they brought a few pairs of socks). My wife or I take this few-kopeck 'fringe' to the market where it is metamorphosed into a 100-ruble bill with which we buy some food and prepare a meal for them. They eat it and again praise Stalin. He has invented a vicious fringe-and-inflationary-100-ruble game indeed which the people go on playing without realizing that they are caught in the middle struggling for their bare existence."

I heard from Sandler many other interesting Hasidic stories, which I hope to tell on some other occasion. It was very late in the night already when we parted and I returned home.

Gelbman rebuked me. "Where have you been that late? I thought the NKVD grabbed you." I told him about Sandler. We talked a while and then he fell asleep. I lay awake for a long while thinking about Nahum Sandler. It was a most rewarding experience. Fate, however, did not will it that we meet again. We exchanged letters during my sojourn in Russia, but I don't know what happened to him afterward. I'll never forget that wonderful wise man, and his captivating stories are still fresh in my memory.

*   *   *

Next morning Sperling took me to his friend. He said that he could solve my problem for 20,000 rubles. I would have gladly given him the money, but I did not have then even one-twentieth of that sum. I told him that I must return home to raise the money and would then come back. He got me a round-trip ticket to Tamak through the *Delegatura*.

Gelbman planned to stay in Orenburg several more days. I, however, had nothing more to do there and, saying my good-byes, left for the station. After the usual difficulties I managed to board a train in the afternoon. Despite my *Delegatura komandirovka* I was fearful of some unforseen mishap, especially since I intended to stop at the Czechoslovak Embassy in Kuybyshev.

I had to change trains twice. About noon the next day I arrived in Kuybyshev. However, when I got to the exit from the station, the militiaman who checked the papers there said that my *komandirovka* was not valid for Kuybyshev and told me to continue my trip to Tamak. I heaved a sigh of relief as I walked away unscathed from that close brush with peril. Nevertheless, the failure of my plan saddened me.

I boarded a train to Ufa. As we pulled out of the station, I wondered sadly whether I would have another chance to be there. Twenty minutes later we stopped at a small station. An idea struck me suddenly like lightning—I grabbed my knapsack and got off.

It would have been foolhardy to go back by train. I walked past the station and proceeded along a dirt road. There were no houses in sight, only vegetable gardens. I asked an elderly kolkhoznik how to get to Kuybyshev. He told me to walk on a few miles to the highway, where I could get a ride.

After two hours I finally managed to get a lift on a truck. I arrived in Kuybyshev safely, but by the time I got to the embassy, it was already closed. I walked around in front of the embassy in the hope of seeing someone going in or out, but nobody did. When dusk came I left in disappointment.

I was now faced with the problem of where to spend the night. Apart from being an important center of war industry, Kuybyshev was then practically the capital of the country, housing many government institutions and the embassies. I therefore concluded that the surveillance here would be very strict.

I sat down in a park. Noticing later a plainclothesman asking the people on the benches for their papers, I slipped away and began strolling through the streets. When I got tired, I sat down in the waiting shed of a tram stop. After some time the old switchman asked me why I was sitting there so long. "I'm an out-of-towner and am waiting here for a friend with whom I'm to stay," I replied. He winked knowingly and whispered, "An NKVD man could become curious. You'd better get on a street-car."

I jumped onto the tram that was just leaving. I had no idea where it was going; but what difference did it make? I kept riding. In order to attract less attention, I changed trams frequently. I must have covered most of Kuybyshev's suburbs. Once we even got close to the Volga.

At 1 A.M. the streetcars stopped running. I was at my wits' end. The only thing left was to walk the streets again. Later I sat down in the park, selecting a strategic corner so as to be ready to leave in case some guardian of the law showed up. I was dead tired and sleepy, but the chill and the drizzle helped me to stay awake. The time dragged on interminably.

The streetcars began to run again at 5 A.M., and I resumed my aimless riding. At least I was now out of the drizzle, and the chill in my bones lessened somewhat. Little by little the trams filled up. I was glad that the trepidation of the night was over and felt safer in the crowd.

* * *

I came to the embassy before eight and walked around in the sun on the sidewalk across the street to warm up a little. To my dismay, before long a militiaman came and placed himself at the embassy entrance. I became worried lest he prevent me from entering.

When the embassy doors opened, I walked over, trying hard to appear composed. The militiaman eyed me sternly and asked me who I was. "A Czechoslovak citizen," I said calmly and rang the bell. The agonizing minute until a woman opened the door and let me in seemed like an eternity. I told her that I wanted a passport. She took me to the secretary. I explained to him that the German Consulate in Riga had taken away our Czechoslovak passport and replaced it with "Protectorate" passports, which then remained at the Riga NKVD.

"I have written you from Tamak; you can find my letter in your files," I said.

"I'm afraid I can't help you. All our files are in Moscow already. We are in the process of moving back there. Only a skeleton staff has been left here to fold matters up," he replied.

I told him that the passport, especially now after my dismissal from the VU, was a matter of survival for us and described the travail and dangers I had gone through to get here. He thought a moment and then told me to file an application.

Tedious paper work began. First I had to fill out a series of long, complicated questionnaires (in five copies each). Then came the writing of a *curriculum vitae,* with a detailed description of where I had lived, studied and worked, names of teachers, colleagues and friends, to which organizations I belonged, and so forth. When I gave it to the secretary, he asked for more data and other apparently irrelevant details.

The labor on my paper work reminded me so much of the whims of the bureaucratic Czech officials prior to our leaving Czechoslovakia, as if intending to make our escape from Hitler as difficult as possible. I had hoped to find the spirit of Masaryk's humaneness in the embassy. Instead, I experienced an atmosphere of icy indifference. Nobody asked me whether I was hungry or had a place to stay. What hurt me most, however, was that none of them even bothered to inquire how we were managing to survive in Tamak and if there were something they could do to help us.

When the secretary was finally satisfied with my paper work, he said, "I'll transmit your application to the embassy in Moscow, and they will get in touch with you by mail." I was very disappointed—I had expected to get the passport the same day. Upon my request, though, he issued me an official paper to the effect that our passport was being processed. (That document, in fact, proved to be very useful to me that same day at the railroad station in Kuybyshev as well as on later occasions.)

I had no particular difficulty in boarding a train to Ufa. It was, however, very crowded, and I barely squeezed in. Later in the evening I managed to get a seat. I had not slept a wink the previous night and soon dozed off.

When I woke up in the morning, I was hungry. I had not eaten anything since the previous dawn in the Kuybyshev park. At the next station I got some *kipyatok* and crumbled into it the few *sukhari* I still had. Though feeling more rested physically now, I was nonetheless fearful. So far, the frequent checking of papers since Orenburg had all passed smoothly. But one could never feel safe from some mishap with the NKVD.

I arrived in Ufa in the afternoon and then changed for a train to Tamak. About midnight, after a ten-day arduous journey, I finally arrived home safely.

FOUR

I woke up the next morning to the dismal reality of Tamak. When my son got up, he welcomed me with joy, as if he had not seen me in ages. He looked at the orange in wonderment and took it along to the *Dyetdom* to show the children "the ball" his Daddy brought him. He played with it, and in several days it was cracked and ripped beyond hope.

The first thing that demanded my attention was the field, and I went there immediately. The early morning was beautiful. The sun in the cloudless sky licked the dew off the leaves with the avidity of a young parched calf. The quiet around me soothed my tension, and I tried to assess my situation. The temptation to move to Orenburg was strong. Yet, how was I to raise 20,000 rubles? The only tangible sum could come from the sale of the potatoes. But the harvest was still a very long way off, and who would buy chickens before they were hatched?

That evening I visited Menikhes. I was glad to see that he was better now, and I told him at length about the adventures of my trip. He listened and then said, pensively, "Your idea of trying to get out of Russia is sound. For the time being, however, it seems to be out of your reach. The Russian muzhiks have a saying that on the way to the tavern, too, one needs a drink. I think you have to get a job in the meantime. Tomorrow we'll go to see a former student of mine who can help you."

Menikhes's landsman, Simkhovich, was the manager of the produce supplies department at the Ishimbay Oil *Kombinat*. He was very friendly but in the end said, "Reb Mendel, handling food is a tempting business. If an employee steals too much, he can get me in trouble too. On the other hand, if he is too honest, his fellow workers will be afraid of him and try to get rid of him. I therefore prefer people who steal within reasonable limits. Our foreigner friend, however, is unfamiliar with our way of life. I'm afraid he is incapable of becoming even a moderate pilferer, and therefore the other employees will give him trouble."

I did not know whether to feel insulted or flattered by his compliment. Anyway, even though I did not get the job, I learned from him a new fundamental rule in Soviet economics—that stealing at one's place of work was taken for granted and was an essential part of one's livelihood. Simkhovich's philosophy was probably shared by the other practical managers. We talked for a long while, and I heard many things from him that afforded me a glimpse into the inner workings of Soviet economic life. One of his stories I would like to relate in brief.

It seems that this laborer in a wood-processing plant got an original idea of how to supplement his miserable wages. Every Saturday he used to fill a handcart with hay that he would pick up around the plant over the week. He told the guards at the gate that he needed the hay for his goat. They would rummage through the hay to make sure that there were no tools or other factory property hidden in it and let him pass.

There was, however, one detail that was overlooked. Only many months later did it occur to one of the guards that the worker never returned the handcart. An investigation showed that he had taken a handcart each week and sold it on the black market. He was arrested by the NKVD.

The trial, which attracted the attention of the local press and radio, caused much embarrassment to the authorities. The laborer said that he could not live on the ridiculously low wages he got and stated flatly that he had not stolen the handcarts but merely taken them as payment from the factory for what was due to him in order to feed his family. Such impudent counterrevolutionary talk could not be tolerated. The court meted out justice and sentenced the poor worker to a 15-year term in a labor camp.

* * *

Gelbman came back from Orenburg a week after my return, and several days later he and his family and the Kutner widow with her only surviving child left for Orenburg. I was glad to see them come a step closer to the hope of getting out of Russia. Between me and that hope, however, stood a high wall of 20,000 rubles, which, at any rate, I could not surmount before the harvest of our potatoes. I had no choice but to go back to the rut of the daily struggle in Tamak.

During this period our friendship with Galya and her parents grew even closer. Since our fields were far from the Belaya that summer, I seldom went fishing there with Volodya. Instead, I used to fish with Yakov in the Sterla River or in the lake. Our catches were meager, only a few trout and some other small fry, yet it was always a welcome contribution to our miserable diet.

The fishing trips with Yakov enriched my knowledge of Soviet reality. His stories about the horrible suffering of people in the Soviet prisons and labor camps curdled my blood. He was well-acquainted with the methods of the secret police, and the things he told me were shocking.

There is a gruesome fatalism in the Russian saying that "one can't escape two things in life—the poorhouse and prison." For in the Soviet concept every citizen is suspect and a potential candidate for arrest. And by the same token, everybody is also regarded as a potential informer.

"The tactics of the NKVD are diabolical indeed," Yakov said. "They have a file on practically everyone. One day you are invited for a visit. The official is polite and even friendly. He inquires if your job and living conditions are satisfactory. Then he drops a few names of your friends or fellow workers and reminds you gently of your duty as a loyal Soviet citizen to be vigilant against 'the enemies of the people.' Before you leave, you are advised not to mention the visit to anybody, including your family."

After such a visit one usually knows what the NKVD wants from him. An opportunist of course sees in it a chance for personal advancement. But many an honest person too may lack the moral fortitude to withstand the pressure; the fear of what might happen to him if he disobeys gives him sleepless nights. Then he recalls grudges—that pushy fellow worker whom the NKVD official mentioned was promoted recently to a higher position for which he himself was best qualified, or this colleague got a new apartment while he and his large family are still living in a small dingy room—and he begins to listen more attentively to the conversations of those friends. It occurs to him that some of their remarks sound "suspicious" indeed, and on his next visit to the NKVD (one can always be sure that another invitation will follow) he tells things to the official, who enters these remarks into the proper files.

The NKVD officials are methodical in gathering information and bide their time. Their slogan is "You just give us the man and we'll build up a case." One night those "enemies of the people" will suddenly be arrested without even being told why and will be shipped off to a labor camp.

Only he who has lived in Russia for a longer period and had a chance to observe life from the inside can fathom the deep demoralization that has been created over the years by the secret police. Friends suspect one another—someone might be a coerced informer. One mistrusts even his relatives. And this is precisely what the NKVD terror is intended to achieve—that people should be afraid not only to talk to each other but also to think aloud.

There is a sad truism in a joke I heard from Yakov—that when you get up in the morning and look at your image in the mirror, you warningly shake your finger and say, "Don't talk to me. I won't tell you a thing. One of us two could be an informer."

Once Yakov told me something that was kept as a strict secret in their family. Galya's first child was a boy, and after the birth Yevsey went on a longer *komandirovka* and told Yakov to arrange the circumcision while he was away from Dnepropetrovsk. Yakov's description of the clandestine atmosphere in which the circumcision ceremony was performed moved me deeply, a sad testimony indeed to the persecution and tragedy of Soviet Jewry. Upon hearing that story my respect for Yevsey grew even more. For I realized what a great risk he had taken with his high position in the Party.

*　*　*

The month of June 1943 brought a sad event. On my last visit to Sonya Plavnik after my return from Orenburg, I saw that she had recovered somewhat from her stroke and that she was holding her own. She was alert and showed a lively interest in what I told her about my trip. Her daughter told me that she was having a hard time keeping from her the bad news that her husband had recently been severely wounded at the front. Toward the end of June, however, she suffered another stroke and died a few days later.

The funeral of the last of the *Kantonist* tribe in Tamak was a moving experience for me. In the course of the period I knew Sonya she had told me many interesting stories about those unfortunate Jews. (I used to take notes on scraps of paper or between the lines of newspapers. Living in constant fear of an unexpected visit by the NKVD, I gave them, along with other notes about my experiences in Russia, to Straus to keep for me. One day, however, there was a sudden rumor of impending NKVD arrests among the Latvian evacuees, and Straus got scared and burned my notes together with many of his own papers.)

After burying Sonya near her husband and parents, I realized that the last link with the extinct Jewish community in that Ural town was gone forever. I walked with Reb Mendel among the *Kantonist* graves. The old Bashkir caretaker who accompanied us sighed. "Ah, they were fine, honest and hardworking people! Now poor Sonya too has been laid to her eternal rest among them. May she rest in peace. She suffered plenty of pain and sorrow in our vale of tears."

Trying to decipher the faded Hebrew inscriptions on the sunken gravestones I came across the names of some of the protagonists in Sonya's stories. I recalled her vivid descriptions of them and visualized those sturdy *Kantonists* rising from their graves to retell their horrible suffering in the Czarist Army. The leaves of the bushes around the fresh grave rustled in the breeze. Maybe they were transmitting the inaudible exchange of greetings between Sonya and her kin.

* * *

In those weeks the Slutskys were busy selling off their belongings to finance their departure for Central Asia. I toyed with the idea of going with them, but the lack of money dashed those hopes likewise—I could not have raised sufficient funds to even buy tickets and food for the long journey, not to speak of the other expenses.

The Slutskys had to overcome many difficulties. One of the problems was their potato field. They were willing to sell it at any price offered. But according to the regulations an allottee was prohibited from selling his plot to an outsider. Instead, he had to return it to the *Dyetdom* with the planted potatoes.

I spoke to Riva, and after some string pulling with the *Dyetdom* manager she succeeded in having the field transferred to her name. (Being unable to take care of the field herself, she made me a one-third partner for attending to it.) Riva gave the Slutskys 3,000 rubles, which was a very good price under the circumstances. They knew that she was doing it to help them out in their need and were grateful to her.

On July 2 we walked with the Slutsky family to the station to see them off. We felt sad at their leaving. The hard times we had gone through together made our friendship very close. "We hope you'll join us before too long," they said as we parted. Yet inside me a question gnawed—will we ever meet these good friends again? Especially moving was Rebecca's saying goodbye to Raphi. The two of them had become very fond of one another, and he missed her terribly later, asking when Granny Becky would come back to him.

* * *

In June Riva's sister, Genya, came to Tamak. Her husband, the director of a construction plant, was evacuated with the plant to Chelyabinsk. The Orshovskys had not seen her since Odessa, and her visit was a happy event for them. I became well-acquainted with her, and once she told me, "There is a camp for prisoners of war near Chelyabinsk. Some of the prisoners work in my husband's plant. We are close friends with the camp commandant. I'm sure you can get a position there as a German interpreter."

Her suggestion appealed to me. I would be able to work in a field related to my training and to escape from the hunger and cold in Tamak. I was no less attracted, however, by the idea of seeing the erstwhile Teutonic conquerors in their new role as war prisoners.

In the beginning of July, shortly after Genya's return home, I received a telegram from her to come for an interview. Chelyabinsk, the second most important Ural industrial city, was only about 350 miles northeast of Tamak as the crow flies, but in order to get there one had to take a very long, roundabout route.

Muleyev helped me get a round trip ticket. I took the midnight train to Ufa and then, from early morning, I attempted in vain to board any train going east. At 9 A.M. I saw the Trans-Siberian Express roll into the station. The authoritative appearance of its sleek cars was familiar to me from Kazan. I knew that trying to get on that exclusive train would be futile. Seeing the other passengers rush to the train, however, I joined them. When I showed the conductress my ticket she snapped, "For regular train only!" She admitted only the chosen ones—Party and government officials; one could recognize them by the self-conscious expression of importance on their faces.

A few hours later I finally managed to get on a freight train. The car had no roof, only low walls. The weather was beautiful, and the ride in the open air turned out to be an interesting experience. The train left the main line and wound its way through picturesque mountain valleys and primeval forests. Ural nature revealed itself in its full beauty.

When night fell, the air became chilly. I lay down on the floor to seek shelter from the wind, but it did not help much. Seeing my neighbors fall asleep and some of them even snore loudly, I once again became aware of my inability to adjust to the hard conditions of Soviet life. I was shivering from cold and was glad when the train arrived at its last stop about midnight.

Some time later I succeeded in boarding a passenger train.

After dawn I was awakened by the commotion and noise of the passengers. "Asia! Asia!" All crowded at the windows. I too stretched my neck and saw a moment later a marker "Europe-Asia" glide by.

Leaving the European continent for the first time in my life was a thrilling experience. I forgot my worries for a while and daydreamed that I was going as a tourist on a pleasure trip to Asia. Soon, however, I remembered that I was now actually in Siberia, the land of the countless slave-labor camps. The train wheels went on ticking out dolefully "Siberia! Siberia!" and the howling wind seemed to be carrying to me the muted sighs of the millions of innocent suffering prisoners.

Recalling the NKVD visit in our Riga apartment and my many close brushes with them later, it suddenly occurred to me that in case of an unexpected encounter with them now they would not have to take me too far.

About noon I had to change for a train due north. After dusk I arrived in Chelyabinsk. It took me some time to find the suburb where the Lidins lived. Genya's husband, Viktor, turned out to be a very friendly and intelligent man and gave me a lot of helpful information about the POW camp. The family made me feel at home, and I had a good night's rest after two sleepless nights.

* * *

In the morning Viktor put me on one of his plant's trucks, which transported building material to the camp. "Going to take a look at the 'Fritz' beasts?" the jovial truck driver said. After 20 minutes we arrived at a vast clearing amid the woods. If not for the high barbed-wire fences and the wooden sentry towers around the place it would have looked like a large suburb under construction, with huge piles of felled trees all around and bull-dozers busy digging long rows of dugouts, some of which were already furnished with low log walls and roofs.

A guard at the gate showed me the way to the commandant's office. Colonel Okun, a broadshouldered man of about 50, greeted me warmly. "Viktor and Genya told me a lot about you. I think you're the man we need." His chest was covered with medals for distinction in battle. The energetic features of his face and his self-assured demeanor betrayed a seasoned command-ing officer. He was particularly interested in my work at the Military College and seemed to be impressed by the letters of recommendation from Ryabov and Glinka that I showed him.

His cordiality made me feel at ease. When I told him about the ordeals we had gone through on our escape from Czechoslova-kia and then later from Latvia, his face clouded. "You don't know how lucky you are. My wife and children remained in Minsk. Who knows what those German beasts did to them," he sighed, pointing at the POW dugouts. "Their atrocities against the Jews are beyond imagination." He fell silent. After a mo-ment his face resumed its resolute military expression. "Want to see them? Come, I'll show you around the camp a little." He rose briskly and we went outside.

The camp had then about 3,000 war prisoners, but they were making intensive preparations to accommodate far larger num-bers. Most prisoners left early in the morning for work in the forests, mines and factories. There was, however, a group of recent arrivals who were being screened, and we went to see them. I must admit that I enjoyed the sight I beheld—lean, haggard "supermen" dressed in a strange mishmash of tattered clothes, from tightly fitting army tunics to odd pieces of women's garments.

"What a far cry from the haughty conquerors of Czechoslova-kia," I said to Okun.

"This is nothing," he replied. "You should have seen those who came in the wintertime from Stalingrad. They were wrapped in stoles and ladies' underwear, with layers of silk stock-ings around their ears. One could not help laughing."

He then showed me the maximum security section for Waffen SS prisoners. Gone were their death's heads and other SS insig-nia. The paleness of their emaciated faces was even more accen-tuated by the black color of their ragged uniforms. Looking at their brutal eyes and masklike faces I recalled the truck driver's utterance and wondered how many innocent victims they had on their consciences.

Okun had to go back to his office, and on the way he in-troduced me to the camp interpreter, a captain in his forties, and told him to let me interrogate several prisoners. The captain was busy with a prisoner, and I had a chance to watch him perform the interrogation. Glancing through the questionnaire, I found it rather stereotyped and decided to use a broader psychological approach.

My first interrogee was a young Alsatian flier. He had a typical German name and his German pronunciation was flawless, yet he brazenly claimed to be a Frenchman whom the Germans had forced to join the army.

"How come they trusted you with a plane?" I asked him. He had no answer.

"*Mais la coeur*—my heart is French," he went on repeating, and asked to be sent to the Free French Air Force Unit that fought at the Russian front.

When I asked him, however, various circumstantial questions about his background and schooling, he realized that I was up to his tricks and he gave up his game.

The next POW was a lieutenant, about 30, from Breslau. At first he was uncooperative, hardly answering my questions. He stared at me sullenly, wondering probably who the strange civilian might be. His puzzlement grew when he noticed that I was taking notes in German shorthand. To break the ice I offered him a cigarette (I did not smoke, but I had borrowed a pack of cigarettes from the captain) and began to chat with him easily about his home town, which I had visited as a student. Before long he became communicative and told me that he had been there on a furlough six months before. I learned from him a lot of information about life and conditions in Breslau and about the mood of the civilian population in the hinterland in general.

My third interrogee, a stocky, middle-aged sergeant, was from Vienna, a city I knew. That moon-faced fellow with a reddish nose and bulging eyes tried to play the simpleton and reminded me of "The Good Soldier Schweik." As soon as the guard brought him in, he clicked his heels, raised his clenched fist in a communist revolutionary salute and shouted loudly "Rot Front!" (Red Front).

He was very talkative and stated at once that he was a Social-Democrat and that he had fought in the uprising of the Austrian *Schutzbund* against the Dolfuss regime in 1934. His favorite refrain was "Hitler kaput," and he kept pouring out curses on the heads of the Nazis. For good measure he threw in, "I helped many of my Jewish friends." However, when I insisted that he give me the names and addresses of those friends and also asked him how come, as a former *Schutzbund* fighter, he had not been persecuted under Hitler, he became confused and dropped his story.

When I finished my interviews, the captain resumed his work. In the meantime I completed the questionnaires and wrote out on separate sheets my personal evaluations of the three interrogees. Naturally, most of the prisoners, as I noticed, volunteered statements that would please their captors. But I nonetheless thought that some of their information might be correct and useful.

Some time later Okun dropped in. The captain showed him my questionnaires. I noticed that he was especially impressed by my individualized evaluations and read them with great interest. I knew that he was pleased, but I still had to pass the grade with the *politkomissar,* who was away from the camp and was expected back in the afternoon.

When he returned, I went to see him. He asked me many questions about my background and even my political views. Then he outlined his program of reeducation for the prisoners in which, he told me, I would have to participate. We talked for a long while, yet at the end I was not any wiser as to his opinion about me; he sounded rather noncommittal and told me to wait until he discussed the matter with the commandant.

In the meantime I went back to the captain to watch him screen the prisoners. It was interesting to observe their behavior. Later I was called to Okun's office. The *politkomissar* was there also. "We are all pleased with you and have decided to offer you the position," Okun said and added, "There is one stipulation though—you'll have to become a commissioned officer." I was taken aback; he had never mentioned it before. I said that I needed some time to think about it.

When the *politkomissar* left, I candidly expressed my fears to Okun. "At the Military College I was a civilian employee. To be an officer in the Red Army, however, could entangle me in a delicate situation that I might not be able to get out of later."

"I can assure you that you'll be free to return home after the war. In the meantime, you'll have a handsome salary with the fringe benefits of a warm, comfortable apartment and food for you and your family," he said. "But I appreciate your dilemma. Think it over and let me know your decision within two weeks."

I thanked that wonderful man for his understanding. As we parted, he told me, "I'd like you to accept the position and do hope to see you soon."

Dusk was already falling as I got on the truck that was to take me back to the Lidins. The rotating projectors began casting patches of eerie light across the camp area. Columns of emaciated and ragged prisoners were returning from work. I felt pity for them. Seeing, however, the hateful glances they cast at the truck driver and me as they passed us, my pity evaporated. "Who has invited these 'master race' murderers here? If not for their lust for war, neither they nor I would be in Chelyabinsk now," I said to myself.

I intended to leave that evening, but Genya and Viktor persuaded me to stay overnight. "Don't hesitate to accept the position. You can trust Okun," they argued. We were up very late discussing the pros and cons of the matter.

It was already midnight when I went to bed, but sleep did not come; I was thinking about what I had seen in the camp. We in Russia had no idea then about the horrible proportions of the Holocaust. The incidental hints in the articles of Ehrenburg and other Soviet Jewish war correspondents revealed only a little about the German mass slaughter of the Jews in the occupied territories.

True, I saw the Teutonic murderers languish in the camp. But no punishment could fit their monstrous crimes. To my mind came Bialik's words "that the vengeance for the spilt blood of one single innocent child Satan has not created as yet." I lay gazing at the Siberian moon and stars to detect in them a sign of divine justice and vengeance. But they remained silent and indifferently poured down their gray light on the tile roofs of the suburban houses.

I finally fell asleep, and before long the Breslau Nazi, the Alsatian pilot and the Vienna sergeant were grinning at me. Then their faces fused into one—that of my Bavarian interrogator at the Brno Gestapo who roared, in his brutal voice,

"You dirty Jew! You thought you could bribe me with your cigarettes!" He began to drag me down to the dreaded Brno Gestapo dungeon. I resisted and opened my eyes with difficulty.
Viktor was shaking me and whispered, "Wake up. You were
crying in your sleep; you must have had a bad dream." I felt the
cold drops of sweat trickling down my spine. I tried to go back to
sleep, but sleep eluded me for a long while.

Early in the morning I said goodbye to my wonderful hosts
and left for the station. During the trip I experienced the usual
difficulties, including one close brush with the NKVD. On the
third day I finally arrived home.

FIVE

On July 5, 1943, Hitler, striving to undo his humiliating defeat
at Stalingrad, launched a large-scale offensive at Kursk. The
initial German successes filled hearts with worry. My mind, however, was preoccupied with my own dilemma. I found myself at a
crucial crossroads. My future depended on the road I would
take, but which was the right one to choose?

Most of my friends in Tamak thought that I was overly fearful
and urged me not to let the lucky chance slip by. I knew that they
wished me well, even though they failed to fully grasp the potential dangers involved.

Sasha, who had legal experience in army matters, analyzed all
points. "You can't circumvent the officer's commission. What
worries me even more, however, is that sooner or later they'll
offer you Soviet citizenship; and if you refuse their 'friendly'
gesture, you'll be in trouble." When I told him that Ryabov had
in fact made that proposal and that I had somehow gotten out of
it unharmed, he said, "You may not be that lucky next time."

Reb Mendel with his Talmudic acumen formulated my problem succinctly when he reminded me of the Rabbinic metaphor
about the bee—"I want neither your honey nor your stings."

Meanwhile, the days passed in agonizing indecision. Inside me
two antagonists carried on a running battle. One argued sarcastically—"You're too cowardly to take a risk and would rather
have your family go on suffering in Tamak." The other would
retort cooly—"That is still better than winding up in a Siberian
labor camp."

Once, when I was working in the field, the sarcastic one grinned at me—"Having trouble with your back again? Remember your last year's hospitalization? Just look at the nasty blisters on your hands. It serves you right! If you were not such a fool, you'd be in Chelyabinsk by now." Fearing lest I eventually succumb to his shrewd persuasions, I decided not to wait the few more days I still had to make up my mind. I interrupted my work and hurried to cable Okun that I could not accept the position. I did it with a heavy heart and still went on brooding over whether I had chosen the right road. But the agony of indecision was over, and I felt great relief.

* * *

I started to look around for a job. Riva knew well one of the directors of the factory where Volodya worked. She spoke to him, and I went to see him. He was willing to give me a position. In the evening I dropped in on the Orshovskys to tell Riva about my meeting with the director. When Volodya came home, he ate his supper in silence, listening gloomily to our conversation. It did not strike me as peculiar—he would often be taciturn and withdrawn. As I was leaving, he suddenly said, "Tomorrow is my day off. Would you like to go fishing?" I gladly agreed.

At the crack of dawn we met at the usual street corner and set out on the six-mile walk to the Belaya. We strode silently along the empty streets. When we reached the dirt road outside the town, Volodya looked around warily. Thinking that somebody was following us, I too turned my head; but there was no human being in sight. I glanced at him questioningly. He shook his head. "You don't know the elementary rules of self-preservation. Stalin's eyes and ears are everywhere. You tell everybody, even in the presence of my children, about your experiences in the POW camp. Your lack of caution will yet get you in trouble." After a while he continued. "Believe me, I'm talking from my own experience," and he began telling me about his past activities in the Jewish Self-Defense organization and the Zionist underground after the Revolution. I had never seen him so talkative. He related episodes that he had never mentioned before, even in our intimate talks during the night watches in the potato field the previous summer.

At the time of his brother's arrest, Volodya lived in hiding with a group of Halutzim, always one step ahead of the secret police. They made repeated attempts to cross the Rumanian border, but each time they were surprised by a Soviet border patrol.

His description of their last attempt was very moving. When they began swimming across the river in the dark of night, the border guards suddenly opened fire. One Halutz was killed, several were severely wounded and then captured. The others managed to escape. Volodya too was wounded in the shoulder. He barely escaped and lay hidden in a barn loft in the village for three months until his wound healed. In the meantime some of his friends finally succeeded in crossing the border, and they went to Palestine. Others gave up trying and dispersed to bide their time in the underground.

The feeling of guilt for Misha's arrest seemed to weigh heavily on Volodya's conscience. He had always avoided talking about it. Now, however, he suddenly said, "It is not so easy to live with a false identity. In the beginning I would not respond to the name Misha. Sometimes I used to forget and introduced myself as Volodya. Fearing lest I'd be unmasked, I moved from place to place frequently."

He was absorbed in his thoughts and sighed. "Misha's languishing in a labor camp for my 'sins' tormented me day and night, and I often wanted to give myself up. But I realized that this would not free him but rather bring calamity on the entire family. When I learned about his 'drowning' I nearly went out of my mind and thought of ending my life too."

Volodya spoke at length about his ordeals over the years. Some of what he told me I had already heard before—without his knowing of it—from Riva and his mother. Most of the things, however, were new to me and gave me a deeper insight into the agonized heart of this present-day Marrano, one of the countless Jewish victims of the Red Inquisition in the Soviet Union. I also understood better now why he had been so alarmed when he learned about my correspondence with Misha.

As we approached the Belaya and noticed the anglers on the shore, he fell silent. We did our fishing and then started out on our way home. When we were at a safe distance from the river,

Volodya once again looked around cautiously and began in a low voice—"You know, I actually did not intend to go fishing today, but I wanted to talk to you alone. Believe me, I'm your friend. You must not take the position in our plant. We manufacture tanks and ammunition. The NKVD will check up on you thoroughly, and when they find out that you're a foreigner, you'll be in hot water. Moreover, you might get me and our family in trouble, too."

I realized that his deep fear made him see the shadows of mountains as mountains, but I did not want to exacerbate his inner agony. "Don't worry; I won't accept the job," I said. He showed great relief and asked me not to tell Riva or his mother about our talk.

The conversation with Volodya, however, left me in a dilemma—the job in the director's office seemed satisfactory, and I had agreed to take it. Now, I had suddenly to think up some excuse for changing my mind. But Riva could not be fooled.

"It it because of Volodya?" she said.

"You guessed it, but please don't make an issue of it."

SIX

The battle at Kursk kept everybody in suspense. On July 12 the Red Army turned the tables on Hitler and went over to the counteroffensive on a wide front. The Germans were routed, and vast regions were liberated. The events caused a joyous stir, especially among those refugees whose home towns were freed. They immediately sent letters and telegrams to relatives and friends who had stayed at home. However, the days passed and there were no answers. Alas, little by little, the bitter truth came out. There was nobody left to reply; the Germans had massacred all the Jews in the occupied areas.

The authorities did not allow the refugees to return to the freed regions. Many of them, however, found a way and set out on their journeys home. It was encouraging to see the stream of evacuation turn in the opposite direction.

July 24 was a happy day—our new Czechoslovak passport finally arrived. True, I had no illusions that it would serve as a talisman against the NKVD; for there was practically no foolproof protection from their clutches. Nevertheless, I hoped—or rather wanted to hope—that it would give us some protection in case of trouble.

At the end of the month Sasha received permission to return to Moscow. He was elated. "Things are looking up. The government institutions have started to move back to Moscow. I'm sure the political climate will change after the war; we're going to have more freedom. Let us keep in touch." I was naturally glad for the Levins and Valeria that their tribulations in Tamak were over. Yet, I also felt sadness as I said farewell to them the next day. My friendship with Sasha was very close, and I missed him greatly later on.

Still sadder was my experience about two weeks later when Reb Mendel left. His departure did not come as a surprise. In June he had told me, "My doctor warns me that I could hardly survive another Ural winter. I plan to move to my older daughter's in Central Asia before the arrival of the cold weather." Recalling how much he had suffered from asthma in the winter, I did not try to dissuade him from leaving.

I was not surprised to see so many people come to say their goodbyes to Menikhes. For he was a steadfast beacon of spiritual guidance to those blown by the war to that Ural backwater. His untiring efforts to create some semblance of Jewish communal life in town gave inspiration to many. I sensed sadly that all of it would fade away after his departure. Who was going to raise funds to maintain the cemetery and to help the sick and needy among the refugees, to organize a *minyan* on a *yahrzeit* or the holidays?

To me, however, his leaving meant even more—the loss of a dear personal friend to whom I felt deep attachment. The ties between us were very close, and they had helped me overcome many a difficult situation. Shortly before the arrival of the train Reb Mendel called me aside and said, pensively, "God knows if we'll see each other again. I have grown attached to you like to a son. Be careful and return home safely. You must tell the Jews in the free world about our plight in this country." I saw tears in his eyes and felt my eyes, too, getting moist.

* * *

About mid-August I went through a traumatic experience. One day, when I came home in the evening, Ida told me that an NKVD plainclothesman had been looking for me; he wanted me to be in his office the first thing in the morning. She was in a state of despair. "Let us leave everything and go at once to the station. We still have the round-trip tickets for Orenburg."

Although, of course, I was very alarmed myself, I tried to calm her. "Running away won't help; they'll find us before too long wherever we may be. Besides," I added, although hardly believing what I was saying, "if they want to arrest somebody they don't come in the daytime but during their 'working hours' after midnight."

I did not sleep all night, racking my brains to guess my "crime." My correspondence and packages from abroad? My selling a piece of American soap in the market occasionally? My visit at the Polish *Delegatura*? Or perhaps, it occurred to me, that I had no job?

Only those who passed through the gates of the Gestapo or NKVD hell can appreciate the trepidation I experienced as I went early next morning to the NKVD District Headquarters. I entered the building and walked, my heart pounding rapidly, to the indicated room.

The NKVD official, his face drawn and unsmiling, began asking me questions about my work at the Military College. I soon realized that he was familiar with my background and that he also knew that I was from Czechoslovakia. I tried to appear composed, but my inner tension was unbearable. Then he suddenly asked, "Do you know Dolgikh?"

Failing at first to grasp what he was driving at, I replied noncommittally. "I do; he was my superior before my dismissal from the school."

"This is not what I'd like to know. I mean, what kind of person is he? Can you describe his behavior to you and to the other people around him?" he said, while pulling a few sheets of paper out of his thick file and handing them to me.

I read them through quickly. First was the *politkomissar*'s report about his meeting with Valeria, Varya and me. Then came Tsitron's lengthy deposition. There was also a handwritten note from a man whose name was unfamiliar to me; I surmised that he was the friend to whom Sasha had spoken about Dolgikh.

"Would you like to add something to these statements?" the official said when I finished reading. I felt now a little bit more at ease and gave him a detailed description of Dolgikh's anti-Semitic remarks and intrigues. "His conduct and actions were hardly becoming for an officer of the Red Army," I concluded.

The NKVD man made no comment; the frozen expression on his face remained unchanged throughout the interrogation. I heaved a sigh of relief when I left his office. Knowing that Ida was waiting on tenterhooks, I hurried to the *Dyetdom* to tell her what it was about.

Everybody knew the cardinal rule that one had to keep silent about his visit to the NKVD. I wondered why the official had not warned me about it—was it merely an oversight or did he assume that it was not necessary to state the obvious? However, I felt that I must talk to Tsitron and went to him at once.

I was very dismayed over my involvement in an NKVD investigation. "There's no reason for fear," Tsitron said. "We only started the ball rolling, but many other people at the VU have complained to the NKVD about Dolgikh, and as soon as his home town was freed, they began to make inquiries about his background. Some surprising facts, far worse than his anti-Semitism, have come to light. I'm not at liberty, however, to talk about it at the present."

* * *

Despite Tsitron's assuagement of my fears, I was worried over my coming to the attention of the NKVD and deemed it prudent to find a job as soon as possible. The opportunity came unexpectedly a few days later. One evening Aleksandr, Reb Mendel's son-in-law, dropped in to tell me that the supervisor of the tenement houses and dormitories at the Ishimbay Oil Trust, an evacuee from Kharkov, was returning home. Aleksandr had spoken to the director of maintenance, and he agreed to hire me.

It certainly was not the kind of work I wanted. But I was anxious to take any job and started to work the next day. The few hundred inflationary rubles a month did not mean much.

But my daily bread ration now increased by 200 grams, and I was also given one soup a day in the Trust *stolovaya*.

I did not have the faintest notion how to handle the job. My predecessor comforted me. "Don't worry. Neither had I when I started two years ago; I'm a librarian. Just use common sense and you'll manage." He took me around to take inventory. In many apartments the furnishings, which all belonged to the Oil Trust, were missing, and I witnessed embarrassing scenes between the librarian and the tenants, mostly refugees. They were hungry and would sell a piece of furniture from time to time on the black market at a high price and report it as "stolen." The Trust used to replace the object and deduct its cost, according to the low state-price scale, from the tenant's paycheck.

Eventually, however, the Trust ran out of supplies and could not keep abreast of the thefts. They then became very strict about it—a second theft usually resulted in the eviction of the tenant. "If you want to survive in this job, you have to be callous. I have learned to remain unmoved even by the tears of a woman tenant," the mild middle-aged librarian said with a sad smile.

Anyway, his bits of information and advice proved to be very helpful to me later on. Work was tedious and unpleasant. Thanks to the Soviet lack of efficiency it was difficult to get a repairman from the maintenance office. I was also often called in the middle of the night to take care of an emergency.

The director offered me the vacated room of my predecessor. I suspected that he was less interested in my comfort than in having me close at hand to be available day and night. Nevertheless, it was hard to withstand the tempting offer of living in a spacious room with gas and electricity, running hot water, an indoor toilet and, above all, central heating. The approach of the cold season made my dilemma even harder. But I was not enthusiastic about the job and hoped that, eventually, something better would turn up. In that case, I reasoned, I would have forfeited my right to the dingy kitchen and would be unable to find a place to live.

August was over, and the Ural summer came to an end. In the beginning of September the long-awaited package from America arrived. Our potatoes were harvested, and the yield was somewhat larger than in the previous year. I figured out that the sale of the potatoes and the contents of the package could bring the 20,000 rubles needed in Orenburg, and I began making plans for our departure. Alas, our hopes were dashed. A few days later I got a letter from Gelbman that he and Sperling as well as his friend in the *Delegatura* had left with a group of refugees for Central Asia.

I mused sadly about my futile attempts during the summer to get away from the suffering in Tamak. I felt helpless and resigned myself to fate. The chilly whiff of fall was in the air already, and there was no choice but to dig in for a third long winter in Tamak.

SEVEN

How often did I hear from communists the same simplistic explanation for even the most typical shortcomings of the Soviet economic system—"They are merely 'survivals of capitalism' and will disappear soon." Yet these defects were inherent in the very nature of the system and created corruption and demoralization at all levels, which generated more and more anomalies.

The most conspicuous was the sad fact that very few people could live on their wages, so that even the most honest person had to resort to means that were against his conscience. An incident, although trivial in itself, may help to illustrate the point.

Shortly after the arrival of our package I went to Galya to give her a cake of American soap as a present. Her family was in a tight pinch then. Their food rations from the factory had been discontinued, and they had to barter their belongings for food. Yakov and Sima, who had experienced many hardships in life, took it in stride. Galya, however, used to the comfort and privileges that came with Yevsey's high position, took it very hard. Yet she could do little about it; the money Yevsey sent could not buy much in the market.

I was very close with the family, and we chatted about our common worries. Then Galya said, "I won't barter the last shirt off my shoulders. I'm going to produce soap and sell it."

"You mean to open a soap factory? Private enterprise is forbidden in the Soviet Union," Yakov joked.

She replied, indignantly, "If they have stopped providing Yevsey's family with food despite the important service he gives them, they can't prevent me from doing it. Besides," she went on philosophizing, "why shouldn't I be allowed to sell the soap I make at home? Isn't it my private property, exactly like the clothes that I barter away?" And then, fingering the piece of American soap, she turned to me, "Can you tell me how your damned capitalists make this stuff?"

Galya was the last person from whom I would have expected such heretical talk, and believing she was merely joking I told her half-jestingly, "Of course I can; I have plenty of experience in this line. While working my way through college in Prague I tutored the son of a soap manufacturer. Occasionally, I accompanied my student to their factory."

I then described how fascinated I was especially by Karlíček, the elderly Czech foreman who called everybody, including the factory owner, by his first name. He would walk importantly from one huge kettle to the other, ladle some of the bubbling soap brew into a big glass tube and examine it carefully. From time to time he would, with the mysterious expression of a Faustian alchemist on his face, put some chemicals into the boiling mass.

She listened to me and then said, "You better stop joking. If you had learned from Karlíček what chemical ingredients and formulas he used, it would be more helpful for your survival now than your university degrees."

Galya had a degree in chemistry and went at it methodically. In the coming days she made analytical tests of the American soap. Then, however, came the most difficult part—obtaining the necessary material and chemicals. I introduced her to Akhmadulin, who knew his way around the plants, and, after much seeking, he got her some.

It was interesting to watch the pampered young woman, a *babushka* tied under her chin, cook the first pot of soap. Seeing the intense expression on her face as she stirred the boiling brew with a broomstick and now and then added some ingredients, I was reminded of Goethe's description of the witches' Walpurgis Night on the Brocken.

Galya had the best intentions to produce toilet soap. What

came out, however, was a coarse mass with a nondescript smell. It lathered very poorly and hardly qualified even as laundry soap. Nevertheless, thanks to the chronic shortage of soap, it sold like hotcakes when Yakov and Sima took it to the market.

To make a long story short, Galya boiled up more pots of soap in the following weeks, and each time it had a different look and smell. But business was brisk. Then Yevsey came for a visit unexpectedly. When he learned about his family's soap trade, he was very upset, and Galya had to promise him that from then on she would produce soap only for their own household.

*　*　*

In September Dr. Hornfeld left for the front unexpectedly. He was a refugee from Riga and came to Tamak with his wife and child shortly after our arrival. Although hardly 30, he soon established himself as a successful surgeon at the City Hospital. We had eventually become friends, and I was very sorry to see him leave. I was mystified by his hush-hush departure, but he was reluctant to talk about it and merely remarked laconically as we said goodbye—"I'll explain it to you when we meet after the war."

However, I learned the answer to the puzzle later from his wife. He was a victim of the unenviable status of the medical profession in the Soviet Union. A physician was not allowed to have a private practice. He was merely an employee of the state, and his salary was small. (This was another striking anomaly of Soviet life. Small wonder, then, that young men preferred the fields of engineering, industrial management, etc., where the pay was much higher. Already about half of the medical students were women; today, they have surpassed the three-quarter mark.)

Unable to live on his salary, a doctor had to find an additional medical job or have private patients on the side. Dr. Hornfeld had private patients. Some time before his departure he was suddenly called to the NKVD. When he went there, he was accused of having private patients. He was surprised. For the authorities, as in other matters where they had to accept the facts of reality, usually closed their eyes to those "transgressions." But he was in for a worse shock—after a while the NKVD man began to interrogate him about his studies in Switzerland. He tried in vain to explain that he had been forced to study medicine abroad because of the anti-Jewish discrimination in fascist Latvia. From the tone of the accusation he sensed that it smacked of a most horrible crime in the eyes of the Soviet regime, namely foreign contacts, which might entail grave consequences. Luckily, some of his private patients were high Party officials, and thanks to their intercession he was not sent to a labor camp but given the choice of going immediately to the front.

"I don't know for sure who informed the NKVD," said Mrs. Hornfeld. "But I suspect that it was a Bashkir woman doctor from the hospital to whom he once mentioned his Swiss diploma. She probably did it out of envy of his superior medical knowledge and success in the hospital."

* * *

The cold rains with the consequent deep mud dragged on. It was much the same as in the previous falls, only that this time it made my misery even worse. My work entailed long walks to the suburbs, and I used to return home shivering with cold, my threadbare clothes soaking wet and covered all over with slime.

On October 19 came the sad news about Ryabov's death at the front. I went at once to pay my condolences to his bereaved family. His widow, a kind woman of peasant stock, spoke with a stoic calm about her late husband. "You know how much Vasily dreamed about going back to Riga. In his last letter he wrote that the division he commanded was advancing fast in the Baltic direction. Alas, his hope of reaching Riga was not fulfilled. Well, at least his death was swift and he didn't suffer."

I saw in Ryabov the epitome of the better side of the Russian character. His friendship to me was genuine. He helped me unselfishly in times of distress, and I owe him so much for our survival in Russia. I mourned his death and cherish his memory to this day.

* * *

Dnepropetrovsk was liberated on October 25. Galya and her parents were happy and reminisced about their home town.

"If only Yevsey were here; he would find some way to get us home soon," Galya said.

"That would not be easy even for him," Yakov remarked sadly. "Besides, God knows what we are going to find there."

I knew that he was thinking about the tens of thousands of Jews in Dnepropetrovsk, once a great Jewish community with many famous leaders in Zionism and other Jewish fields who were annihilated by the Germans and their willing Ukrainian helpers.

I did not have a chance to see Yevsey a few days later, when he stopped over for several hours between flights on his way to Kuybyshev. Yakov told me that he had been summoned suddenly to the Komissariat of Heavy Industry. Yevsey did not know what it was about, but he suspected that he was to be given some new important assignment. His family waited anxiously to hear from him.

November brought more worries and also some exciting events. One evening Tsitron dropped in unexpectedly. He looked very agitated and whispered as soon as he entered, "Dolgikh was picked up by the NKVD last night!"

"At last! I already gave up hope that it would ever happen," I exclaimed.

"Oh no. You can depend on the NKVD. Sometimes it takes them longer, but they usually do a thorough job," he smiled. "Now I can tell you the surprising facts they have found out. Dolgikh was an officer in the White Guards and fought against the Reds in the civil war. After the final victory of the Bolsheviks he changed his name, using the papers he took from a fallen Red officer, and lay low for some time. Then he managed somehow to join the Red Army."

I lay awake for a very long time, thinking about the unexpected ending of the Dolgikh affair and hoping that I would not be bothered anymore by the NKVD. In my head ran the sage saying "Rejoice not when your enemy falls . . ." (Proverbs 24:17). Nonetheless, I could not help feeling satisfaction that well-deserved retribution was finally meted out.

EIGHT

Toward the end of October one of my wounds suddenly began to suppurate again. The last straw was probably my job, which turned out to be much more strenuous than I had expected. Riva sent me to Dr. Veksler, a refugee from Odessa who worked at the hospital. He examined my back and advised me to stay there for treatment for a week or so. I knew that he was right. Fearing, however, that it might turn into a protracted hospitalization, I had to reject his advice. He drained some fluid from my spine and bandaged me up, and in the following weeks I once again experienced the ordeal of going to the hospital for torturous fluid drainings and treatment. I had to make superhuman efforts to carry on my work in order to win the struggle for the survival of my family.

It was in the midst of these difficulties that I had a grim experience on my job. Upon the outbreak of the war all the Germans of the so-called Volga German Autonomous Republic were deported to Siberia and kept in detention camps. (The Soviets had good reasons to distrust them because of the acts of sabotage and espionage that apparently had occurred in that republic.) Shortly after starting my job at the Oil Trust, about 200 Volga Germans were brought to work there from a camp. They were housed in a large shed, which was converted into a dormitory of sorts, and I had to take care of it. It lay several miles away on the outskirts, and the long walks there made my work still harder. At first I entered the shed with a strange feeling, but I had to get used to it.

One morning when I went there for my usual inspection, I beheld a horrible sight in one of the rooms—a man was hanging from a rope fastened to a hook in the ceiling. I was petrified. After a moment, however, I pulled myself together and cut the rope with my penknife. I tried to revive him, but he did not stir at all. I ran through all the rooms to find somebody to help me, but there was nobody in the building; all the detainees were at work.

I rushed outside and waded with difficulty through the deep snow to a tool shop across the field. "A man is dying, come to help him," I called out as I entered. Two workers came along with me. When the older one took a look at the man, he said curtly, "You could have saved us and yourself the trouble. Can't you see that the 'Fritz' has been dead for a long time?"

All I could do now was go to the maintenance director and tell him what had happened. The militia investigation showed that the German had reported sick in the morning, apparently in order to remain in the shed alone and carry out his suicide.

The sight of the hanged German haunted me as I was walking home through the *purga* in the dark of evening. Was it the despondency over his deportation that made him do it? But I told myself that his ordeal was nothing in comparison to the untold suffering that his "master race" had inflicted on us Jews. Before my inner eye appeared the horrible scenes of Jewish mass graves, about which the refugees who had returned to their freed home towns had written to Tamak.

That night my sleep was disturbed by a weird nightmare—I was alone in a huge building with many hanged men dangling on ropes from the ceiling, and then I was standing amidst endless rows of open mass graves filled with massacred Jewish men, women and children. In their motionless, horror-stricken eyes I could still read the question they had directed to Heaven in their last moments—"Why?! Why?!" I woke up bathed in cold sweat and seemed to hear the question reverberating in the howling of the snowstorm outside.

* * *

In that period Osip was in a predicament similar to mine. His hopes of leaving Tamak were dashed also. Planning to expand the Ishimbay oil output, the authorities did not allow the Caucasian oil workers to return home. The impractical intellectual that he was, he also had a hard time keeping above water.

When I told him about my experience with the hanged German, he said, "There is a chance to get rid of your job; a colleague of mine in the Mathematics department is going to leave for the army. I think you can get his position." He went with me to his school principal; he was willing to hire me. But it was not a simple matter to be released from my job. In the land of socialism one may not quit his job; he can only be fired. In order to persuade my boss to let me go, I had to bring a statement from Dr. Veksler to the effect that my ailing back did not allow me to walk around much.

Though my salary and daily bread ration were smaller now, and I forfeited the privilege of the daily soup in the *stolovaya*, I was glad to return to teaching. I brushed up on my mathematics, and the principal seemed to be satisfied with my work.

Before that, my teaching in the Soviet Union had been on the college level only. Now, however, I got to know the teenage groups, and it was an interesting experience. During my sojourn in Russia I had ample chance to observe both the positive and negative aspects of Soviet education. The lack of space here prevents me from sharing my impressions with the reader. I'd like, though, to tell in brief about the type of school I taught at then—the Vocational Training School of the Oil Trust.

The emphasis on the middle-school level in general was on the productivity of the youth and industrialization. Therefore, apart from the various public trade schools, every large plant had its own industrial school to train cadres of skilled workers. Our school had about 400 boys, aged 13 to 17, who got free room and board in a dormitory, stipends and other fringe benefits from the Oil Trust. In the first two years the student occupied himself only with classes and homework. After that he started to work in the plant three hours a day; the rest of his working time he spent in theoretical instruction in his specialty. At 18 he was put in the plant on the same footing as an adult worker.

The student body was a colorful ethnic mixture. About one-half were refugees. Under normal circumstances few of them, because of their intellectual level, would have attended an industrial school, but the difficult economic situation prompted their parents to send them there. This category of students usually showed little interest in their work and often presented discipline problems.

On the other hand, the students from the indigenous nationalities caused problems of another sort. Many of them hardly understood Russian and were unable to keep up with the class. And their behavior and etiquette in general also left much to be desired. Once as I stood with Osip reading an announcement on the school billboard, a bunch of Bashkir students from

Osip's class passed by. One of them jostled him and exclaimed, "Learning to read, teach? Just try hard and you may become literate." And then he and his pals burst into laughter. It was exacting work and not easy at all. But it was still better than the constant walking outdoors in the bitter frost and snowstorms of my previous job.

* * *

I used to buy our daily bread rations in an Oil Trust store near the school. The manager, Anton, was a "landsman" of Osip, and they lived in the same building. On his way to work Osip would give him his and my ration coupons, and after classes we picked up our bread. This way we avoided standing in line for hours.

In this store bread was the only thing one could get. There was at the Oil Trust another store where all ration coupons were honored, but it was inaccessible to plain mortals—it was reserved only for high-echelon management personnel and select specialists. In our store they would only very seldom, usually before a national holiday, issue a piece of frozen fish, a jar of pickled cucumbers or suchlike.

Once in a blue moon, if I chanced to come to our store before the small supply was gone, I could buy a few needles, a wick for a kerosene lamp or some other trifle. Having learned the way of Soviet life the hard way, I knew by now the basic rule—Buy anything that is on sale, regardless of whether or not you need it; for you would always be able to barter it for food.

One November afternoon I noticed in the back of the store a box with ladies' summer gloves. Summer gloves for the winter? I mused. But I should not have been surprised at this anomaly in Soviet commerce. I remember how baffled I was at first when on a sultry summer day I saw cotton-padded pants offered for sale but not a single piece of summer wear; and then later in the wintertime there would appear on the shelves straw hats and swimming trunks and no trace of winter clothes.

Anton sold me five pairs of gloves. I walked home happy with this rare stroke of luck. In the evening, however, I saw that all the gloves were for the left hand. Assuming that Anton made a mistake, I brought them back to him the next day to get the right hand gloves. To my great surprise, however, I learned from him something new in the Soviet system of distribution. "In order to reduce thefts," he explained, "the factories ship only one of any paired items—like footwear, gloves, etc.—either lefts only or rights only. This time you got the left hand ones; in the next shipment you'll get the matching right hand ones."

But the other shipment never arrived. Thanks to the "efficiency" of the Soviet supply system it was probably sent to some other store in the Urals or Siberia where the right-hand gloves, like their left-hand counterparts in Tamak, remained lying useless.

* * *

The epidemic diseases among the refugees, triggered by the long rains and nasty swamps, took their toll, and many refugees died. There were cases of typhus in the *Dyetdom* too. One day Raphi became sick. He developed a high fever, and Riva told us to take him to the hospital. We went through a frightful time. Fortunately, the typhus alarm proved to be false, and he was discharged ten days later.

As if to make the measure of suffering full, Ida too fell ill and was bedridden for a number of days so that I had to take Raphi to the *Dyetdom* in the morning and then pick him up after work. We had had similar experiences in the previous winters, and I did my best to go on. But this time all of this combined with my heavy work load wore me down completely. My hope that we would manage to pull through the winter somehow faded with each passing day; I felt that my stamina was at an end, that I could not carry on much longer.

Looking at it in retrospect, I realize that it was this dead-end situation that prompted me to attempt something that can be termed, at best, as sheer frivolity.

9

Exodus from Tamak

ONE

ONE EVENING IN November Straus dropped in unexpectedly. "I have brought you something very interesting," he said, handing me a clipping from an army newspaper. I read it; it was a writeup about the Czechoslovak Military Unit formed in Russia, and it described mainly the Unit's feats at the front. Knowing that even the location of a railroad bridge, for instance, was considered a military secret, I was surprised at the mention of the town, Buzuluk, in the Orenburg Province, where the Unit had its base (I also recalled that Gottwald had refused to give me the address of the Unit).

Straus was in a dismal mood. "Recent rumor has it that the VU is to remain in Tamak for good; I'll hardly ever see my family again," he sighed. I felt sorry for him and for myself also. True, after Ryabov's death my prospects of returning to the VU became slim. Nevertheless, a faint spark of hope still glimmered. Had not Glinka promised to rehire me later? Now, however, even the dim hope of leaving Tamak with the VU was gone.

The article stirred memories of Czechoslovakia, of a life that seemed to be a distant dream by now. I saw that Ida too was excited. "The best thing for us would be to get to the Czech Unit," I said. "If Muleyev were still here"—he had left for the front some weeks before—"he could have gotten us railroad tickets. Now, however, I'll have to ask the *voyenkomat* (military registration office) to help us."

Ida cast a surprised look at me. Straus was thoughtful a while and then said, "You'd better be careful. Once you come under

304

the *voyenkomat's* jurisdiction, they might send you off alone, not giving a damn if your family is left here to perish."

I hardly slept that night, pondering what to do. In the morning I went to the *voyenkomat*. I finally managed to see the head of the office, a lean, gray-haired major. Handing him the newspaper clipping, I began to tell him what I wanted, but he interrupted me. "A Czechoslovak? You fellows gave us a good thrashing in the civil war." (He meant, of course, the Czech Legions that had fought at the Russian front in World War I. After the Bolshevik Revolution the Legions set out on a unique military venture, fighting their way eastward through war-torn Russia and Siberia to the Pacific Ocean and from there went home by ship.)

The major related his experiences in the skirmishes of the Reds with the Czech Legions that held sway over vast stretches of territory in European Russia and in Siberia along the railroad lines. (I glanced at his maimed hand and wondered whether it was the result of one of those encounters.) He spoke with emotion; it apparently triggered off memories in him. There was, however, no bitterness in his words, but rather respect for the military prowess of the Czechs.

His stories were interesting. But I was anxious to present my request, and when I had a chance to put a word in I said, "Please help me and my family get to the Czech Military Unit," adding jestingly: "Rest assured that this time the Czechs won't leave via the Urals and Siberia, but will proceed westward shoulder to shoulder with the victorious Red Army."

There was a faint smile on the major's face. "Your request is somewhat unusual. Why don't you go alone? We'll take good care of your wife and child here."

"No. I could not leave without them," I replied emphatically.

He thought a moment and then said, "Let me look into it; come back in three days."

When I came back, he told me that my request had been approved, and he sent me to the medical commission. "Just a routine procedure," he remarked. Recalling, however, Straus's warning about getting under Soviet military jurisdiction, I became apprehensive. Yet I had no choice in the matter.

The doctor checked my eyes, ears and mouth; everything

seemed to be alright. Then he told me to undress. When he took a look at my back, however, he did not even bother to use his stethoscope; he merely felt my swollen calves and called out to the other commission members—"Rejected!" When I tried to argue that my back ailment was only temporary and that it would pass before long, he remarked sarcastically, "I'd advise you to go to the hospital rather than into the army."

I left the *voyenkomat* deeply disappointed—that avenue of escape from the misery of Tamak was cut off. But I did not give up. I knew one of the ticket clerks at the railroad station from whom Muleyev used to get a ticket for me whenever I needed one. I told him my predicament. The elderly Bashkir listened to me and said, "I can sell you the tickets, but you'll hardly get to the Czech Unit. You have to travel on the main Trans-Siberian artery, and without an official *komandirovka* they'll simply throw you off the train at some station. It is too risky now in the winter, especially with a small child; you might get stuck somewhere and perish. You'd better wait for warmer weather."

I realized that he was right. There was no choice but to return to the daily grind. The struggle for sheer survival became harder every day. The prices of food kept soaring. We had bartered away practically the entire American package by now and also most of our own things. I was at my wits' end.

* * *

On the forthcoming market day of the Umnovs I went to see Glasha and told her my woes. "Come with me to Tishina today, and we'll help you buy some produce at a reasonable price," she said. I gladly accepted her suggestion, but I had very little money left. I got from Yakov several cakes of their homemade soap and sold some badly needed pieces of our clothing and set out on the 25-mile ride in the kolkhoz sleigh.

The beauty of the winter scenery captivated me, despite the bitter cold. The trees on the wooded hills, as if wrapped in white prayer shawls, stood in silent devotion. The bushes along the road were coated with ice crystals that reflected the oblique rays of the frozen December sun. Now and then a hare, frightened by the approaching vehicle, jumped from behind a bush and dashed off like an arrow.

We arrived in Tishina toward dusk. Umnov was pleasantly surprised by my unexpected visit. I was glad to see him walking without a cane now. Since Dunia was visiting her in-laws that day, Glasha went with me to their friends to help do the bartering.

I chatted with the Umnovs until late in the evening. They too had their share of trouble; their son had been reported missing in action some months before and had not been heard from since. Once again I had a chance to observe Umnov's unfaltering faith in God. Glasha was tormented by anxiety, but he exhorted her, "The Lord is merciful and will keep our son alive."

The kolkhoz sleigh picked me up before dawn. The temperature outside was around 50 below zero. My fellow riders had sheepskins, but my worn clothing was hardly adequate to protect me from the bitter cold and icy wind that penetrated to the marrow of my bones. Nevertheless, I was warmed inside by the feeling that I was bringing home this small supply of dairy products and vegetables that would help us tide our child over the next few weeks.

TWO

On the eve of 1944 I reflected on the outgoing year. It looked pitiful indeed—a series of futile efforts to get out of Tamak. A few days earlier I had received a letter from Gelbman, and I sat down to answer him. He wrote about their hopeful prospects of leaving for Iran before long. I envied him and for a moment imagined myself being there too. But the snowstorm outside tore me out of my dreaming and brought me back to the sad reality. (As it happened, Gelbman and his family never managed to go to Iran. After the war they returned from Central Asia to Poland. In 1946 I met them unexpectedly in Czechoslovakia. After many tribulations they had finally succeeded in leaving Poland with the help of the *Bricha*—an underground railroad to rescue the surviving remnants of East European Jewry—and they were on their tortuous way to the Jewish Homeland.)

When I finished my writing, I put out the *koptilka* and went to bed, but I could not fall asleep. I lay thinking about what the coming year had in store. More of the same suffering? But how long would we be able to hold out, I asked myself sadly. I did not bother to guess where we would be a year from now.

The days of January were bleak, with nothing to look forward to. And then—a ray of hope! I believe that almost everybody, at one time or another, must have had a similar experience in his life. To me it happened on several occasions—call it the hand of Providence or blind Fate, if you wish. But when the horizon looked its darkest, there suddenly appeared a ray of hope from an unexpected source that changed the situation radically. It was then that the pendulum of events began swinging in the direction that marked our last chapter in Tamak and led eventually to our exodus from Russia.

After his last stopover in Tamak, Yevsey stayed in Kuybyshev. To the great surprise of his family he was evasive in his letters about the nature of his new assignment, intimating merely, "I'll tell you about it when I come home for New Year." But he did not come. Then, toward the end of January, he arrived unexpectedly. I was eager to see him and went to their place in the evening. Yevsey was not at home. Galya said cheerfully, "You can congratulate us; we are going back home soon."

Thinking she was joking, I said, "Has Hitler capitulated? Come on, pour the champagne!"

"It is too early for that toast," said Yakov, "but she is not kidding you."

I was pleasantly surprised to hear that Yevsey was to be sent to Dnepropetrovsk to rebuild his factory and to help in the reconstruction of the city's industry, which had been destroyed by the retreating Germans. He had come to Tamak to select from the factory a team of specialists he wanted to take along as soon as his reconstruction plan was approved by the *Komissariat*. As for his family, they were either to go with him to Dnepropetrovsk or to follow him shortly afterward.

Galya and her parents excitedly discussed their preparations for the trip. I was, of course, happy for them that their woes in Tamak would be over before long. Nevertheless, I could not help feeling sad about our own hopeless situation.

Yevsey came home late. We were happy to see each other, and we chatted a while. I learned from him a lot of news about current events. One of his observations was very interesting and proved to be prophetic: "The Soviet government has learned its lesson that the concentration of industry in the western regions made the country too vulnerable to a German attack. The evacuated factories will, therefore, remain where they are in order to create new industrial centers deeper in the hinterland, out of reach of potential invaders."

He asked me how things were with me. "Much has happened since we saw each other last," I said and started to tell him about my dismissal from the Military College. He showed great interest in the Dolgikh story.

"It is incredible that this could happen 25 years after the Revolution."

I then told him about my trips to Orenburg and Chelyabinsk and about my unsuccessful attempts to get to the Czech Unit.

He listened to me and then said with his compelling logic, "I'm afraid you are bound to be stuck in Tamak for good if you don't make some move. Why not leave together with my family? I can include you in our factory *komandirovka*. Buzuluk lies on the route of our travel, and you can get off there."

He paused and then continued. "In case the Czechoslovak Unit doesn't accept you, you'll come along to Dnepropetrovsk. I'll find you a position there. It is important for you to be closer to the western border. Before long the Red Army is going to pour across the frontier and there will be a chance for you to make your way home safely."

I thought I was dreaming. Could it really be true that our rescue from Tamak was in sight?! I felt tears welling up in my eyes.

We talked until very late. As I was about to leave, Yevsey said, "I don't know when all the necessary arrangements for our departure will be completed. It may take a month or so, but it could also be much sooner. I'd therefore advise you to begin your preparations immediately in order to be ready for the long journey on short notice.

It was already midnight when I walked home. The frozen moon cast a dim yellowish-gray light over the town and made it an eerie sight. The biting frost made my eyes tear, and the droplets on my lashes froze into fine ice crystals before I managed to wipe them off with my glove. But I hardly felt the bitter cold. I was warmed inwardly by the happy feeling that the way out of the vale of tears called Tamak was finally opened.

I woke Ida and whispered to her the glad tidings. But she hardly grasped what I was saying, muttered "yes, yes" and fell asleep again. I always envied her capacity for sound sleep. In those unhappy days it was good to be carried off on the wings of the angel of dreams to the happier past. For it was only the past that was left to dream about; the future was only a dark question mark.

* * *

The gray, wintry daybreak that glimmered faintly through the ice flowers on the window seemed brighter to me the next morning. When Ida woke up she said, "What was it you started telling me about Yevsey last night?" I smiled and retold the whole story. She was naturally happy, but after a moment she sighed, "Where will you get the money? How are we going to travel in this bitter cold?" She surely was right.

I too was tormented by the same questions. "We'll manage somehow; we have to," I replied.

We began to take stock of our clothes and other belongings. There was precious little left by now, and we needed each piece badly. But we made the painful decision to sell everything that was not absolutely indispensible for the journey. "At least we won't have to worry about traveling light," I mused sadly.

It was time to hurry to work, for in the meantime the crushing burden of daily life had to be carried on as usual. When my first class was over, I told Osip the good news. He was very glad for me. "Don't let this rare chance slip by," he urged. Among the other difficulties that lay ahead was also the problem of how to quit work, because leaving a job without permission was punishable by a term in a labor camp. "Don't worry now; we'll think of some plausible reason when we speak to the principal," Osip said as the bell called us to our next classes.

It was now a race against time to be ready when Yevsey returned. The sale of our things brought about 700 rubles. I calculated that after buying our train tickets I'd have only about 250 rubles left. But what about provisions for the trip?

To buy some substantial food for the money I had was out of

the question. All I was thinking of was *sukhari*. Anton agreed to sell me some bread under the table. The absolute minimum my family and I would need was 20 pounds, for which he wanted 900 rubles. It was cheaper than in the market. But what was the use? I did not have the money.

I racked my brains. There was only one choice left, and I made it with a heavy heart—to sell Ida's watch (mine had been sold long ago, shortly after our arrival in Tamak). Despite Akhmadulin's endeavors, however, the fine Swiss watch brought only 1,200 rubles. "The kolkhozniks seem to have acquired in barter plenty of watches from the evacuees," he explained.

Then Yakov with his sense for practicality came up with a suggestion. "Better let us buy flour together and bake the bread and then the *sukhari* ourselves." But flour was not available in the market, and once again Akhmadulin helped out. He sent us to an acquaintance of his who was an overseer in a mill. Yakov and I bargained hard, yet the overseer remained adamant, and we had to give him 1,800 rubles under the table for a *pud* (about 36 pounds) of flour.

Saturday evening I went with Ida to Galya's place, and all of us set to work. Yakov and I kneaded the dough under Sima's guidance, working hard until late in the night. Then the dough was put on the oven to leaven overnight. We returned early the next morning and work began again.

The baking of the *sukhari* reminded me of the baking of the Passover *matzot* in my youth. And the occasion was appropriate indeed—our exodus from the long suffering in Tamak.

We worked all through the day and the evening. Yakov's idea proved to be very practical. Our share of the grayish bread—the flour did not turn out to be exactly wheat as the overseer had assured us—was about 45 pounds and cost me much less than I would have had to pay Anton for the same quantity of gluey, tasteless black bread.

Fearing the temptation to nibble the *sukhari* before leaving Tamak, we left them in Sima's safekeeping. I went to sleep with the happy feeling that if Yevsey arrived unexpectedly, we could take off at once and survive the journey somehow on *sukhari* and *kipyatok*.

We all waited anxiously to hear from Yevsey. Around mid-

February a letter finally came. "I'll come as soon as everything is arranged here," he wrote laconically. Yakov suspected some unforeseen snag in the bureaucratic machinery of the Komissariat. To be truthful, despite my eagerness to leave I was rather glad for the delay. There was still much to be done before we could be prepared to leave. The most difficult problem I faced was our room. We had a few pieces of furniture and some household articles, most of it junk, hardly worthwhile bothering with in normal circumstances. But such were the conditions in the communist paradise that even this junk could bring some money in the *tolchok*.

The trouble, however, was that we needed everything until the day of our departure. And more importantly—what if we sold the furniture and our journey did not come off? In that case we would be left with an empty room. The only way to solve the dilemma was to find someone who would agree to buy our things for the privilege of taking over our room after we left. In our case, however, there loomed one huge obstacle—Nusia. She had long since gotten over her loss of "Uncle" and found solace with another "landsman" of hers. She did not, however, have him move in with her. He was merely a regular nocturnal visitor, and we got along somehow. However, she never gave up her claim to our room. I was therefore sure that if she should get wind of our leaving, she would do everything to prevent me from letting someone move into "her" kitchen.

THREE

At this time came the sad news of Reb Mendel's passing. I was deeply shaken. In his last letter to me a few weeks earlier he had written that he was feeling well.

I went to pay my condolences to Anna and Aleksandr. She told me that he had suffered a heart attack on February 14 and died the next day. We reminisced about him. I too mourned him genuinely. He was an unforgettable part of my experience in Tamak. Now he too became an indirect victim of the cruel war and found his eternal rest in Alma-Ata.

"I wonder if your father would have approved of my journey?" I said to Anna.

"I believe he would," she replied.

But somehow I could hear him say, "Don't undertake such a risky venture; stick it out in Tamak."

Then on my way home I recalled his last words to me at the station—"Return home safely to tell the Jews in the free world about our suffering in this country."

* * *

The solution to the problem with our room came about unexpectedly. Toward the end of February there was a letter from Mikhael (the last one I got from him in Tamak). I hurried to take it to the Orshovskys. When Esfir finished reading the letter, she said with tearful eyes, "God knows if I'll ever see Mikhael again."

Meaning to console her, I said, "The political climate will be different. . . ." But then I could not find it in my heart to tell her trite words that I did not believe myself, and I stopped.

But the old wise woman could not be fooled. As if reading my thoughts she sighed, "No. Nothing is going to change here after the war. And now that you're leaving, I probably won't even hear from my son again."

After a moment she continued, pensively. "I'd like Mikhael to have some heirloom from us. Can you get this to him?" she said, taking off her neck a thin golden chain with a locket. I felt a twinge in my heart as I opened the locket—it held a small faded photo of her and her late husband.

"I hope to give it to him in person and tell him all about you and your family," I replied.

She made me feel at home, as was always her wont, and said, "I have come to consider you and your family as part of our own family and will miss you very much. Do keep in touch with us in the future."

I carry in my heart to this very day the fondest memories of that wonderful family. No words would suffice to describe my gratitude to them for their unselfish help in times of hardship; and especially to Riva. For it was largely thanks to her untiring efforts that we were able to pull our son through his frequent illnesses and hospitalizations in Tamak. The sad story of the Orshovsky brothers—as supplemented by what I heard later in Israel from Mikhael about his ordeals in prison and in labor camp, and particularly his heroic escape—epitomizes the tragedy of Soviet Jewry. It is indeed stranger than fiction and deserves to be told in all its dramatic details. I hope to do so someday.

Riva came home as I was about to leave. "I ran into Yelizaveta Blikh today and told her about your room. She is interested. I meant to drop in on you soon and go together to talk with her, but since you're here, we might as well do it right away."

We started out, and she briefed me about Yelizaveta. Her husband fell at the front in 1942, and she and her old mother lived with a Bashkir family whom they paid with part of their bread rations for a dark room corner. "I think she is the proper candidate for your room. Even such an unscrupulous shrew as your Nusia would not dare to make trouble for a war widow. There is one thing though I want you to know. Yelizaveta can't afford to pay much for your things."

"Don't worry; I'll give her a price that is practically a giveaway," I said.

We spoke to Yelizaveta, and she came the next day to take a look at our room. She agreed to pay the 1,000 rubles I asked. I was happy that the last major obstacle in the way of our exodus from Tamak was overcome.

* * *

Yevsey arrived at long last on March 9. To our great surprise, however, the travel plan was changed. Instead of all of us going by train, Yevsey and most of his assistants flew to Dnepropetrovsk two days later. His family and mine and four men from his group were to leave by a factory truck on the morning of March 14. I was not too happy with the change. The train would have given Raphi more shelter from the cold. But I had no choice in the matter.

The release from my job was smoother than I expected. The principal, himself a refugee, understood my situation and even gave me a flattering letter of reference.

Only our closest friends knew about our leaving, and we said our goodbyes to them. We had lived through so many hardships together, and it was sad to realize that I would probably not see any of them again in my lifetime. Especially moving was the parting of Esfir and Riva from Raphi, whom they loved so much.

I hardly slept the night before our departure. What if something went wrong, I thought, and imagined the NKVD knocking on our door at any moment. Persecution mania? No; or not quite, at least. For I did have my bitter experience with the NKVD. The fear of them was deep in my bones and never left me until I got out of Russia.

I was awake before dawn. As soon as Nusia and her lover left, we got up, dressed in a hurry and bundled up our sleeping child. I waited on tenterhooks for Yelizaveta. The 1,000 rubles I was to get from her was practically all the money we would have for the journey. What if she changed her mind at the last moment? I drew a sigh of relief when she finally arrived.

Before leaving we sat down for a while, looking around the dismal kitchen in which we had experienced so much hunger and cold. We walked out of the house quietly lest some neighbor notice us. The temperature outside was below zero. We dragged on, Ida carrying Raphi and I with a burlap sack with our belongings and a rucksack that held special food for Raphi (all I could afford to buy was a dozen hard-boiled eggs, several bottles of milk, some melted butter and pot cheese).

The truck, with a tarpaulin roof above its walls, already stood in the yard of Galya's place when we arrived. Our four traveling companions busied themselves with the engine. Yakov and I loaded our things, and when Galya finished dressing her two children, we all got into the truck and pulled out.

We drove through the town. I took a last look at it; I still could not believe that we were leaving it for good. When we crossed the solidly frozen Sterla River, I gazed involuntarily at the cemetery. A heavy mist hovered over the eternal resting place of so many Jewish refugees and friends. My lips silently muttered thanks to God for helping us get out of Tamak alive.

Before long the last houses of Tamak disappeared. We drove on slowly through the deep snow on the slippery dirt road, and after some time we got on a highway leading south. The children woke up eventually and were given something to eat.

Toward noon we hit on a wayside *stolovaya* and stopped. Arkady, who was in charge of the truck, presented our official *komandirovka* and managed to get thin vegetable soup. We crumbled *sukhari* into it and gulped it down. Before resuming our drive Arkady suggested that we rearrange our luggage, which, anxious to start out early, we had loaded rather haphazardly, and there was then more room in the truck.

With the rearrangement, however, the practical Arkady had intended as well to camouflage the steel barrel of gasoline. It was our "iron ration," to be resorted to only in an emergency. Realizing later how extremely difficult it was to get gasoline at the gas stations, I understood why the barrel had to be out of sight of unwelcome eyes.

The truck wound its way slowly through the Ural hills. The dreamy wintry view of the scenery was enchanting. Before dusk we began looking for a place for the night. We came to a Bashkir village. At first the kolkhoz chairman was not impressed by our *komandirovka*. Only when Arkady lectured him about "Party discipline" and mentioned that he would complain to the Party secretary of the district did he relent and accommodate us in five different huts.

Our hosts were not hospitable at all. The three of us were put up on bare wooden benches without blankets, and we froze during the night. For that and a plate of buckwheat porridge for Raphi and *kipyatok* for us in the evening they were not ashamed to charge 100 rubles. The others had similar experiences.

We left early in the morning, but the gasoline began to run low. After repeated and vain attempts along the road, Arkady finally succeeded in buying some. Before noon we stopped at a *stolovaya*. All we could get there, however, was unsweetened tea of a nondescript taste. We drank it with *sukhari* and resumed our drive.

Later the scenery began to change. The rolling hills remained behind, and we were descending into a wide flatland. The snow became shallow, and large bare patches of brownish soil were visible, frozen and wrinkled like wrought iron. I felt the air getting gradually warmer. The Ural winter seemed to be loosening its grip.

* * *

We continued south in a nearly straight line, the Kazakhstan steppe stretching endlessly in all directions. The sun began sinking low; it was time to seek a place to sleep, but there were no villages in sight. Then we saw some huts to our right, and we headed there. It was a Kazakh cattle kolkhoz, and we were in for a strange experience, which is symptomatic of the "love" of the Asian peoples for their Russian conquerors. The elderly chairman, a tall man in a black sheepskin which he wore inside out, hardly spoke Russian. He did not even bother to look at our *komandirovka*. "*Naplevat!*" (I spit on it), he yelled and to demonstrate what he meant, he in fact spat in a wide arch. "No place in huts!" he grumbled.

Arkady then asked him to let us sleep in the hay in the loft of one of the kolkhoz stables, but he cast a hate-filled glance at us and shouted, "*Poshol von, Moskaly!*" (begone, Muscovites).

"The old man apparently fought in the Kazakhstan anti-Russian uprising of 1916 and seems to continue the fight," Arkady remarked as we left. We drove on, scouting the horizon in vain for a hamlet or at least a hut. Then we noticed a cluster of trees ahead of us. We were somewhat surprised; since reaching the steppe we had seen no woods, only sparse bushes and lonely trees here and there.

"We can't drive in the dark anyway. We might as well stop here," said Arkady as we came to the scanty grove. Dusk was falling. We all got busy gathering brushwood and lit a fire to warm up a little. Then we boiled *kipyatok* and had something to eat. The children were naturally thrilled with the campfire and did not want to hear of "going to bed." But it was getting late for them, and the women took them to the truck.

We kept the fire going. Yakov and our travel companions discussed the itinerary. Listening to their conversation I realized that Arkady knew what he was doing in heading south. It would have been extremely difficult to travel along the snowbound icy roads of the north. What would have happened, I thought with horror, if we had had to stay in the truck overnight there? To be sure, here too the cold was sharp at night. But it was a far cry from the below-zero Ural temperature. It was pitch-dark all around, not a single light far and wide; we were in the middle of nowhere. Then the moon sailed out, pouring out a pale silvery shine on the steppe. We sat around the fire and chatted until very late and then climbed into the truck and went to sleep.

We got up at dawn and started out immediately. Soon I beheld a fascinating sunrise—a red ball ascending in a blue cloudless sky, so different from the amber-colored sun in Tamak. Some time later the truck began to develop trouble and then stalled. Petya tinkered with the engine and started it again, but it was not running smoothly. "We'll have it checked in the next town ahead; it's only about 25 kilometers away," said Arkady.

When we reached the town, I found to my surprise that it was Orsk, where our former subtenants were. How very badly I could use the 1,250 rubles they owed me! But I did not bother to look for them; I knew that even if I managed to find them, they would not repay me even a single kopeck. We drove around for quite some time until we finally found a garage where they were willing to repair the truck. But they said that they could do it only the next morning. After greasing the manager's palm Arkady was promised that it would be done soon. However, by the time the truck was repaired, the sun was setting; it did not pay to resume our trip that day.

It was impossible to get a place for the night in that town; it was crowded with refugees. The only alternative left was the railroad station. We drove up there, but seeing the overcrowded waiting room, with people lying or sitting on the floor, our travel companions preferred to sleep in the truck. We, however, wanted the children to be in the warmth and decided to stay.

Galya and Ida with the children tried to find a place at the so-called "Children's Corner." Yet once again it was the same experience Ida had had so often before—"No vacancy!" We had no choice but to put up with sitting through the night on the floor, with the children lying in our laps. To me, of course, this was not new. I recalled the many nights I had spent at the station of Kazan and numerous other towns whose names I have long since forgotten.

In the morning we continued to drive south through the steppe. In the afternoon we got on a highway going west. We were in the middle of nowhere when night fell and had to sleep in the truck again. Only this time there was no wood available;

we could collect barely enough to boil some *kipyatok*. The temperature dipped sharply in the night, and we froze.

Petya had some difficulty in starting the truck in the morning, but after that we drove on without stalling. In the afternoon we noticed that both the landscape and the flora began to change; little by little we left the exotic steppe behind us. Some time later we left Kazakhstan and were in the territory of the Russian Federated Republic.

We drove by some villages; the area here seemed to be more populated. We also finally hit on a *stolovaya*. We had not had anything warm since the previous night, and the watery *lapsha* soup we managed to get tasted delicious. Arkady also succeeded in getting gasoline. With all this "luck" our mood improved.

Later we came to a crossroad. Arkady looked at his map and said, "This is the road leading to Buzuluk." We got on that highway. We had no particular difficulty in finding lodging for the night in a kolkhoz. I don't want to sound repetitious in describing our experience there. It was much the same as three nights before—including the bedbugs that sucked our blood in the night and the miserly hosts who robbed us with their extortionist prices.

Day was breaking as we started out, and we were now only about 70 kilometers from Buzuluk. My suspense grew with every kilometer we came closer to the town—would I be accepted at the Czech Military Unit there or would we have to continue our difficult journey to Dnepropetrovsk?

FOUR

And so, on the sixth day of our arduous journey, we got off, exhausted and worn out, at the Czechoslovak barracks. The truck needed some repair, and the gasoline was running low. They therefore decided that instead of waiting to see how we would fare inside, they would go in the meantime to find a service station and then return.

Noticing the Czech lion, the national emblem of the Republic, on the caps of the sentries at the entrance, my heart began to beat faster. How long had it been since I saw it last? Five years? No. Much longer than that. It seemed like a century at least.

Strangely enough, at the same time I was also overcome by indifference—a kind of feeling that follows long anticipation and tension. I suddenly recalled Esfir's words as we said good-bye—"It is the foremost duty of every Jew to survive; the Germans have murdered so many of us." As was her habit, she illustrated it with a folk saying—"He swam and swam but drowned near the shore." And waving her finger she admonished me, "You have managed to swim across such turbulent waters. So try to stay alive and don't become a dead hero."

We went inside the barracks and were taken to an office. A lengthy procedure of interviewing and filling out questionnaires began. When it was over, I went for the medical checkup. I undressed. The doctor, himself with the sickly pallor of one released from a forced-labor camp only recently, looked at my gaunt body—it was only skin and bones.

He began to examine me. My heart was filled with worry—what would he say about my back? When he looked at it, he asked me how it had started. I told him. To my surprise he made no particular fuss about it; he was apparently used to examining human wrecks like me. "We'll put you in a reserve unit to give you time to get back on your feet gradually," he said.

I took off the odd mixture of my threadbare, grimy looking clothes and donned the military outfit I was issued. I looked at myself in disbelief—am I really a soldier now? Raphi did not recognize me at first when he saw me in the Czech military uniform.

The truck returned in the afternoon. We unloaded our belongings. Yakov, Sima and Galya were naturally happy with our success. I was, however, moved to tears when they reminded us again—"If something should go wrong here, you are always welcome to stay with us in Dnepropetrovsk."

Our parting with these close friends, thanks to whom our exodus from Tamak was made possible, was emotional. I still could not believe that we were saying goodbye for good. When the truck pulled out, I waved my last farewell to them, wondering sadly whether it was destined for us to ever meet again.

Epilogue

W<small>ITH OUR ARRIVAL</small> in Buzuluk I conclude the story of my experiences in Russia. Not that our plight was quite over then—by no means. We still went through many tribulations before succeeding in getting out of the Soviet Union about a year and a half later.

I had of course to live in the military barracks. Ida and Raphi stayed with a Russian family, living in a corner behind a curtain partition, for which they paid with part of the one meal a day they got from the army kitchen. So, in order to survive, it was necessary to buy food in the kolkhoz market. Making ends meet continued to be difficult. Nevertheless, for the first time since coming to Russia I felt some relief from the haunting nightmare of how to get a piece of bread or a few potatoes for our mere survival.

Soon I saw that some other soldiers too had families with them. After the Nazi invasion of Czechoslovakia they had fled with their families to Poland, Rumania or to the Baltic countries, and upon the Soviet occupation of these territories the NKVD shipped them off to Siberian forced-labor camps. Some of them were eventually released to go into the Czech Army.

Unlike on the shores of the Belaya River and in the other places where I had lived constantly in the midst of Soviet people, made friends and studied daily life and society "from the inside," so to speak, I was now, as a member of a foreign army, very cautious in my contacts with Soviet citizens. The more so, since I found out soon enough that even in the army one had to be careful because we had NKVD informers among us—young, hard-boiled communists sent in the prewar years to the Soviet Union by the Czech Communist Party to be trained there as propagandists. In spite of looming dangers from informers inside and outside the barracks, however, I continued to be in

321

touch with Soviet people and to research the various aspects of Soviet society. My ample experience in this respect taught me the art of caution—and I was lucky.

I have tried to relate here as objectively as possible my own experiences and the conditions of life in Russia in general, as well as to depict in brief the untold suffering and horrible tragedies of Jews and non-Jews, inflicted by the inhuman secret police. These unfortunate people, whipped to resounding silence by the knout of communist terror, confided their woes to me and asked me to retell them to the free world.

Have I told everything? Not at all! For it is rather impossible to describe it in all its horrible details. Only a Dante would be equal to the task.

In conclusion I would like to say this. All through my sojourn in the Soviet Union, whether on the shores of the Belaya River or in the many cities and villages to which fate took me, I searched in vain for the *Homo Sovieticus,* the so-called New Soviet Man, who is supposed to be idealistic and selflessly devoted to the commonweal of his fellow men. The Communist propaganda boasted so much about having created this ideal type of man, but I never found him. Instead, I saw everywhere only people intimidated by terror and demoralized by a political system they despised who have become cynical and callous to the suffering of others. To be sure, there are also many who have not lost their human kindness and are willing to help their fellow men, but alas!—they constitute only a tiny minority.

The military unit I was assigned to went through a tough basic training. What with my bad back it was a trying ordeal, but I made strenuous efforts to keep abreast, and the service in the army afforded me many interesting experiences.

A few months later we were all loaded on a long freight train—I was on my way to the Russian western front. Life at the front was a series of constant dangers, and I had many traumatic battle experiences (I disregarded Esfir's admonitions, after all). I was lucky indeed to get out of it all alive. As much as I would like to describe my experiences in the army, and especially at the front, it cannot be included in this book. For to do so even in brief would fill a volume.

On V-Day in May 1945 our military unit reached the Moravian town of Olomouc. An official celebration of the end of the war was held, to which we too were invited. There was jubilation all around. But what did *I* have to be jubilant about? The crematoriums and gas chambers and the countless mass graves of slaughtered Jews all over Europe? Little by little the bitter truth about Auschwitz, Maidanek, Dachau and other German death camps became known. The proportions of the Holocaust were horrible and paralyzed the mind. In Czechoslovakia too only very few Jews survived.

The course of political developments in postwar Czechoslovakia—as in the other countries overrun by the Red Army—is well known, and I need not elaborate on it. The red handwriting was legible enough, and it should have been clear to anyone that it spelled Soviet subjugation. But people hoped against hope that "President Beneš would straighten things out somehow."

What amazes me most in retrospect is the fact that even we, the returnees from the Soviet Union who had seen the naked truth there, were stricken with blindness. Very few of us were wise enough to leave the country in time.

I don't seem to have been endowed with the precious gift of sober foresight. For if I were, I would not have missed the opportunity to escape from Europe before the war and could have saved myself a decade of untold physical and mental suffering that has left a painful imprint on my memory.

And so, thanks again to my lack of foresight, I settled down in Prague after my demobilization from the army in the hopes of rebuilding my wrecked life and starting anew. But our hopes were soon dashed. After the communist seizure of power by force in February 1948 I escaped by the skin of my teeth from Czechoslovakia together with my wife and son, leaving everything behind—the clothes on our backs constituting all of our possessions—and reached Paris. I was a refugee again, for the second time in less than a decade.

In June 1948 we arrived in the United States and settled in New York City.

Glossary

Avoska (Russ.)   Net shopping bag

Babushka (Russ.)   Grandmother; triangular scarf tied under the chin

Banya (Russ.)   Public baths

Black Hundred   Paramilitary organization set up by the Czarist government, with the blessing of Nicholas II, to carry out pogroms on Jewish communities

Drang nach Osten (Ger.)   Drive toward the East; traditional Eastern expansion of Germany

Dyetdom (Russ.)   Children's Home

Eiruv (Heb.)   Wire strung on the circumference of a town to classify it as enclosed private property within which objects may be carried on the Sabbath

Evakpunkt (Russ.)   Evacuation Center

Fritz   Russian pejorative term for a German during World War II

GPU (Russ.)   Soviet Secret Police, from 1922 to 1934 (known as KGB today)

Heder (Heb.)   Religious school

Kipyatok (Russ.)   Hot, boiled water

Komandirovka (Russ.)   Permit for an official business trip

Kombinat (Russ.)   Group of interconnected industrial enterprises

Kopeck (Russ.)   A coin, 100th of a ruble

Kulak (Russ.)   Landed peasant

Lapsha (Russ.)   Broad, dark noodles

Lepyoshka (Russ.)   Flat cake of rough meal

Makhorka (Russ.)   Rough, homegrown tobacco

Mikveh (Heb.)   Public ritual bath

Militia (Russ.)   Soviet term for police in general

Minyan (Heb.)   Quorum of ten men necessary for public worship

NEP (Russ.)   New Economic Policy, introduced by Lenin in 1921 and abolished by Stalin in 1928

Nichevo! (Russ.)   Never mind; it doesn't matter

NKVD (Russ.)   Soviet Secret Police, from 1934 to 1943

Ochered (Russ.)   Line for bread, etc.

Pirogi (Russ.)   Pastry turnovers filled with meat, cheese, etc.

Politkomissar (Russ.)   Political commissar in the Red Army

Politruk (Russ.)   Political instructor in the Red Army

Purga (Russ.)   Snowstorm

Sabra (Heb.)   A native-born Israeli

Stolovaya (Russ.)   Public kitchen; cafeteria

Sukhari (Russ.)   Dried slices of bread

Tolchok (Russ.)   Kind of flea market

VU   Voyennoye Uchilische (Military College)

Yahrzeit (Yid.)   Anniversary of the death of a parent or other member of the immediate family

Yevsektsia (Russ.)   Jewish Section in the Communist Party before World War II

Yevsek   Official of the Yevsektsia